RICH WHERE

"A praiseworthy book that reveals how you can prosper in what truly matters and pass on a principled legacy. Charlie Douglas does an outstanding job of demonstrating that we need both spiritual and financial capital to realize the American Dream."

—Ken Blanchard, Ph.D.,
Bestselling Coauthor of *The One Minute Manager*®

"It has often been said that no one on their deathbed wished they had spent more time at the office. Relationships are what truly matter—both human and divine. This book's chronological historical analysis through this lens is fascinating and insightful, and consistently shows that happiness is truly never found in the wallet, but rather lies within the heart."

—Dr. Stephen Covey, Author, *The 7 Habits of Highly Effective People*

"God created us to be successful, but true success cannot be measured by dollars alone. Charlie Douglas puts readers in touch with what it means to be successful, and how to pass on a meaningful legacy. In the past few years, many people have been troubled by the lack of business ethics, but there is no such thing as 'business ethics' there are only personal ethics and they are the underpinnings of the American Dream."

—S. Truett Cathy, Founder of Chick-fil-A

"Charlie Douglas offers rich insights for reassessing our paths to success based on the basic principles and bedrock spirituality upon which our nation was founded. A timely book that will challenge you."

—Sonny Perdue, Governor of Georgia

"As a free nation, Americans have the opportunity to reach for their dreams based on the right to life, liberty, and the pursuit of happiness. This timely book serves as a powerful reminder that the foundation of the 'American Dream' depends upon values, virtues, and the Creator who endowed us with our inalienable rights."

—Zell Miller, United States Senator

"In the rush to capitalize on ever-expanding financial markets, many people neglected the truly important things. Charlie Douglas exposes the cost of that thinking, and reveals the joy that flows from filling the voids in your spiritual and personal life. He makes it plain that morality and markets can and should be intertwined."

—William J. Bennett, Bestselling Author of *The Book of Virtues*

"Impossible, but here it is all in one volume: inspiration, education, history, theology, and mini-biographies of the giants that shaped our great country. Tremendous!"

—Charlie "Tremendous" Jones, Bestselling Author of *Life Is Tremendous*

"Charlie Douglas has tackled, head on, two of the most important issues facing America: how have we so massively lost our way and what role spirituality and religion can play in fashioning values that will right us."

—**Charles B. Knapp**, Former President of the University of Georgia

"Charlie Douglas warns us that 'we are losing touch with the need to develop lasting wealth based on enduring values.' Right on! He reminds us that the American Dream has never merely been about the acquisition of wealth—but about living lives of virtue, faith, and service to our fellow man. A timely message in an age of corporate scandals."

—**Ed Feulner, Ph.D.**, President of the Heritage Foundation

"*Rich Where It Counts* is right on the money!"

—**Dyan Cannon**, Actress

"A powerful and much-needed examination of the true American Dream, Charlie Douglas's book couldn't be more timely. America needs this book; we need to rediscover and celebrate the majesty of the American capitalist system, and fully appreciate the financial and spiritual freedoms we enjoy. An absolute, one-of-a-kind must-read for every American, regardless of political persuasion."

—**Doug Wead**, Former Special Assistant to President George H. W. Bush, Author of The New York Times Bestseller *All the Presidents' Children*

"Charlie Douglas's new book is a must-read for all who want to be successful by leading a value-centered life. It is a virtual manual on how to do well and do good by living a life of integrity."

—**John R. Seffrin, Ph.D.**, CEO, American Cancer Society

"Charlie Douglas is an extraordinary person, and his book reflects that. After reading it, I came away feeling like I could go and start my life all over again, and do it better, with more love for my fellowman—even at this late age. It's a book you'll want to read, reread, and pass on to your children and grandchildren."

—**Shirley Jones**, Academy Award Winning Actress

"There is a widespread belief that making money is somehow at odds with making a connection to the higher aspects of life. In this book, Charlie Douglas leaves readers literally more awake, more able to see clearly that succeeding in business is not the goal but rather a part of the journey."

—**Gavin de Becker**, Bestselling Author of *The Gift of Fear and Fear Less*

"This book would make a good gift to Christian business students or those graduating and ready to enter the fray."

—**CBA Marketplace**, Official Magazine of the Christian Booksellers Association

"Charlie paints a wonderful kaleidoscope of the true American Dream. He shatters the 'Madison Avenue Myth' and enthusiastically articulates the Real American Dream: Being excellent stewards of God's resources to accomplish His purposes. A must-read for 'Serious Dreamers.'"

—**Steve Franklin, Ph.D.,** Author, *TV Commentator,*
and Sr. Vice President of New Business Development, Wells Real Estate Funds

"A must-read for anyone looking for a roadmap to achieving their dream and creating an unstoppable legacy."

—**Cynthia Kersey,** Bestselling Author of *Unstoppable*

"*Rich Where It Counts* is a superb book that offers a sweeping historical, cultural, political and economic perspective on America—and then hones it into an intensely personal philosophy. Combining sharp analysis and gentle insight, Charlie Douglas challenges each one of us to establish our spiritual priorities even as we pursue the blessings of free markets."

—**Dr. Judy Shelton,** Economist and author of *Money Meltdown*

"In this book, author Charlie Douglas has re-established, and with considerable style, the proper continuity between God, personal integrity, and true wealth. By weaving together an entertaining history of our country's economy and its best-known business moguls, with an equally fascinating chronicle of American morals and values, Douglas achieves a portrait of contemporary America that not only clearly defines our dilemmas, but also reveals practical solutions already built into our way of life. And most importantly, he shows how belief in God and God's influence over individuals, when welcomed, can lead us to a future prosperity—not only a prosperity of goods, but a prosperity of spirit. This book will engage your interest and enlighten you, from beginning to end."

—**John F. Donoghue,** Archbishop Emeritus Atlanta, GA

"Charlie Douglas has done a great service for American culture by writing Rich *Where It Counts.* We are all called to be good stewards of the gifts the Lord has given us. Charlie masterfully weaves together nuggets of wisdom from our shared history and our common faith bonds that effectively guide readers in their lifetime journey of stewardship."

—**Philip Lenahan,** President, Veritas Financial Ministries

"The American Dream is accessible to anyone who understands the basic values and principles upon which the American republic was founded. In this book, Charlie Douglas provides deep, enriching insights and ideas that make you want to pursue the vastness of the Dream with renewed vigor. It is an inspiring and uplifting tribute to all that is good and great in America."

—**Brian Tracy,** Bestselling Author of *Maximum Achievement*

"I met Charlie Douglas by pure chance. That encounter led me to his inspiring book. He describes some disheartening trends in American society, but he also offers an uplifting message by weaving together a fabric of a financial, spiritual, and value-laden American Dream. Parents and teachers should tell our youth to turn off the television and rap music and read Charlie's book. They will learn valuable lessons."
—**Major General William K. Suter,** U.S. Army (Ret.)

"....addresses a very timely subject."
—**Steve Forbes,** President and CEO of Forbes Inc.
and Editor-in-Chief of *Forbes Magazine*

"A thought-provoking and inspiring read. This book nicely weaves wisdom from various key fields of study. Charlie Douglas presents a clear, consistent vision that informs and uplifts."
—**Jeff Rosensweig, Ph.D.,** Associate Dean at the Goizueta Business School of Emory University, Author, *Winning the Global Game: A Strategy for Linking People and Profits*

"The work of Charlie Douglas in *Rich Where It Counts* should be mandatory reading for every American. Balanced, honest, and carefully researched, Charlie has written a book which may literally change our nation's perception of 'the American Dream' in a most profound and positive way."
—**Linda Forsythe,** Publisher, *Mentors Magazine*

"What an enlightening and provocative perspective on the character of America and the American Dream. Charlie does an extraordinary job of painting a picture that allows one to self discover his/her ability to contribute (or not) to the 'richness' of America today. This is one of those rare books where the content meets and exceeds the cover!"
—**Shaun Rawls,** Multiple Office Owner, Keller Williams Realty

"Financial planner and motivational speaker Charlie Douglas surveys the religious and cultural history of the U.S. to chart how we reached the state of moral confusion in which our society finds itself today. Then he draws on his analytical and counseling skills—along with his deep Catholic faith—to arrive at some specific recommendations for leading a life of purpose, value and commitment to God. *Rich Where It Counts* is well worth reading, filled with penetrating insights and sound advice."
—**Thomas S. Monaghan,** Founder, Domino's Pizza

"Charlie Douglas has written a most timely book. Anyone who wants to live the American Dream and make this world a better place will need to read it. His message will resonate with everyone who cares about this country and wants to see it get closer to God."
—**Dr. Robert H. Schuller,** Crystal Cathedral Ministries

"Our nation is facing some pivotal questions that will define our country for the next hundred years. This book makes plain that the answers cannot be found in money alone or apart from God. Charlie Douglas makes a compelling case that America's well-being still very much depends upon its Judeo-Christian roots, traditional values, and the moral character of a free people."

—**Sadie Fields**, Chairman, Georgia Christian Coalition

"Taking principles of faith and fact to the front lines of American legal policy struggles is the basis for our work at Southeastern Legal Foundation. Sound, reasoned, and faith-based approaches to personal and national management are keystones on which Charlie Douglas highlights success for Americans across the board."

—**Shannon L. Goessling, Esq.**,
Executive Director, Southeastern Legal Foundation Inc.

"Capturing the spiritual to be successful in today's world is essential. In this book, Charlie Douglas captures it in a way that is applicable to everyone who desires to have an impact and succeed."

—**Herschel Walker**, Former NFL Running Back and Heisman Trophy Winner

"If you put your political party above your country then you won't like *Rich Where it Counts*. In particular, Charlie Douglas speaks frankly that budgets and deficits are more than just numbers. They are moral statements about how we live and what we value. As we strive for the American Dream today, we cannot afford to pass on swelling debts to the next generation. Read it and write your Congressman!"

—**Phil Smith**, National Grassroots Director, The Concord Coalition

"The American Dream is becoming the American Nightmare for many people in today's society. My good friend, Charlie Douglas identifies the key element of restoring the Dream's true success as he traces how possessing the freedom to pursue our God-given dreams can result in a fulfilling life of enrichment."

—**Dr. Ike Reighard**, Executive Vice President/Chief People Officer, HomeBanc

"The relationship between faith, business and national character is a delicate matter. Some claim that these critical components are unconnected and belong to separate realms. Charlie Douglas demonstrates from history, current events, and thought leaders that this is not the case. In fact, as he shows, one cannot be considered without taking account of the others."

—**Rev. Jerry Zandstra**, Acton Institute

"It is a tremendous book. I learned many things about the Founding Fathers that I did not know, but its real value is in how well it connects spiritual values and a belief in free markets to everyday life in our materialistic world."

—**Kelly McCutchen**, Executive Vice President, Georgia Public Policy Foundation

"This book demonstrates that values and faith are the foundations of inner peace and the prosperity of purpose."

—**Johnny Isakson,** United States Senator

"In *Rich Where It Counts,* Charlie Douglas does a wonderful job of exploring the 'success idea' in America, God's vital role, and how you can apply foundational principles in your family life for a lasting legacy. It is a book I wholeheartedly endorse and recommend."

—**Thomas Rogerson,** Senior Director of Wealth Management, Mellon Bank

"In his terrific book, *Rich Where It Counts,* Charlie Douglas reminds us where true riches are found. This is a must-read for anyone who seeks to put wealth in its proper perspective and desires to make a difference in the world."

—**David A. Williams,** President & CEO, Make-A-Wish Foundation of America

"I have the privilege of knowing Charlie Douglas and I have seen his passion for communicating the elements of true success. He is a very gifted man who has a vital message for our generation. It is a privilege to recommend *Rich Where it Counts.*"

—**Ron Blue,** Bestselling author and CEO of the *Christian Financial Professionals Network*

"Charlie Douglas does a magnificent job of pointing out that each of us must slow down long enough to honestly evaluate ourselves and our priorities if we are to ever become truly secure—a security that comes only when our values come to rest in a Creator; not in the things He created."

—**Jeff Scroggins, J.D.,** LLM, Scroggins & Associates, LLC

"Charlie Douglas truly connects you with the power of the American Dream, your life purpose and the values necessary for fully living it out. For those working on getting the most from their life plans, this is mandatory reading."

—**Hugh Massie,** President and Founder of Financial DNA® Resources, Inc.

"America's Godly heritage may have been lost if not forgotten by most American's today. Thankfully, Charlie Douglas has written a book that restores America's conscience to true riches—the same riches that our many of founding fathers came in search of."

—**Jerry Black,** President, Legacy Planning Group

"Charlie Douglas does a great service. In this timely book, he dispels the myth that business is inherently corrupt. He proves that by keeping all things in perspective— from your spiritual life to your relationship with your family—you can make money, live a full life, and leave a lasting legacy. Investors should read this book, if for no other purpose than to keep themselves grounded in those fundamental principles upon which our nation was founded."

—**Jack Kemp,** Former Presidential Vice Presidential Candidate

RICH
WHERE IT COUNTS

Create Lasting Wealth by
Cultivating Spiritual Capital

CHARLES V. DOUGLAS, J.D., AEP, CFP®

RICH WHERE IT COUNTS

Rich Where It Counts:
Create Lasting Wealth by Cultivating Spiritual Capital/Charles V. Douglas.
Based on the book Awaken The American Dream by Charles V. Douglas

1. Capitalism—Religious aspects.
2. Capitalism—Moral and ethical aspects—United States.
3. Wealth—Religious aspects.
4. United States—Economic conditions.
I. Title.

Manufactured in the United States of America

ISBN: 1-60037-074-8 (Hardcover)

ISBN: 1-933596-63-5 (Paperback)

ISBN: 1-60037-075-6 (Audio)

Published by:

MORGAN · JAMES
THE ENTREPRENEURIAL PUBLISHER™
Morgan James Publishing, LLC
1225 Franklin Ave Ste 325
Garden City, NY 11530-1693
Toll Free 800-485-4943
www.MorganJamesPublishing.com

Habitat
for Humanity®
Peninsula
Building Partner

Interior Design by:
Michelle Radomski
One to One Creative Services
www.creativeones.net

This book is dedicated to
all of those virtuous individuals who have
gone before us, whose selfless spirits have long
served as a guiding light for countless others
in their pursuit of the American Dream.

And especially to my young daughter,
Elizabeth, I hope this adds something special
to your heritage as you leave your own legacy,
one day at a time.

ACKNOWLEDGMENTS

To the many people who have helped me along the way with their willingness to listen to my ideas, lend their support, and read "one more" draft. The list of those who assisted me in this journey is far too long to mention, but a few special people come to mind: Leo Grant, Phil Turner, Linda Forsythe, David Hancock, Ally Beasley, Terry Ford, Steve Levy, Joe Kilbarger, Dennis and Jayne Horn, Dee and Greg Cabana, Harold Metzel, Harold Gourgues, John Maiers, Janet Althouse, David Pace and Gavin de Becker. So many others gave their heartfelt input too—please know that I am sincerely grateful.

To my wife, Lori, thank you for the gift of believing in me. To my parents, thank you for your many years of loving support. And to God, whose spirit of inspiration helped me to finish this race.

CONTENTS

"The American Dream is the liberty to pursue your dreams as our Creator intended. Or put another way, it is having the freedom to follow those inspired dreams that God entrusted to us—not merely for the sake of self-interest, but also to promote the common good for the collective benefit of others."

—Charlie Douglas

1

WHAT IS THE AMERICAN DREAM?

"Blessed is the Nation whose God is the Lord..."
—*Psalm 33:12*

The American Dream has lost much of its meaning. Today, Americans too often grasp for fools' gold, while allowing the "Dream's" true riches to slip through their fingers.

Having long exploited and taken the American Dream for granted, the Dream has become a shadow of its former self. As it stands now, the Dream will not survive the next few generations of Americans unless we act swiftly to restore its true essence.

The Dream may appear to be richer than ever during this time of unprecedented wealth. But appearances can be deceiving. Leading richer lives does not mean that we are living richly in what truly matters. Like any book, we cannot correctly judge the Dream by its exterior cover.

Since America's promising beginnings, various generations have lived out the American Dream in different ways. But the true essence of the Dream has not wavered. *The American Dream is the liberty to pursue your dreams as our Creator intended.* Or put another way, *it is having the freedom to follow those inspired dreams that God entrusted to us—not merely for the sake of self-interest, but also to promote the common good for the collective benefit of others.*

For many today, the fundamental meaning of the American Dream seems to be unclear and uncertain. The Dream is commonly confused with becoming the next *American Idol,* winning the lottery, or owning the house of your dreams.

Looking back, the term "The American Dream," was first used by James Truslow in his book the *Epic of America* (1931) and was described as "that dream of a land in which life should be better and richer and fuller for everyone, with opportunity for each according to ability or achievement."

Yet Truslow was careful to point out that the American Dream was not expressly about material wealth. It was not merely a dream of motor cars and high wages. It was a dream that unequivocally demonstrated that all men and women could attain their fullest stature regardless of their birth position in life.

The actual inception of the American Dream, however, began centuries prior to the phrase. It originated with the settling of the New World by the spirited Pilgrims and thereafter appeared etched in the Declaration of Independence with the words: *"...all men are created equal, that they are endowed by their Creator with certain unalienable rights, that among these are life, liberty, and the pursuit of happiness."*

The Dream Finds a Home in a City upon a Hill

America, along with the Dream, began as "a City upon a Hill," as poetically expressed by John Winthrop, a preeminent public figure of early New England. Winthrop preached that "the eyes of all people would be upon us" to see if we would prosper and endure in a new land that was to be a model of Christian charity. Our country offered the promise of both economic opportunity and religious freedom for those who were disposed to embark on a journey of great labor and great faith.

Scores of settlers considered themselves to be a new chosen people in a new promised land. Government in early America was more than a social contract among self-interested individuals. Instead, government embodied a covenantal bond between God and individuals inspired by Judeo-Christian principles. It offered visionary pioneers the liberty to worship their Creator through inspired enterprise, yielding prosperity grounded in faith, virtue and the common good.

President Ronald Reagan often referred to America as the "Shining City on the Hill." He once remarked, "I believe this blessed land was set apart in a very special way, a country created by men who came here, not in search of gold, but in search of God. They would be free people, living under the law with faith in their Maker and their future."

Like many of the Founding Fathers, Reagan believed the American Dream to be a country where "every man must be free to become whatever God intends him to become;" and where the Dream would only be realized by "keeping faith with the mighty spirit of free people under God."

For most of America's history, the American Dream was seen foremost as a by-product of a well-ordered and virtuous life. The emphasis was on building *spiritual capital—utilizing God-given resources as a faithful steward, where one acts with enlightened self-interest in accordance with one's unique calling.*

The primary emphasis was on creative enterprise, believing that our Creator would provide enough financial capital along the way to meet one's needs. It was a vision rooted in the words of Jesus: "Seek first His kingdom and righteousness, and all these things shall be yours as well" (Matthew 6:33).

Who Moved the American Dream?

Over the many years since America's auspicious beginning material wealth became the hallmark of capitalism and the primary focus of the American Dream. To be sure, material wealth is not contrary to the America Dream; it is an essential component. Yet, money and possessions were not meant to be the Dream's sole measure of success and significance.

Picture for a moment an image of an immense iceberg. The part that lies above the water is financial capital or material wealth. It is this part that we so often strive to possess, consume, feel and touch. However, that material aspect is only the "tip of the iceberg." By far, the largest part of the iceberg lies below the surface and represents spiritual capital.

The #1 International Bestseller, *Who Moved My Cheese?* by Spencer Johnson, M.D., describes a world where mice and mouse-sized humans react differently when the cheese they love is moved to another part of the maze. But what is cheese? As Ken Blanchard, Ph.D., describes in the foreword, cheese is "a metaphor for what we want to have in life, whether it is a job, a relationship, money, a big house, freedom, health, recognition, spiritual peace, or even an activity like jogging or golf." Cheese symbolizes the notion of freedom in pursuing what we truly believe will bring sincere happiness to ourselves and to others. In this sense, cheese represents the freedom and richness of the American Dream.

The freedom to pursue worthwhile dreams demands great courage in a world that has been badly shaken since the new millennium began. A brutal bear market, September 11th, the ensuing War on Terror, Hurricane Katrina, and a host of scandals have collectively chipped away at the core of our institutions. From Enron's implosion, to missing weapons of mass destruction, to the United Nation's Oil-for-Food debacle, to disconcerting investigations of corporate and elected officials, we have sought reassurance from unsteady institutions in many cases.

Gerald Celente of Trends Research Institute in Rhinebeck, N.Y., recently said, "We have never seen anything like this before. So many people have lost so much trust in so many institutions at the same time."

The dwindling spiritual capital of our ailing institutions has caused some to question if we are still "One nation under God." Feelings of fear and envy, rather than love and charity, often reside within us in a world increasingly focused on materialism.

Too often things have taken God's place in our hearts. In fact, materialism is now the DNA of capitalism and the driving force of the American Dream. This limited view, however, is proving to be detrimental.

Consider the disturbing observation made in a recent issue of *Fast Company* magazine: "Between 1970 and 1999, the average American family received a 16% raise (adjusted for inflation), while the percentage of people who described themselves as 'very happy' fell from 36% to 29%... We are better paid, better fed, and better educated than ever. Yet the divorce rate has doubled, the teenage suicide rate has tripled, and depression has soared in the past 30 years. The conclusion is inescapable: Our lifestyles are packed with more stuff, but we lead emptier lives. We are consuming more but enjoying it less."

Madonna, the "Material Girl," now middle-aged, recently reflected on the short-sightedness of her view of the American Dream: "Take it from me. I went down the road of 'be all you can be, realize your dreams,' and I'm telling you that fame and fortune are not what they're cracked up to be. We live in a society that seems to value only physical things, only ephemeral things. People will do anything to get on these reality shows and talent contests on TV. We're obsessed."

Unlike the majority of bestselling books that deal with wealth, this book is not written for the purpose of helping you become financially rich. To be candid, wealth planning involves a lot more than just money planning.

This book's primary purpose is to awaken within you the notion of true riches, to revitalize the fundamental American Dream, and to help you reconnect with your life's purpose. Humankind has never been able to live by bread alone and living a rich life depends upon a lot more than making money. Moreover, this book seeks to preserve and protect our revered heritage in order to pass on a principled legacy to the next generation.

It is anticipated that this book will be openly shared and discussed in small groups and especially among grandparents, children and grandchildren. We must have a grassroots effort, starting with caring families and concerned communities, to rescue the American Dream and to restore patriotism in our weakened institutions.

Keep in mind that our heritage is not hereditary; it must be deliberately nurtured and passed on from one generation to the next in order to survive. This is not a small matter to be taken lightly.

For example, more Americans today can identify the names from the cartoon family, *The Simpsons,* or specify the judges from the *American Idol,* than can name a like number of freedoms as guaranteed by the First Amendment (freedom of speech, religion, press, assembly and petition for redress of grievances).

More significant than glancing at selected highlights from history in several of the chapters to follow, is reconnecting with and reflecting upon a fundamental part of our tradition. Although the targeted message of this book is not fully realized until its conclusion, the brief historical sections that appear from time to time are essential toward building an informed perspective within a related framework.

In truth, a heritage is much grander than arbitrary historical events. More accurately, a heritage serves as a cohesive blueprint for effectively building upon the efforts of preceding generations.

Without a heritage, each successive generation must begin building from scratch. President Woodrow Wilson once remarked, "A nation which does not remember what it was yesterday, does not know what it is today, nor what it is trying to do. We are trying to do a futile thing if we do not know where we came from or what we have been about."

The Toil of Trying to Serve Two Masters

For over 20 years, as both a lawyer and financial advisor, I have been counseling people about monetary wealth. I offered what I thought was comprehensive planning by recommending prudent financial and legal vehicles to help clients achieve their material goals. However, I began to realize my services were too limited since they often ignored the behavior, core values and dreams of those I sought to help. Yet these intangible elements are precisely what are needed to drive the whole planning process.

Born near the end of the Baby Boom, I have arbitrarily chased after bits and pieces of the American Dream for most of my life, unaware of the Dream's true essence. It seemed as though Jesus in Matthew 6:24 had spoken His words of caution directly to me: "No one can serve two masters. He will either hate one and love the other, or be devoted to one and despise the other. You cannot serve God and money."

I can assure you that I had noble intentions even though they did little to dispel Jesus' warning. But when I set my sights squarely on achieving financial prosperity, I often felt uneasy. My pursuit and realization of material gain did little to satisfy the restlessness stirring in my soul. The more financial success I had, the more I became aware of the rumpled person outside my car window—the one with the dog-eared cardboard sign that read: "Homeless. Will work for food."

On the other hand, when I pursued my spirituality foremost, my ego frequently sounded the alarm that reminded me that I was letting others in the material world pass me by. I frequently felt torn, trying to live a spiritual life in a material world. I could relate to the plate-spinner on *The Ed Sullivan Show*—caught between two poles precariously placed at opposite ends of the stage, frantically running back and forth to keep both plates spinning.

Phillip Yancey, editor of *Christianity Today,* captured my sentiments well: "I feel pulled in opposite directions over the money issue. Sometimes I want to sell all that I own, join a Christian commune, and live out my days in intentional poverty. At other times, I want to rid myself of guilt and enjoy the fruits of our nation's prosperity. Mostly, I wish I did not have to think about money at all."

I have struggled often in my journey between balancing God and money and there is still much work to be done before journey's end. It is not enough for any writer to simply proffer principles, point to crying injustices and utter prophetic criticisms. For the most part, writers themselves, most especially this one, need to continually learn the challenging lessons of the message they seek to offer to others. With God's grace, however, I hope to make a difference for you in your journey toward a richer, more meaningful life.

To accomplish this, you, the reader must earnestly examine yourself to see what you have done up until now in your pursuit of the American Dream and what you ought to do in your journey ahead. Keep in mind that words, no matter how poetically expressed, will always lack real weight unless we earnestly commit ourselves to living out transcendent truths.

As you read this book, reflect on the relative importance of financial and spiritual capital. Take time to complete the review questions at the end of each chapter and note the key [⚷] presented for creating *lasting wealth—those enduring riches that help bear fruit that will last* (John 15:16) *and store treasure in heaven* (Matthew 6:20, Luke 12:33).

Ultimately, each of us must decide whether our life's energy will be spent pursuing dreams that are more money-driven or more purpose-driven. Even so, balancing spiritual and financial capital as depicted on this book's cover is not easy.

In Michelangelo's world-famous fresco, *The Creation of Adam,* we see that the touch of God's hand awakens a naked Adam and thus begins the life of humankind.

Today, however, a modern-day Adam is often unsettled between reaching out for God's divine touch and grasping for money that ironically proclaims: "In God We Trust." Yet, it is difficult to connect with the breath of life when we are at odds about whether to be more like Donald Trump's "Apprentice" or the Lord's "Servant."

Faith and finances have always been interrelated to some degree. Every financial decision is in part a spiritual one—a moral and cultural statement about how we live. Therefore, morality and the marketplace need to stay allied.

Private profit and public virtue are by no means mutually exclusive. But doing well for ourselves and doing good for others many times requires that our investments of time and economic resources be in those undertakings which foremost help promote life, human dignity and the common good.

The Dream's Light is in Danger of Burning Out

Like the brilliant torch of the Statue of Liberty, the American Dream has long burned brightly for the Shining City on the Hill as a beacon of hope and inspiration to millions of people in search of a better way of living. While still visible today, the Dream's guiding light is in danger of burning out. Little by little the light has grown dimmer, as if by its own accord.

The reality is, however, that we are largely responsible for the muted appearance of the flame. There are a host of reasons for the dimness of the Dream, but three in particular are worth mentioning.

First, we have mired the Dream in massive economic debt, both private and public, that will need to be paid later in time. Future generations can now look forward to inheriting a downsized Dream comprised of higher taxes, smaller institutional benefits and a reduced standard of living. Economic opportunities that have been readily available since the inception of the Dream will not be available in the not so distant future due to substantial economic burdens in an increasingly competitive global marketplace.

The thought of this is discomforting, but not enough to mandate sacrifice and immediate economic reform. We hear superficial rhetoric from those in our Nation's capitol about being "good stewards" over the economy and taxpayer dollars as reckless federal spending continues unabated. While freely inheriting the American Dream from the spirited efforts of the generations gone before us, we are far less concerned about being patriotic stewards, and passing the Dream on intact to future generations.

Second, the American Dream is caught up in the midst of an intense culture war between religious and secular values. This war's battlefield is broad and includes the courtroom, the media, the public square and even late-night barbs exchanged between Bill O'Reilly and David Letterman. This culture war may not dominate the headlines on a daily basis, but its' outcome is just as important as the War against Terror.

At stake is the role that God will play in our country's future. The question arises, will the Judeo-Christian principles under which America and the Dream were founded and prospered under play an important part in our nation's future? Or, will a more secular and subjective agenda (as shrewdly advocated by the ACLU) increasingly take its place?

Perhaps the most profound question at stake in this divisive culture war, and one that America and the Dream have sought to answer since their beginning is: Will a free people endure, prosper, and successfully govern themselves?

For the majority of our nation's existence that answer was affirmative and to a large degree depended upon the industrious nature and religious faith of our predecessors. But today we are looking far less to God for our moral prescriptions and more to individual and secular opinions.

More and more, materialism is replacing our daily dependence upon God. For most of humanity's history, however, people were concerned about survival and depended in no small way upon Providence. Yet, daily survival in the industrialized West is no longer a daily concern for most. As a nation, we appear to be acting as though we do not need God since we already have our daily bread. While we may still place our eternal hope in God, our daily hope is frequently found in the world.

As today's culture war rages on we are increasingly secularizing our democracy and losing our inner bank of common morality. For example, the "Theory of Evolution" is no longer a hypothesis to be critically considered; it has become today's gospel. Our children in public school are now being taught that everything is without direction and order and can be neatly summed up by a materialist philosophy in science.

It is not possible for any nation over the long term to maintain its moral compass without the guidance of religious faith. Without God there are no transcendent truths. When each person defines what is right in his or her own eyes there can be no cohesive moral foundation in building a better society. Instead our efforts, no mater how sincere, will fare no better than those of the builders of the Tower of Babel from the book of Genesis.

The third reason for the Dream's faintness is that we have lost sight of what the Dream really is, and what it was that allowed the Dream to endure and prosper. Having lost touch with our heritage and enduring values, we have become estranged from the Dream. Although not in need of an "extreme makeover;" the Dream could use a proper unmasking.

At the inception of the Dream early settlers in America were heavily influenced by the Protestant work ethic where one's life was to serve as God's instrument through diligence, profit, and the primacy of work. America's settlers were not encouraged to amass material riches for consumption or pleasure. Instead, they were commanded to be stewards of God's bounty and multiply wealth through work, saving and reinvestment.

During the Colonial period, Benjamin Franklin's *Poor Richard's Almanac* pragmatically embodied much of the Protestant ethic and stressed wealth through frugality and industry. Franklin's international best-selling essay, "The Way to Wealth" was a masterful treatise on virtue, prosperity and financial commonsense. Throughout Franklin's works the notion of private profit and public virtue went hand-in-hand.

With the coming of the industrial revolution the Protestant ethic was further secularized and the definition of "success" more narrowly defined to individual merit and material wealth. During a time of wealthy industrialists, Horatio Alger's rags-to-riches tales became a cornerstone of American society. Stressing an "up by your bootstrap" mentality and a rugged individualism of overcoming adversity through industry, perseverance and self-reliance, anyone could achieve wealth and the American Dream if they were willing to adopt the right character traits and work hard.

Today, however, an entirely new ethic has emerged. The American Dream is now about getting rich quickly. Fundamental precepts that allowed the Dream to endure and prosper over hundreds of years are in danger of perishing. Being God's steward, promoting public virtue and advancing the common good through industry and hard work are frequently disregarded in favor of finding the best vehicle that allows one to cash in with the least effort.

Recent bestsellers proffer a much different picture. David Bach's bestseller *Automatic Millionaire* offers a finish-rich wisdom "that makes you rich automatically—without a budget, discipline or painful sacrifice." Similarly, Mark Victor Hansen and Robert Allen show us the short way to climb the millionaire mountain because we "Want it FAST!" in their bestseller, *The One-minute Millionaire.*

The primary aim of the American Dream has become the short term pursuit of one's own material wellbeing. Our quality of life is now essentially measured by consumerism, physical beauty and pleasure. The more profound spiritual and religious dimensions for our existence are often overlooked.

The quest for the Dream finds many of us at the service of economic activity, which is seen less as a source of brotherhood and a sign of Providence. Increasingly, businesses are looked upon as a "society of capital goods," instead of a "society of persons."

Those who control capital in America today, particularly large corporations, frequently forget their obligations to employ their productive power in ways that serve the common good, beyond serving the bottom-line and self-interest. More and more, material goods and the way we develop them are seen as ends in themselves instead of God's gifts of creation.

Likewise, developed nations, especially the United States, are consuming the resources of the earth in an excessive and disordered way. President George W. Bush recently denounced America's "addiction to oil" and suggested we turn to technology and alternative energy sources to reduce our dependence and improve our environment. But God's resources are more than just commodities to be consumed; they are gifts for the benefit of all.

The Dream is progressively being lived out in a culture where "having," takes precedence over "being," where "things" are valued over the "person," and where "others" are seen as "rivals"—not brothers and sisters to be loved for who they are.

As the Dream's light grows fainter we are losing sight of how we have been created—from the earth and from the breath of God. Believing that economic activity and technology alone will supply the raw material for human advancement we are, in some cases, ignoring the fact that they are powerless to achieve it. Only the Creator of us all can advance humankind.

The American Dream is Not a Gated Community

As a nation, Americans have long enjoyed a high standard of living. Even at the time of the Revolutionary War America's standard of living was the highest of any people in the world. Today, however, the great wealth of our country may be hindering our ability to see the poverty of more than 40 million Americans and the destitution of hundreds of millions of people in other parts of the world. In reality, America's promise of liberty and justice for all is not readily available to the poor and the oppressed.

Historically, the American Dream has endured and prospered precisely because millions of immigrants courageously came to our nation in search of a better life. The vast majority of these immigrants came here legally and were willing to acclimatize to a new culture in America's melting pot. Over the years, however, America's melting pot has become tepid as more immigrants not only reside in America illegally, but they also are much slower to assimilate to American culture.

According to government and academic estimates, there are somewhere between 10 to 20 million illegal immigrants living in our nation, with nearly an additional 1 million more gaining unlawful access every year through our poorly protected borders. Like the vast majority of Americans I, too, strongly believe that illegal immigration should not be encouraged and our borders need to be shored up.

At this time there is a great need for patriotic immigration, which emphasizes educating new immigrants on American culture. Nonetheless, tightening immigration laws, reinforcing border control systems, and familiarizing recent immigrants about America's heritage are not the sole answers.

All immigrants, legal and otherwise, deserve to be treated with respect and dignity, and not seen as afflictions upon society. The people on the other side of America's borders are not second or third class human beings without dignity. They are our brothers and sisters, too, who share a common Creator. And lest we forget, we cannot wall off our economy from all immigrants because the economy needs them to operate.

The American Dream should not be a gated community. All people should have the right to pursue and possess a piece of the Dream—the right to life, food, clothing, shelter, religious freedom of expression, rest, medical care, education and employment, as long as each is willing to work for it.

As Cain from the Old Testament discovered, we cannot escape and hide from the responsibility for being our brother's and sister's keeper. Solidarity must not become a feeling of vague compassion or shallow distress at the misfortunes of others, both here and abroad. Solidarity must remain a firm and pressing determination to commit oneself to the common good because we really are in this journey together.

At its core, the fundamental nature of the American Dream should never be contrary to the common good. In justice, the Dream cannot long endure unless it promotes the common good. The Dream's ability to sustain itself requires baseline social conditions that readily enable people from all walks of life to reach their God-given potential.

The Light of the Dream Lies within our Reach

Take heart, the Dream has not yet burned out. It can still be rekindled if we clearly see it for what it is and take immediate action. Despite one Mortgage Company's proprietary claim of being, "The Proud Sponsor of the American Dream," the American Dream has never confined itself to ownership of residential real estate.

The Dream is too splendid, too vast, to be confined to a narrow definition. Furthermore, Americans are beginning to see the light that makes itself known that the earnest pursuit of the fundamental Dream necessitates faith, moral values and transcendent truths.

The presidential election of 2004 noticeably revealed that the soul of America is thirsting for moral values—the one issue that mattered the most to many voters. That thirst is profound and prevalent—in our leaders, in the workplace, in our communities, and in our own homes. The election also made apparent that the so-called "religious right," was more often than not mainstream America.

Although many of our public institutions suggest that we are a secular nation, Americans are still a religious people. According to recent Gallup Polls, 90 percent of Americans believe in God. More revealing is the fact that 77 percent of Americans believe the overall health of the nation depends a great deal on the spiritual health of its people. George Gallup, director of the Gallup International Institute, recently said, "You cannot really understand America if you do not understand her spiritual underpinnings."

Enduring principles by which to live are in many cases tied to religious principles. In the mega-bestseller *"The 7 Habits of Highly Effective People,"* Stephen Covey shares his own personal conviction concerning the source of correct principles. "I believe that correct principles are natural laws, and that God, the Creator and Father of us all, is the source of them, and the source of our conscience." He goes on to add, "To the extent that we align ourselves with correct principles, divine endowments will be released within our nature in enabling us to fulfill the measure of our creation."

The fact is there are no new moral principles, habits or secret techniques of success to discover, although book publishers would have us believe the contrary. There are only enduring principles and eternal truths that are repackaged and marketed in countless ways each year.

Being highly effective in the present does not depend upon our turning the clock back in time. Rather, our effectiveness is found through reconnecting with those faithful guideposts for our journeys ahead. In particular, religious principles have the power to form effective habits, alter mindsets, and instill objective truths that testify to the greatness of God and the human person.

God intended us to prosper in what truly matters and to live courageously in the pursuit of worthwhile dreams. But if we think we can achieve the American Dream without help from God and others, then we can be assured that we are not realizing the American Dream. The reality is that realizing the Dream is far greater than our own individual efforts and what we may end up owning as a result of them.

Be assured, the radiance of the American Dream rests well within our reach. Still, if we are to succeed in what truly matters and preserve the Dream for future generations, we must be wary of *The Millionaire Fixation* as explored in the next chapter.

CHAPTER QUESTIONS

1. What is your definition of the American Dream?

2. Does achieving your dreams depend more upon spiritual capital or financial capital? Is it really money or in God we trust?

3. How can we achieve our life's purpose if we are primarily concerned with making money?

Living rich is having the liberty to pursue our dreams as our Creator intended. It is having the freedom to follow those inspired dreams that God has entrusted to us for the common good of all.

"It is not wrong to want to live better; what is wrong is a style of life presumed to be better when our actions are directed towards 'having' rather than 'being,' and which wants to have more, not in order to be more but in order to spend life in enjoyment as an end in itself."
—*Pope John Paul II*

2

THE MILLIONAIRE FIXATION

"For what does it profit a man to gain the whole world, and forfeit his soul?" —Mark 8:36

Fixations are usually not apparent or easy to admit in the moment. Intently focused on the matters at hand, we are often too busy in our daily pursuit to take notice of our attachment to the outcome. With hindsight, however, fixations frequently reveal themselves with much more clarity.

As the 1990s drew to a close, I recall beginning each day with a 6 a.m. workout at a nearby gym. The bull market was charging ahead, fueled by venture capital and the perceived bright future of the Internet's new-economy stocks. In those days, morning workouts were actually kind of fun.

Most days I would begin my routine with a half hour of cardiovascular exercise on the treadmill, while watching CNBC's *Squawk Box* on the television set overhead. Everywhere I looked people were working out and watching some type of financial program. There was electricity in the air surrounding the capitalization of the Internet and how much IPOs (Initial Public Offerings), like eToys, would appreciate on the first day of trading.

I would listen attentively as CNBC's Maria Bartiromo described market conditions before the opening bell. She often said, "Once again folks, it's all about technology as the sector is set to open higher." During those golden days, I would say to myself, "What an opportunity to be living and investing during the build-out of the Internet's infrastructure."

Even so, I never really believed in the dot.coms. I reasoned there was a gold-rush mentality surrounding the new-economy stocks and figured that most who "panned for gold" were sure to come up empty-handed. But the infrastructure, or backbone, to the Internet—now that was a different story. After all, during the 1849 California Gold Rush those entrepreneurs who supplied pickaxes and shovels made a healthy return.

With blue-chip companies like Dell, Cisco, Lucent Technologies, Oracle, Intel, Microsoft, AT&T, Sun Microsystems, Nokia, WorldCom, and a host of others, how could anyone miss over the long-term? These were real companies with solid earnings, viable business plans, and capable leaders. Besides, Wall Street pundits and analysts were adamant that we should be buying the stock of these types of companies as it was just the first inning.

A seven-year-old caller to CNBC wanted to know the outlook for Lucent Technologies, which is trading in the mid-sixties. Everyone on the program smiles and remarks how wonderful it is that a child is getting such an early start at building her financial acumen. Of course, they confidently tell her it is definitely a buy over the long-term.

I stop the treadmill and ask myself if anyone has the common sense to say to her—"Hey, kid, what are you doing calling us? Shouldn't you be in school, out playing, or watching cartoons? You're only seven."

As I stand motionless, I recall that when I was seven, my limited financial insight consisted of prematurely yanking out a baby tooth so the benevolent tooth fairy would grace me with 25 cents. I thought that was particularly shrewd thinking, as it was all the money I needed to buy a comic book and catch up with my superheroes, *Spiderman* and *Superman*.

I wipe the sweat from my face as I look around the gym. People are slurping their bottled water as the treadmills quickly turn underneath their feet. I whisper to myself, "Wow! We look just like Pavlovian rats running on our wheels, waiting for the next stimulus of pleasure from green up-arrows, as we mindlessly stare at the moving ticker tape on the TV screen."

Many of us were more physically fit on the outside than we were on the inside. Perhaps we were spending a lot more time at the gym than at our places of worship? I began to wonder, "Is this life for the body or the soul?"

I ask myself two daunting questions: "Am I merely a material being? Or am I an eternal soul that has temporary use of this material body?" As I think about the answer, I start feeling uncomfortable. I try to avoid the issue by quickly moving to the bicep machine and cranking out ten reps.

Let's Create Something versus *"Show Me the Money"*

As I watch my biceps in the mirror, which have gone nowhere in 20 years, I thought about an article I had recently read in *Forbes* about Silicon Valley. The writer told of a luncheon he had in Palo Alto with a forty-something CEO who said flat-out, "Ten million dollars is chump change…I don't know anyone who thinks one million, five million, or ten million is enough!" The article ends with some thoughts from a venture capitalist who says, "The newer people are motivated by wealth. It's troublesome. It's 'What's in it for me?' instead of 'Let's create something.'"

I ask myself, "If we are no longer interested in collectively creating something, then what's in store for America?" My mind is no longer on my workout as I leave the curl machine to begin tricep extensions. The well-known line from the movie, *Jerry McGuire*, "Show me the money," seems to be turning into a way of life.

Had engaging in virtuous, creative enterprises taken a back seat to accumulating economic wealth? So many people seemed fixated on the idea of becoming millionaires. They were trying to lasso the benefits of belonging to a club where America's affluent seemed to enjoy power, higher social status, and economic freedom.

Although there has always been a fascination with people of extraordinary wealth and power, there seems to be something different this time around. Yesterday's intrigue with marquee names such as Vanderbilt, Carnegie, and Rockefeller appears to have given way to a fixation on how to become more like Bill Gates, Donald Trump, and Warren Buffet. Further support of the allure included a growing number of top-rated TV shows and bestselling books endorsing the theme of becoming a millionaire.

Everyone Wanted to Become the Next *Millionaire Next Door*

Early in the new millennium, *Who Wants to Be a Millionaire?* quickly became our top-ranked TV show. Long gone were the days when shows like

The $25,000 Pyramid offered what seemed to be an outrageous amount of money to keep us tuning in. Night after night we religiously watched Regis Philbin and vicariously experienced the thrill of what it would be like to become an instant millionaire. Armed with the right answer to the final $1 million question, we each pictured ourselves as a gracious winner in front of a national audience.

In February 2000, we witnessed the marriage of two complete strangers on the *Who Wants to Marry a Multi-Millionaire?* TV show. That night, 22 million Americans watched a jazzed-up version of *The Dating Game* from the 1960s as fifty attractive bachelorettes competed for the top spot. For her efforts, the winner received a $35,000, three-carat wedding ring, and an all-expenses-paid honeymoon on a Caribbean cruise with her new multi-millionaire husband. Yet, when the ship docked, the honeymoon was over. Simply put, they were "two people who could not get along in real life."

Three years later, "reality TV" would present 20 single women jetting off to France on Fox's *Joe Millionaire*. Each one had been duped into believing that the bachelor was a millionaire. In real reality, he was a construction worker with an annual income of $19,000. And NBC's *For Love or Money* made it clear that a charming bachelor could not compete with $1 million dollars—the woman he erroneously chose for love picked the money instead.

At local convenience stores, people willingly stood in long lines and eagerly threw their hard-earned money away on an infinitesimal chance for the lottery's most recent jackpot. And why not? After all, somebody eventually was going to have that winning ticket and, in America, it could happen to you!

Then there were the day-traders who used options and margined accounts to place large bets on momentum stocks trying to time the market's next direction. Still others put up with jobs they really did not like so they could cash in on stock options. It was often the case that these people sacrificed their happiness, hoping their options would have significant value by the time they vested.

The majority of us, however, were intent on becoming affluent the old-fashioned way—sensibly, over time—and we became students devoted to the process. We made books like *The Millionaire Next Door* and *Rich Dad, Poor Dad* runaway bestsellers as we tried to catch glimpses of who the wealthy were and how they made their fortunes.

We also scoured magazines, trade publications, and other references for the keys to unlock the secrets of financial success. In October 1999, *Forbes* put out an issue titled, "The Billionaire Next Door." It revealed that of the then richest four-hundred Americans more than half were billionaires!

A new classification of wealth appeared to be emerging. New-sprung definitions for affluence and social status were published in *Forbes* as follows:

Classification	Income	Wealth
Superrich	$10 million+	$100 million+
Rich	$1–$10 million	$10 million–$100 million
Upper-Middle	$75,000–$1 million	$500,000–$10 million
Middle	$35,000–$75,000	$55,000–$500,000
Lower-Middle	$15,000–$35,000	$10,000–$55,000
Poor	$0–$15,000	$0–$10,000

The stock market had been on a tear for nearly two decades, with the P/E (price-to-earnings ratio) quadrupling from 8 in 1980 to 32 in 1999. Other well-respected magazines like *The Wall Street Journal's Smart Money* and *Newsweek* captured the growing sentiment of what the American Dream had become for many. They adorned their respective covers with "*RETIRE TEN YEARS EARLY—It's America's newest obsession!*" and "*The whine of '99— everyone is getting rich but me.*"

During the 1990s alone, the stock market increased by $10 trillion. Some people were making obscene amounts of money from new economy stocks, many of which did not have either profits or products.

Merrill Lynch's Henry Blodget was the most widely read analyst of the day. He needed only to predict that Amazon.com would have a price target of $400 someday, for the stock to be in great demand. Little did we know that Blodgett in private was scoffing about some of the very stocks he was recommending to the public.

Most other analysts on Wall Street also were bullish too and hardly a bear could be found. Prudential Securities' technical analyst, Ralph Acampora, as late as March 2000, was pounding the table with the misguided belief that the NASDAQ would hit the 6000 mark by the end of the year. Even the

Federal Reserve Chairman, Alan Greenspan, reassured Congress, "Beneficent fundamentals will provide the framework for continued economic progress well into the new millennium."

Founders of Internet start-up companies like Global Crossing's Chairman, Gary Winnick, made billions of dollars in a matter of months. John D. Rockefeller, on the other hand, worked 25 years to make his first billion. The brightest minds graduating from our universities were frantically developing business plans to secure venture-capital financing for new-economy companies in order to cash in on the bonanza. Who had time to pursue a conventional MBA? In those days, two years seemed like a lifetime.

"Having" More Rather Than "Being" More

Underneath the shiny exterior of material gain things just did not seem to be quite right. A growing number of investors were counting on double-digit returns for the long-term and expecting to retire by the time they were 40. Still others, who were already retired, focused primarily on how to protect their financial wealth from unwarranted creditors and the obtrusive reach of Uncle Sam.

As an advisor who routinely helped others achieve their financial objectives, I found myself thinking of singer Peggy Lee's famous line, wondering "Is that all there is?" It became clear to me that many of us had lost touch with our reason for being and the founding spirit that has made America a great nation.

Pope John Paul II put it well for me when he said, "It is not wrong to want to live better; what is wrong is a style of life presumed to be better when our actions are directed toward 'having' rather than 'being,' and which wants to have more, not in order to be more but in order to spend life in enjoyment as an end in itself."

CHAPTER QUESTIONS

1. If you approached each day as an eternal soul that had temporary use of a body, would you live it differently? If so, how?

2. Are you more driven by "creative enterprise" or by "show me the money?" Is your answer in line with your life's purpose?

3. Is "having more" of greater importance than "being more?" Are you seeking to spend your life in enjoyment as an end in itself?

*Lasting Wealth is more than becoming a millionaire;
it is becoming who God intended you to be.*

"If we are to win this war
—sure to last into our children's futures—
we have to reweave the rituals of God and
country into our institutions. We can't expect
our children to understand and defend a
heritage they have never been given."
—Kathleen Parker

3

THE PARTY ENDS BADLY
AS THE BUBBLE BURSTS

"Trust in the Lord with all you heart,
and on your own intelligence rely not;
in all thy ways be mindful of him,
and he will make straight your paths."
—*Proverbs 3:5–6*

In some cases, the greed and envy that accompanied the chase for material gain were getting out of hand. During the late 1990s, it was not uncommon to read about a Wall Street analyst who had received an anonymous death threat from an enraged stockholder after downgrading a particular stock.

A few hundred yards from where I lived in Atlanta, day-trader Mark Barton, who lost $105,000 in the stock market in a little over a month and $500,000 altogether, went on a shooting spree. He took nine lives and left thirteen people wounded at several day-trading firms.

Barton was described as a typical nice guy who was always on the phone with his kids. Most likely he was just an extreme example of someone who was emotionally unstable and finally snapped under pressure. On the other hand, a computer-generated suicide note found in Barton's apartment rationally touched upon the dark side of materialism—"I have come to hate this life in this system of things. I have come to have no hope."

Many were too busy enjoying the party to notice the telling signs of its coming demise. Some even took the party to new extremes. Ex-Tyco International CEO, Dennis Kozlowski, used company funds to throw a million-dollar party for his wife on the Italian island of Sardinia. A memo from a Tyco employee detailed the festivities of the party: "The guests come into the pool area, the band is playing, they are dressed in elegant chic. Big ice sculpture of Michelangelo's David, lots of shellfish and caviar at his feet. A waiter is pouring Stoli vodka into the statue's back so it comes out its penis into a crystal glass."

Our Financial World Changed

The party ended badly in March 2000 as the bubble burst. Although it was not the Federal Reserve's job to burst the stock market's bubble, its policy of tightening short-term interest rates in 1999 and 2000 cannot be defended otherwise. Besides rising oil prices, there had been little or no evidence of inflation.

After the bubble burst, my morning trips to the gym noticeably changed. There were still a few loyal watchers of CNBC but Bartiromo's pre-market mantra was altogether different. Post-bubble she began many opening bells by telling us—"Well folks, technology and telecom shares are once again preparing to take it on the chin today." Over the next few years, the S&P 500 would be cut in half, and the once high-flying NASDAQ was twice cut more than half.

Altogether the market, at its 2002 low, lost some $8.5 trillion—the worst bear market since the Great Depression. And high-priced market pundits like Goldman Sach's Abby Joseph Cohen, a perennial bull, lost enormous credibility. In the post-bubble environment, stock analysts downgraded the very stocks and sectors that, not long before, they said were strong buys.

For many investors it was an agonizing time. I often thought of the cute voice of the seven year old who called about Lucent and was told it was a no-brainer as a long-term buy. In the fall of 2002, Lucent traded for under $1 per share, having lost over 99 percent of its value. But Lucent had a lot of company, during those days, as a hungry bear devoured many blue-chip stocks during its reign on Wall Street.

There were far fewer green arrows along the ticker tape in the post-bubble environment, and many days it just looked like a sea of red. It was astounding how long it took to earn money, and how quickly it could slip through your fingers. I recall the guy on the treadmill next to me saying, "Can't we watch something besides CNBC? For God's sake, this is a gym! You guys ever heard of ESPN?"

Creating Something May Require Us to Risk It All

A few people cashed out handsomely during the Internet's boom without creating anything at all. Others who had the courage to create something in the new economy were in some cases left empty-handed.

For example, eToys's founder and CEO, Toby Lenk, at one time was worth almost $1 billion on paper. However, he wanted to create and run a respectable business so he didn't sell any of his stock. Under Lenk's committed leadership, eToys became a profitable company and the third most-trafficked e-commerce website on the Internet.

Those impressive results meant little, however, to callous investment bankers who jumped ship when the Internet sector started heading south. Having relied on the promises of its financial backers, eToys was in the middle of a significant build-out and could not recover once investment bankers pulled the plug.

Toby lost all of his equity in eToys and walked away with only a modest salary after running the company for four years. Some said Lenk was foolish for not having taken most of his chips off the table far sooner as many others in his situation had done. But I think Toby Lenk was rich in character—he endeavored to create something worth believing in.

In some key ways, Lenk was just like many Americans before him who risked everything for their dreams. Many successful entrepreneurs, like Wal-Mart founder Sam Walton, risked it all more than once. Even though they could have just cashed in, they continued forging ahead. They had bigger dreams and believed they could make a greater difference by not sacrificing their long-term vision for short-term gain.

9/11 Was a Reality Check

Wall Street's woes were put in perspective during those sobering events that occurred the morning of September 11, 2001—the day the War Against Terrorism began. I recall a *USA Today* story describing American Airlines Flight 11, with ninety-two people onboard, hitting Tower One at 8:45 a.m. Minutes before the horrific impact, Norbert Pete, 42, had just made his first delivery in Tower One.

As the building shook violently and a deafening explosion was still ringing in his ears, Pete, who was near a 79th-floor elevator, quickly pressed the down button. When the door opened, a blast of hot air and smoke shot out from the shaft. He thought of his seven-month-old son. "Okay, God, it's up to you and me now. You've got to help me get through this," he prayed as he headed for the stairs.

Brave firefighters made their way up congested stairs, hauling hoses and other heavy equipment. Upon seeing the firefighters, people began to cheer and applaud not knowing these same men would all be dead in a matter of minutes. "Keep going down," the firefighters yelled as they marched up into the towering inferno. A woman remarked how good-looking they were— such fine young men.

Pete encountered the firefighters and offered to help. He made his way to safety only after a commander thanked him and shouted, "Get the hell down the stairs!"

In the South Tower, executive Robert DeAngelis started down from the 91st floor but returned after hearing everything was okay. He called his wife, Denise, and told her that he did not believe what he was seeing—"My God, people are jumping from the windows of the North Tower." Denise screamed on the other end of the line, "Robert, there is another plane coming! Get out of that building!" She watched helplessly as United Airlines Flight 175, carrying sixty-five people, slammed into Tower Two at 9:03 a.m. near her husband's floor. The phone went dead.

It is hard to imagine ever being put into a situation where you would have to choose one of two dreadful ways to die—in a fire burning at more than 1,000 degrees or by jumping from an unfathomable height. It is difficult to see a loving God in the midst of a great injustice, and the suffering and loss of thousands of innocent human lives.

Perhaps there is comfort in remembering the selflessness of the seven crew members and thirty-three passengers on United Flight 93, which crashed near Shanksville, Pennsylvania that same day. They were all strangers who began a routine flight, yet bound together with a self-sacrificing courage that began with the words, "Let's roll!"

The terrorists were deliberate in two of their chosen targets—New York's Twin Towers. To the terrorists, the Towers symbolized America's prideful arrogance of might and wealth in a world of economic disparity. To many of us, they represented the freedom of capitalism and a long line of Americans who dared to reach for a part of the American Dream.

But what struck me most about 9/11 was that Americans all across the land looked to God and their country for reassurance. For a time, people were markedly kinder to one another. There were no Republicans or Democrats for the moment, just Americans banded together for a common cause. Out of tragedy came selflessness reminiscent of America's founding spirit.

We showed great compassion toward others. Many donated money while others gave blood in the vain hope that more people would be found alive. We bought American flags everywhere they were sold and proudly displayed them from our homes and cars. America's leaders asked us to pray, and we responded like "One nation under God."

President George W. Bush addressed us from the Oval Office on the evening of 9/11 and said, "Tonight I ask for your prayers for all those who grieve, for the children whose worlds have been shattered, for all whose sense of safety and security have been threatened. And I pray that they will be comforted by a power greater than any of us, spoken of the ages in Psalm 23: 'Even though I walk through the valley of the shadow of death, I fear no evil for You are with me.'"

It is, however, only natural for us to reach out for God, country, and each other in the face of terrorist led tragedies or natural disasters like hurricanes or tsunamis. Yet, our greatest challenge going forward is to maintain that selfless spirit as we interact with each other in everyday life.

Our Ailing Institutions

As we looked hopefully to our nation's institutions for comfort after 9/11, it was obvious that some had become weak from years of neglect. The moral sustenance our institutions once provided had declined. Should we have been surprised? After all, we had progressively excluded God from our public domain and further distanced ourselves from the patriotic principles that once bonded us together as a nation.

After the terrorist attack, syndicated columnist Kathleen Parker recalled watching the memorial service at the National Cathedral on television. As the audience sang, "The Battle Hymn of the Republic," she joined in from the back of the family room. It occurred to her that her son, as well as most American children, didn't know the words to that song or a half-dozen other patriotic tunes that are imprinted on older Americans' brains. In that moment, it dawned on her that many young people today have been and are being dramatically influenced by godless institutions within a culture that has lost touch with the importance of patriotism.

Be that as it may, virtues and values need to be continually nurtured if they are to be responsibly passed from one generation to the next. Parker writes, "If we are to win this war—sure to last into our children's futures—we have to reweave the rituals of God and country into our institutions. We can't expect our children to understand and defend a heritage they have never been given."

In our quest for material wealth, we have increasingly lost touch with our foundation and have misplaced meaningful values that promoted a sense of community and common identity. Today, although we continue to enjoy a level of personal independence and affluence unprecedented in America's history, it has come at a cost. There has been a decisive deterioration of our relationships with each other as well as with our Creator. According to a Gallup Poll completed the day before September 11th, 55 percent of the citizens of the wealthiest, most powerful nation in history were "dissatisfied with the way things were going in America."

To a large degree, we are living off the waning spiritual capital entrusted to us by previous generations. In the long-run, however, our institutions cannot thrive apart from the virtuous principles upon which they were created. The dignity of individual human beings and the common good must always be the cause and end of every institution.

A Wake-Up Call for a Better Future

The terrorist attack of 9/11 was certainly painful, but even more misfortune was soon to follow. Enron, the sixth largest company in America, shocked the nation as it scandalously imploded and became the biggest case of consumer fraud in American history. While September 11th and massive corporate scandals have not dispelled the emotions of greed and envy from occurring, it can serve as a wake-up call for us about the direction in which our nation may well be heading.

After another morning workout, I noticed a front-page story in *The Atlanta Journal-Constitution*. Ironically, it was about another day-trader, Fred Herder, who had been wounded in Mark Barton's shooting spree of 1999. While Herder, a retired chef, managed to survive the attack, a bullet remained lodged in his back that doctors could not remove without risking danger to his spine.

In the article, Herder's ex-wife described him as a guy who did not like to spend freely. She said, "He never paid credit card interest; he researched cars for months before buying one; and he believed Christmas should be limited to only one nice gift."

Herder, who had been given a second chance at life, however, returned to day-trading at the very same firm he had sued for failing to provide adequate security during the Barton episode. Tragically, within a matter of months, Herder's life ended in much the same way Barton's did. Herder's suicide email to his girlfriend read:

My dear Shirley!

As you know by now, my life came to an end and I lost in excess of $400,000 in the last three years. Most people who "day trade" lose money. I never had the necessary discipline, and most of the time I took on too much risk. Nobody else but myself is at fault. Certainly, I should have quit a long time ago when I still had some money left, but I was determined to make this work. I did not want to go back to the very stressful business world as an employee... I could write a book about what went wrong in my life but that would not help you understand my action.

To some extent, the heartrending events of the last few years changed our world and the way we view it. They also presented us with windows of opportunity to uproot our complacency and to begin anew, provided we had the courage to act in accordance with the wisdom forged from difficult times.

Be that as it may, life for the most part would return to normal in due course. The bursting bubble did not destroy the economic resolve of the American people. The stock market would make a strong recovery and real estate would develop a bubble of its own.

Millionaire books soon recaptured their place atop the bestsellers list because the bottom-line is that getting "rich" is still a major aspiration for most of us. Type in the word "millionaire" into Amazon's search engine and you will discover over 1,300 "millionaire" books to choose from.

Still, if we are to reconnect with our country's founding spirit and our reason for being we cannot afford to lose sight that our primary purpose is to love God and others as ourselves.

CHAPTER QUESTIONS

1. What are you willing to risk for your dreams? Is the potential price to be paid worth paying both here and in the hereafter?

2. What things have you placed your trust in only to have your bubble burst?

3. In what ways is life different for you after the bubble burst and the events of 9/11? What can be learned from those calamities that will help us live and plan for a better future?

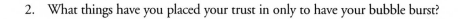

Lasting Wealth is found in having the courage to act with the wisdom forged from difficult times.

"There can be only two basic loves:
the love of God unto the forgetfulness of self,
or the love of self unto the forgetfulness
and denial of God."
—St. Augustine

4

OUR REASON FOR BEING

"A new command I give you: Love one another.
As I have loved you, so you must love one another."
—John 13:34

Throughout history, man has looked to God and religion to answer fundamental questions regarding the human condition. Who am I? What is the purpose of life? Where should I go to find true happiness? For most of the Christian era, people believed that God and salvation were humanity's primary concerns. What was accomplished and possessed during one's lifetime was secondary to living life in accordance with godly principles and virtues.

In contemporary times, however, many of us have been looking far less to God and religion to answer those fundamental questions. What we do for a living, consume, and possess essentially define who we are today. Psychoanalyst Eric Fromm observed of our modern era—"Today, life is strictly separated from religious values in that it is devoted to striving for material comforts, where man's happiness lies in the satisfaction of consuming."

Mark Twain took it one step further and cautioned that mankind's purpose and concept of God dramatically changed in the modern era: "What is the chief end of man?—to get rich. In what way?—dishonestly if we can; honestly if we must. Who is God, the one and only true? Money is God. Gold and Greenbacks and Stock—father, son and ghosts of same—three persons in one; these are the true and only God, mighty and supreme…"

God's Role and God's Concerns

Today, many of us turn to God as a resource to help us achieve personal success. But how many of us turn to our Creator for the grace to live in accordance with selfless virtues? With consideration of God's paramount role in our lives and in all of creation, we are led to ask a few more poignant questions.

Does God fret about how financially successful we can become? Or is our Creator more likely to be concerned that we often lack faith and may not have enough love in our hearts for others? Should God be overly troubled if we do not retire 10 years early because of a corporate downsizing or a bear market? Or is it more likely that God may be offended by our materialistic actions if we make financial wealth our main goal, and seek happiness primarily from what we consume and possess? At the end of our earthly days, will God be more concerned with our store of material goods or the state of our souls?

In our efforts to answer these questions truthfully, many of us may painfully discover that the spiritual life we desire is inconsistent with our attitude toward the material world in which we live. Historian Arnold Toynbee observed, "...religious founders disagreed with each other in the pictures of what is the nature of the universe, the nature of spiritual life, the nature of ultimate reality. But they all agreed in their ethical precepts.... They all said with one voice that if we made material wealth our paramount aim, this would lead to disaster."

In our western culture, we need to put into perspective just how much we consume in comparison to the rest of the world. Recently, a United Nations Development Program study found that 26 percent of the world's people in high-income countries, such as the United States, consume 86 percent of the world's goods.

The $8 billion annually that Americans spend on cosmetics could provide basic education to the world's poor—with $2 billion left over. The $11 billion Europeans spend on ice cream nearly equals the $12 billion cost of universal access to water and sanitation. Imagine what could be done for humanity with the hundreds of billions spent worldwide on cigarettes and alcohol. Sadly, the report concluded that it is not likely the world could arrive at an equitable distribution of goods and services. Unless drastic measures are implemented millions of people will die needlessly during the next decade, according to the United Nations.

The United Nations Environment Program also released a recent report that predicted more than half of humanity will be living with water shortages, depleted fisheries, and polluted coastlines within 50 years because of a world-wide water crisis. Over 90 percent of the severe problems are in developing nations where they have poor irrigation and water supply practices due to impoverished economic conditions.

Does God really provide blessings of economic assistance to some while withholding them from others? Or is it more likely that we need to take more responsibility for the economic inequality that exists in our world today? Have we loved well if we have not given well? The New Testament reminds us, "But whoever has the world's goods and beholds his brother in need and closes his heart against him, how does the love of God abide in him?" (1 John 3:17)

Not long ago *USA Today* published a distressing story of an Ethiopian family. They were forced to leave their village because an unrelenting drought had nearly exhausted the stores of water and food. The family of five had to trek through 110-degree heat across a desert to reach a tiny settlement where thousands of people clamored for the donated food being handed out by local officials.

During the journey, the family lost their one-year-old son on the first night, the three-year-old daughter the next day, and the two-year-old son that night. With each death, the family had little choice but to dig a simple hole, chant a prayer, and move on. When they reached the settlement, only the two parents and the donkey were still alive. They secured two bags of grain and began their three-day walk home—past the little mounds of their deceased children. The father, a very religious man, said only, "I suppose Allah thought their time had come."

Was it really their time, or was this a painful example of humanity's unwillingness to share? Mankind's progress has been so profound in so many different aspects of life. But as President Franklin Roosevelt once said, "The test of our progress is not whether we add more abundance to those who have much; it is whether we provide enough for those who have too little."

God Is Love

Many religions, including all Christian denominations, agree that God is love. "The one who does not know love does not know God, for God is love" (1 John 4:8). What often separates us, however, is found basically in the manner and theology of expressing that common belief.

Philosopher Bernard Lonergan said, "All religious experience at its roots is an experience of an unconditional and unrestricted being in love." Our Creator is the source of all love from which we draw our supply. God loves divinely and unconditionally—not humanly and conditionally. The obvious virtue being extolled by God and religion is love. So what is love?

Pope Benedict XVI in his first papal teaching letter *(God is Love)* poetically expressed that love is central to the Christian faith and is not a result of an ethical choice or a lofty idea, but results from an encounter with God. Love comes from God and unites us to God, where love of God and love of neighbor are inseparable. The Pope further acknowledged that "love" is a single reality, but has different dimensions at different times.

C.S. Lewis's *The Four Loves* offered four Greek words for the different dimensions of love: *Storge*—affection for things; *Philia*—friendship or brotherly love; *Eros*—romantic love; and *Agape*—charity or Divine love.

In our contemporary culture, we love that special person who causes our heart to race. We are continually bombarded with romantic books, movies, and TV shows that drive home the message that love is a magical feeling of affection.

For example, ABC's *The Bachelor* and *The Bachelorette* help promote the notion that true love can somehow be manufactured through physical attraction and surreal dates with a flock of willing suitors. Some of us may spend a lifetime searching for that special someone to arouse that feeling of passion or affection within us. Still others may end marital relationships, entered into under the promise of "until death do us part," primarily because that feeling is gone.

Aside from that romantic someone, we generally love our children, parents, siblings, pets, and a few close friends. In addition, we often love and have a strong affection for what we can buy and consume—we love big homes, new cars, stylish clothes, fine foods, exciting entertainment, and exotic vacations, to name but a few.

The Bible says, "Do not love the world or the things in the world. If any one loves the world, the love of the Father is not in him" (1 John 2:15–17). Yet, advertisers spend billions of dollars each year directly or indirectly telling us that if we buy their products or services, we will secure greater love for ourselves or others.

Selfless Love Is Easy Only in Theory

Rarely does the western world's definition of love mention the word God, nor does it imply that to love means to live with a charitable heart where we act out of concern for others. Jesus gave us a daunting commandment— "Love each other as I have loved you." But how many of us today love our neighbors to the extent of laying down our lives and possessions for them?

To love well is one of life's greatest challenges. With over 50 percent of marriages failing, it is obvious that many of us find it difficult to love even at home. Journalist G. K. Chesterton was right when he said, "It is not that Christianity hasn't been tried and found wanting. It has been, and found difficult."

For over two thousand years, Jesus' countercultural call for "love" has challenged billions of followers to take up their cross daily; to die to self; to act sacrificially; to turn the other cheek, to care for one's enemies, to forgive those who have trespassed against them; and to put their trust solely in God and not in the things of this world.

Although we may sincerely wish for warm feelings of faith, the true measure of faith is found in times of adversity. In the end, love is a choice and a decisive act. Love should not be based on how we feel since feelings can vary. Rather, love emanates from having a relationship with God and from our will which controls our actions. St. Augustine put it well when he said—"There can only be two basic loves: the love of God unto the forgetfulness of self, or the love of self unto the forgetfulness and denial of God."

CHAPTER QUESTIONS

1. How do you define love? Is it a feeling? A decision? An act? To meet your definition, what should matter the most for you to accomplish each day and over a lifetime?

2. In what ways, if any, does God determine those who have (materially) and those who do not have? In what ways, if any, does mankind make those same determinations?

3. Responding to the call to love often requires sacrifice—can we love well without giving to others?

If we have loved well then we will have lived a rich life.

"Give enough money to your kids
so they can do anything, but not enough
so they can do nothing."
—Warren Buffet

5

MONEY CAN'T BUY ME LOVE

*"...for though one may be rich,
one's life does not consist of possessions."*
—Luke 12:15

In the 1960s, the Beatles sang, "Can't Buy Me Love." The song embodied the simple truth that just because you have money does not mean you can buy love. For those who have attained financial wealth, has their ability to love been enhanced or hindered in the process of acquiring and possessing riches? To help answer that question, we need to look at a few of America's wealthiest individuals whose stories have endured over the decades.

Legacies of Great Possessions with Little Love Passed On

The first three examples of extraordinary financial achievement were truly exceptional businesspeople. Each person was the richest man or woman in America at that time. Sadly, however, they all left undersized legacies of love.

Cornelius Vanderbilt was the wealthiest industrialist of the Gilded Age. He accumulated extraordinary financial wealth by providing transportation. His first fortune was ultimately built with the steamboats that handled roughly 75 percent of America's commerce as they traveled through New York's harbors. A subsequent fortune was made by investing in railroad stocks and consolidating New York's rail lines.

Like other successful businessmen of that era, he was tough and often took matters into his own hands. Vanderbilt once said, "My God, you don't suppose you can run a railroad in accordance with the statutes of New York." On another occasion, he told a troublesome competitor, "I won't sue you for the law is too slow. I'll ruin you!"

Mark Twain wrote to Vanderbilt, who was never known for his philanthropy, and recommended that he do one worthy act before it was too late. Mainly due to the insistence of his second wife, a 33-year-old cousin from Alabama, Vanderbilt, near the end of his life, gave $1 million to a small southern college that was renamed after him.

At his death in 1877, he was the richest man in America with an estate worth more than $100 million—more money than there was in the U.S. Treasury. He left no money to charity, paid no estate taxes, and even though he had thirteen children, he bequeathed 90 percent of his estate to his eldest son, William Henry. Remarkably, the son doubled the family fortune within seven years.

Vanderbilt's deathbed wish was, "Keep the money together and keep the New York Central our road." Yet the Vanderbilt empire was dramatically weakened over the next two generations due to lavish spending, family lawsuits, and subdivisions among grudging heirs.

In the end, the Vanderbilts were unable to keep the money together, and they lost the New York Central. When eldest son William Henry was asked by a reporter whether the railroads should be run for the public benefit, he replied, "The public be damned." At that point, the Vanderbilts lost a lot of the public's respect and admiration as well.

Gathering at Vanderbilt University in 1973 for the first family reunion, less than 100 years after Cornelius's death, not even one of his 120 descendents was a millionaire. The Vanderbilts lived out the adage often heard regarding wealth: "The first generation makes money, the second generation holds the money, the third generation spends the money, and the fourth generation starts over."

Hetty Green was the richest woman in America and perhaps one of the most detested. Known as the "Witch of Wall Street," she became a player in the financial markets shortly before the beginning of the Civil War. It was a time when Wall Street was for men only.

In remarkable fashion, she turned a $1 million inheritance into $100 million. Her investment philosophy was simple, yet potent, "I don't much believe in stocks. I never buy industrials. Railroads and real estate are the things I like. Before deciding on an investment, I seek out every kind of information about it. There is no secret in fortune making. All you have to do is buy cheap and sell dear, act with thrift and shrewdness, and be persistent."

Although Hetty was in many ways a financial genius, she was also an unscrupulous and uncompassionate businesswoman. But most of all, she was an implausible miser. On one occasion, she spent half the night looking for a two-cent stamp that had fallen off a letter. On another, she carelessly took a crowded street car to make an enormous deposit in bearer bonds. When her bankers questioned her on why she took such a risk and chose not to take a private carriage, she responded, "A carriage indeed! Perhaps you can afford to ride in a carriage but I cannot."

Spending a great deal of time on Wall Street and in greater New York, Hetty did everything she could to avoid being considered a resident since she did not want to be subject to taxation. She resorted to staying in rooming houses and cheap hotels, and often used an empty desk at her bank as her office. Perhaps the most pitiful example of her tightwad manner was when she refused to seek medical attention for her son's leg, considering a visit to the doctor to be too expensive. Regrettably, her son had to have his leg amputated.

If *Forbes 400* had existed when Hetty died, she would have comfortably been within the top twenty. Nevertheless, her millions had largely been stockpiled away where they simply collected interest and accumulated dust. Although she left no money to charity, her legacy has not been forgotten. She remains listed in the *Guinness Book of World Records* as the "Most Miserly Woman in the World."

When **John Paul Getty** discovered the largest oil reserve in the world in Saudi Arabia, he established himself as the world's richest man. Yet, for Getty and his family, his money brought greater problems than it could solve.

Until the age of 64, Getty remained virtually unknown to the public; however, he became an international figure when a Paris gossip columnist leaked to *Time* magazine word of Getty's inordinate wealth. As Getty became better known as a public figure, the word cheapskate did not quite do justice for some who encountered him. For example, if you wanted to make a call from his home, you had to use a pay phone. If you stayed for dinner, he determined your worth beforehand and served you accordingly.

To the man who discovered the largest oil reserve in the world, he paid a meager $1,200 a month for six months and then cut him off. In a tragic family incident, he refused to pay the ransom to his grandson's kidnappers, the Italian Mafia, even after they sent the grandson's bloodied ear in the mail to show they meant business. When Getty finally acquiesced and loaned his son $1 million dollars as a part of the ransom price, he promptly charged the son interest.

Getty was married and divorced five times. Of his four sons who reached adulthood, only one survived relatively unharmed. One committed suicide, and one became a drug-addicted recluse before eventually finding new life in philanthropy. The third had to bear the life-long stigma of being disinherited in childhood because his mother had negotiated such a tough divorce with Getty.

When he died, Getty left a mere pittance for twelve women who had befriended him, each one believing she would be the lucky one to receive a ticket to a life of luxury. The bulk of Getty's remaining estate was left as a memorial to himself in the form of a bequest to the Getty Trust, the centerpiece of which is the Getty Museum.

During the construction of the world's most expensive museum, Getty even refused to pay for the museum director's electric pencil sharpener, threatening to fire him for such extravagance. Aside from contributing to the arts, Getty's legacy is rooted, above all, in oil and the money it produced. Unfortunately, his billions brought little in the way of love to others or himself.

Selfless Philanthropy or Selfish Promotion?

Our next two examples of extraordinary financial wealth are from the same era, and they may well be America's most noted philanthropists. They had tarnished images, but humanity still owes them a great debt of gratitude for their generosity. It will forever be debated how much of their philanthropy was done out of love and how much was well-timed self-promotion to improve public perception.

Andrew Carnegie fought his way out of the slums of Pittsburgh to amass a great financial fortune. He invested in rail cars, telegraph communications, oil, and steel bridges. Just after the Civil War had ended, at 33, he was worth $400,000 (nearly $5 million in today's dollars) and had a guaranteed annual income of $50,000 (practically $600,000). Nevertheless, he was troubled by his wealth and wrote a letter to himself promising that he would stop working in two years and pursue a life devoted to education, writing, and philanthropy— "To continue much longer overwhelmed by business cares…must degrade me beyond hope of permanent recovery." Yet like many others of great financial wealth, Carnegie did not leave the game when his two years were up.

In many ways, Carnegie was a Jekyll and Hyde. He amassed a fortune by crushing his competitors and exploiting his workers. He paid his steelworkers a miserly $2.50 a day for working twelve hours a day, seven days a week. He also used drastic methods to break unions when his workers united to strike against intolerable working conditions. Surprisingly, he championed philanthropy by giving away the vast bulk of his wealth.

Carnegie, an atheist, espoused some impressive views on philanthropy in *The North American Review* in 1889 in an article titled, "The Gospel of Wealth." Carnegie viewed the accumulation of wealth in the hands of a few as a very good thing. He was a Social Darwinist who believed in natural selection and survival of the fittest. On the other hand, Carnegie also believed that a man of great wealth should "become the sole agent and trustee for his poorer brethren, bringing to their service his superior wisdom, experience, and the ability to administer—doing for them better than they would or could do for themselves."

Carnegie was adamantly opposed to leaving wealth to family members— even to the first son—as was common practice at the time. He stated that "great sums bequeathed more often work for the injury than for the good of the recipients." He added, "The parent who leaves his son enormous wealth generally deadens the talents and energies of the son and tempts him to lead a less useful and less worthy life than he would otherwise."

Carnegie further said, "A rich man who dies rich dies in disgrace." Therefore, he was very much against waiting until death to leave wealth for public uses. He believed that the community in the form of the state should not be deprived its proper share. He felt that by taxing estates heavily at death, the state marks its condemnation of the selfish millionaire.

When he sold Carnegie Steel to J.P. Morgan in 1901 for about $400 million, Carnegie was the richest man in the world. Yet, by the time of his death in 1919, he had given away over $350 million to public causes. Overall, Carnegie made good on his word and gave away roughly 90 percent of his fortune during his lifetime.

John D. Rockefeller became the richest man in the world and its first billionaire. Near the turn of the 20th century, his company, Standard Oil, controlled over 90 percent of the oil-refining industry. He sincerely believed God had given him his money and that the power to make money was a gift from God. Rockefeller saw it as his duty to make money and still more money—and to use the money he earned for the good of his fellow man.

He was impressed by Andrew Carnegie's *The Gospel of Wealth* and personally wrote Carnegie—"I would that more men of wealth were doing as you are with your money, but be assured your example will bear fruits, and the time will come when men of wealth will more generally be willing to use it for the good of others."

Rockefeller, a devoted Baptist, likewise became an outstanding philanthropist giving away more than $500 million to charitable endeavors before he died. The Rockefeller Foundation was established to "promote the well-being of mankind throughout the world" and was initially funded with $250 million. Today, it has a market value in excess of $3 billion and has given more than $2 billion to grantees worldwide.

But Rockefeller was often unscrupulous in his business practices, leading Senator Robert LaFollete to call him "the greatest criminal of the age." Cartoonists often portrayed Rockefeller as a hypocrite who would give away coins with one hand and steal bags of gold with the other. He frequently received kickbacks and drawbacks as he forced railroads to pay him a portion of the shipping fees they collected from his competitors. As he continued to increase market share within the oil-refining industry, he offered his competitors a simple choice—either receive stock in Standard Oil in exchange for their business or be put out of business.

Teddy Roosevelt viewed Rockefeller as the worst of the "malefactors of great wealth" and used the Sherman Antitrust Act to break up Standard Oil. Ironically, this served only to bring Rockefeller even greater riches as he was part owner of the 34 companies that originally made up Standard Oil.

Before he died, Rockefeller gave his son, John D. Rockefeller Jr., virtually all of his remaining fortune—close to $500 million—in order to avoid estate taxes. Junior, who had earlier suffered a nervous breakdown working in his father's business, spent the rest of his life in the role of the good steward. With philanthropic integrity, he did his best to dispense the money his father aggressively made.

Two Legacies Rich in Financial and Spiritual Capital

The next two examples of exceptional business success were people of great character and integrity. They made their mark not only by the tremendous financial wealth they amassed but, even more so, by the love they passed on to others.

J.C. Penney was reared to believe that life was to be lived in accordance with the Golden Rule (Luke 6:31)—"Do unto others as you would have them do unto you." Good intentions, however, do not always meet with good results. Penney failed at his first business when he lost a major account simply because he refused to throw in a bottle of whiskey as a premium. For his principled conduct, Penney lost his business and all that he had saved.

Prophetically, Penney next worked for the Golden Rule Store, which he eventually bought and renamed after himself. His dream was to provide low-priced quality goods all over America. To help reach his dream, he brought in thousands of junior partners all of whom were handpicked by J.C. on the basis of business ability and integrity.

All during his life, Penney had his share of troubles and relied heavily on his faith for strength. His wife died when he was just 35, leaving him a widower with two children. For a time, Penney battled against thoughts of suicide.

In 1929, his troubles continued when he pledged a large amount of Penney's stock, then worth $40 million, as collateral to obtain bank loans. The loans were not used to run his business but, instead, to further charitable endeavors at Penney farms. The farms essentially allowed the economically disadvantaged to have land of their own if they committed to working it for one year.

With the market crash of 1929 and the ensuing Depression, Penney stock dropped from $120 to $13, and J.C. lost everything. He was broke at age 56 and checked into a mental hospital. In time, his faith and a recovering economy provided a way for him to recapture his peace of mind and financial wealth.

As the world of retail modernized and competition intensified, J.C. Penney was still unwilling to compromise his values. In the 1950s, credit cards were introduced and were an instant boon to retailers, allowing customers to buy now and pay later. Penney, however, was against the use of credit cards and held firm on his cash-only policy until he was outvoted by the board. Penney's reasoning against allowing customers to use credit cards was simply that he thought it would result in people being oversold; a concept J.C. felt was not in keeping with the Golden Rule.

Milton Hershey became the real-life Willy Wonka of the chocolate factory that bore his name. En route to becoming the chocolate king, however, he failed at his first two businesses. His relatives, who had earlier been willing to support him, refused to provide additional support. Hershey, though, had a unique ability to rise up from failure. He lived in a time when chocolate was available only to the wealthy, but his dream was to make quality chocolate affordable to the masses. He believed that if you gave people quality, it was the best advertising and surest way to succeed.

Hershey used the proceeds from the sale of a caramel business to build a chocolate factory in what is now known as Hershey, Pennsylvania. But he built much more than just a factory. Like the care he put into making quality chocolate, he had quality homes constructed for his workers, while planning and developing a model community. In rapid succession, he built a bank, department store, school, churches, golf courses, zoo, an amusement park (the now famous Hersheypark), and a trolley system to transport workers. His own home, modest for a man of his means, was built near his chocolate factory.

While other businessmen were trying to survive the Depression, Hershey hired workers and expanded his business. Even though the community of Hershey had been well-established for years, he started a second building boom during the Depression. He kept men at work constructing a grand hotel, community building, theatre, sports arena, and a new office building for the chocolate factory. When the strikes that took place against nearly all industrialists eventually found their way to the Hershey factory, they were very short-lived because of Hershey's character and generosity. His ceaseless labor and concern for others were an inspiration to all who worked for him.

Hershey had a strong religious upbringing and believed that individuals were morally obligated to share the fruits of their labor. Deeply saddened that they were unable to have children of their own, Milton Hershey and his wife, Catherine, founded a school for orphan boys in 1909—the Milton Hershey School. In 1918, three years after the death of his beloved wife, Hershey gave his entire personal fortune to the school they had jointly envisioned and established. The 9,000-acre campus now houses, nurtures, and educates 1,300 boys and girls in social or financial need with the same goal today of teaching and developing their skills to prepare them for meaningful, productive, and successful lives. Hershey's personal convictions regarding wealth, his company, and the town he founded continue to be, like his chocolates, sweet experiences for many.

Today's Rich and the Legacies They Plan to Leave

What about some of today's richest people and their views on wealth? **Bill Gates,** the world's richest man, with an estimated wealth of about $50 billion, has said that he would give each of his children $10 million and donate the rest to charity. He thinks that too much inherited wealth is detrimental to one's well-being. In fact, Bill Gates recently said of being the world's richest man, "I wish I wasn't. There's nothing good that comes out of that."

Regarding charity, Gates and his wife, Melinda, have established the world's largest private foundation which has an endowment in excess of $29 billion. Among other things, the foundation focuses on improving health in the world's most vulnerable populations, equipping libraries in poorer communities with computers, and offering scholarships for ethnic and racial groups that are currently under-represented in higher education.

Investment magnate **Warren Buffet** has also voiced concern over the potential negative impact of his sizable estate on his children. As an investor who has accumulated his wealth looking for value, Buffet also believes a child's development is not facilitated by starting a 100-yard dash at the 50-yard line. In line with this thinking, he and his wife are reportedly planning to give away 98 percent of their estate to the Buffet Foundation, as well as to other charities. Buffet's philosophy is simple—"Give enough money to your kids so they can do anything, but not enough so they can do nothing."

Born Rich and Our Greatest Challenge

A recent documentary called "Born Rich" gives credibility to Buffet's prudent words. Created by Jamie Johnson of the Johnson & Johnson pharmaceutical fortune, this documentary discusses the burdens of inherited wealth from 10 young adults, including the likes of Ivanka Trump (daughter of Donald Trump) and Georgina Bloomberg (daughter of Michael Bloomberg). Johnson's motive in making the film was kindled by his concern that those with money refuse to talk about it and avoid thinking about wealth.

The lives of the very wealthy time and again prove, as the Beatles reminded us, money can't buy you love. Material wealth will never be able to satisfy the longing of the human soul. But material wealth provides those who have it greater choices, resources, and responsibility to effect positive change. Charity, philanthropy, and prudent economic investment can all be empowered to benefit mankind through material wealth.

More than any amount of money we may acquire, however, it is the spiritual capital we dispense and our concern for others that ultimately determine whether we have lived a rich life. But the biggest obstacle we face has nothing to do with money or what it can or cannot buy. Our greatest challenge is to learn how to love others and cultivate an eternal perspective related to wealth.

CHAPTER QUESTIONS

1. In what ways can striving for and having money hinder our ability to love others? In what ways can it enhance it?

2. All of the "wealthy" individuals mentioned in this chapter were materially rich. But what makes the difference in living a life that's rich?

3. Is it spiritually better to desire poverty over riches, riches over poverty, or neither? Why did you answer the way that you did?

More than any amount of money we may acquire, it's the spiritual capital we dispense that ultimately determines whether we have lived a rich life.

"A person finds identity only to the extent that he commits to something beyond himself, to a cause greater than himself."
—Victor Frankl

6

WE ARE NOT BORN LOVING

"The way we came to know love
was that he laid down his life for us;
so we ought to lay down our lives for our brothers."
—1 John 3:16

We are created in the image of a loving God, but we are not born loving. Rather, we are born narcissistic. Babies demand that their own wants and needs be satisfied first. They want to be held, fed, burped, changed, and entertained on demand.

As we get a little older, we want to play with and not share our toys, stay up as late as we want, and eat as many sugar-filled snacks as we like. But mostly we want to be the center of our parents' attention and have their world revolve around us. As we move into adulthood, many of us carry that need for special attention and recognition into our families, communities, and workplaces.

Learning to Love and Our Capacity for Love

The ability to respect ourselves and love others needs to be taught and nurtured through effective role modeling, instruction, and encouragement. It is from our institutions, starting with our family of origin, that we begin to learn that love, among other things, is sharing, commitment, forgiveness, and treating others compassionately.

As we move from adolescence into adulthood, we become more affected by other institutional forces such as religion, school, business, and government—each one playing a role in the development of our values. We will spend our entire lives learning how to grow in love, while dealing with an ego that continually says, "Hey, world, stop and look at me."

At the same time, we are created with a tremendous capacity to love. A few standouts like Gandhi and Mother Teresa have demonstrated remarkable acts of love and have exemplified our potential for it. They extended their acts of kindness beyond family members, close friends, and the so-called "desirable" people in society. Both of these courageous figures embraced unwanted strangers and even foes.

Gandhi and Mother Teresa were so successful at encouraging love, because they practiced it tirelessly. They did not withhold love, saving it for a particular group. They helped Hindus become better Hindus, Muslims become better Muslims, and Christians become better Christians. As Gandhi said of love as it relates to Christianity—"If Christians were to live their Christian lives to the fullest, there would not be one Hindu left in India."

EGO Means—*Edge God Out*

What keeps many of us from realizing our potential to generate love? Frequently, it is our ego—that childish voice that we carry within that is intent on convincing us of the way things should be. The ego stresses self-importance and wants to boast, judge, and condemn.

It is our ego that gets attached to ideals and notions of justice and fairness. It covets and becomes jealous as it wants to be rewarded and remembered. The ego believes that we are what we do, what we have, and what others think of us. Therefore, the ego needs to be recognized as special and stand apart. It continually looks up and down but never at the same level. It has to have the right physical attributes, degrees, and possessions to be on top.

The ego erroneously believes that more is better. It prevents us from understanding that if we are not grateful for what we have in our lives today, we probably will not be content with what we receive tomorrow. When we allow the ego to be in charge, we never seem to achieve enough to keep it satisfied for long. The novelty of whatever we have accomplished quickly diminishes and leaves us with an empty sense of longing. Life's journey and the station where "we will have finally arrived" constantly remain in the distance from the train we are riding.

The worst part of the ego, however, is that it can prevent us from connecting with God and the Divine Voice within. The ego is often like a thick cloud layer that keeps us from experiencing blue skies and the warmth of the sun. Although God, like blue skies, is always there, the ego can edge God right out of our lives.

Love, Marriage, and Children

Many of us begin to understand what love is only when we marry that special someone and give up the freedoms of being single. We discover that love is more than an affectionate feeling as we learn about commitment, forgiveness, and consideration of another person's wants and needs. No longer able to just do solely what pleases us, we need to search for things in common with our spouse and make reasonable compromises. Once married, what we do, how we spend or invest our money, and with whom we share our time all change in many ways as we focus on another and not just ourselves.

Bring children into the picture and we surrender more of our freedom. Yet, despite the inconveniences, both marriage and children can provide some of life's most joyful and fulfilling experiences. It is ironic that the loss of some of our personal freedom as a result of these commitments is what frees us to experience love. In fact, it is through commitment and concern for others that we encounter love and find our purpose. Victor Frankl said, "A person finds identity only to the extent that he commits to something beyond himself, to a cause greater than himself."

But is it possible to balance fulfilling careers and material wealth with happy marriages and well-adjusted children? Or, do we deceive ourselves by trying to serve too many masters?

I once traveled to the Greek Isle of Rhodes and met a local woman who did not allow her children to play with modern toys. This woman explained that she wanted them to use their imaginations and develop their ingenuity with "old-fashioned toys." When asked if she felt her children were deprived because of the lack of modern, "high-tech" toys, she responded with an emphatic, "No!"

Her philosophy was simple enough—"We provide food and shelter for our children, and they do not want for any necessities. But most of all, we spend a lot of quality time with our children and give them love. We think they are very rich!"

Are our children today being given the love and attention they need? Mother Teresa offered the following opinion—"Children have lost their place in the family. Children are very, very lonely! When children come home from school, there is no one to greet them. Then they go back to the streets. We must find our children and bring them back home.

Mothers are at the heart of the family. If the mothers are there, the children will be there too. Everybody today seems to be in such a terrible rush, anxious for greater development and greater riches. Children have very little time for their parents, and parents have very little time for their children and each other. So the breakdown of peace in the world begins at home."

Our Mission is to Love Others

What will become of our culture and the American Dream if we continue down a materialistic road that increasingly distances us from God, virtues, and the development of spiritual capital? What will be the fate of our nation should we reach the point where we no longer see others as part of ourselves? If we lose touch with our mission to love, will we be left as spiritually hollow people with narcissistic motives? History has shown, time and time again, that unchecked narcissism inevitably leads to a society's downfall.

History repeatedly demonstrates that long before any fallen society began to experience the effects of an external breakdown, there was first a gradual but deadly decay of love-centered values.

Will we have to endure the tormenting lessons the ancient Israelites experienced over and over again? Every time the Israelites focused on things that took them away from God and toward idols, they suffered terrible hardship. Contemporary America may be falling into the same trap; only our golden calf is the almighty dollar.

More than 200 years ago, a professor named Alexander Tytler wrote, "The average age of the world's greatest civilizations has been only 200 years." Moreover, Tytler pointed out that these civilizations all passed through similar cycles "… from bondage to spiritual faith, to great courage, to abundance, to selfishness, to apathy, to dependency and back to bondage," where the cycle begins again. Could it be that America is running on borrowed time?

If we are to understand our heritage and revitalize the American Dream, looking at our past can well provide answers as to how to live a better present. Therefore, it is important to revisit the birth of the Dream when America was first colonized in accordance with the Protestant work ethic. Likewise, it is essential to reexamine the crucial role that our institutional environment played in shaping the heritage entrusted to today's Retirees, Baby Boomers, and Generation Xers as variations of the Dream have been passed on from one generation to the next.

Though categorizing people into particular generations and making broad generalizations have limitations, it is, nevertheless, indicative of our changing values and the direction in which we are heading. Winston Churchill once said, "The farther backward you look, the farther forward you'll be able to see."

CHAPTER QUESTIONS

1. In what ways does your ego edge God out?

2. In what areas of your life have you made commitments that have allowed you to experience the freedom of love?

3. At this point in time, what is one thing that you can do today to better live out your capacity to love?

Lasting Wealth is found in the freedom of making worthwhile commitments to matters greater than oneself.

"For everyone had prepared a calling, which he
should profess and in which he should labor.
This calling was God's commandment to the
individual to work for the divine glory."
—Max Weber

7

THE RISE OF THE PROTESTANT WORK ETHIC

*"Whatever you do, do from the heart,
as for the Lord and not for others,
knowing that you will receive from the Lord
the due payment of the inheritance..."*
—Colossians 3:23–24

America is the financial capital of the world—the wealthiest nation on the planet. We have experienced tremendous prosperity since our humble beginnings some 230 years ago. Why?

Our prosperity can be explained in part by a society devoted to capitalism and the technological advancements of the Industrial Revolution. Capitalism, however, was born out of European philosophical thought while the Industrial Revolution was confined largely to Britain. These catalysts of economic and cultural change were more readily available to other parts of the world and could have been better exploited by other nations who were wealthier than America at the time. So why did capitalism blossom in America?

Unique to America was the combination of industrialism, capitalism, and limited government, all of which were energized by the resourceful spirit of the Protestant work ethic. Americans had considerable incentive and resources to build the greatest, freest country in the world, and they eagerly worked toward that end.

The Role of the Catholic Church Prior to Protestantism

Before the sixteenth century, Protestants were non-existent. At that time, today's oldest and largest Christian institution, the Catholic Church, dramatically influenced the spiritual and temporal affairs of Western civilization. This profound religious and cultural influence took flight in the fourth century after the fall of the Roman Empire, and was driven by the fact that the Church was the largest and most stable institution left remaining. The Catholic Church simply expanded its role to fill the power vacuum that had been formed.

For many centuries under the Church's guidance, economies were stable but grew very slowly. Most people worked as necessary to support only their immediate needs. Like the ancient Greeks before them, higher social classes viewed work as an activity to be avoided—left instead to serfs and peasants. For the most part, work was perceived as punishment by God for man's original sin and held no intrinsic value.

Aristocratic wealth was rooted in land and inherited affluence, while wealth that was earned through commerce or manufacturing was often frowned upon. Frequently, the best and brightest became priests and part of the Church's growing bureaucracy. At the same time, the Church was increasingly composed of those who were often better skilled as politicians and lawyers than as trained theologians.

Over the centuries, the Church dramatically increased its power base and became an integral part of governing states throughout Western Europe. It held a significant role in formulating the political policy that was ultimately carried out. Toward the end of the eleventh century, Pope Gregory VII recognized the potential pitfalls of this fusion between Church and State and tried to separate the two by making distinct the spiritual and temporal powers in the Episcopal office. But he was strongly opposed and died in exile.

In some ways, the Church had grown too powerful and had become too entrenched in states' affairs, making some of its leaders vulnerable to the corruption that misuse of power often brings. Power is never easy to use wisely or to relinquish—not even when the members of an institution are dedicated to carrying out the divine mission of spreading God's love.

The Most Important Religious Event to Affect America

In the early part of the sixteenth century, the most important religious event to ever affect America took place. The Protestant Reformation began when an Augustinian monk named Martin Luther openly challenged questionable practices within the Catholic Church.

Luther had no intention of founding a new church. He thought that by questioning and then openly challenging the Catholic Church on some of its doctrines and the Pope's supremacy that the Church would reform itself. Although the Church would make reformative efforts at a later date, it was not willing to alter its long-held traditions in order to appease Luther, and he was excommunicated.

One of the most far-reaching technological developments ever invented greatly aided the rise of Protestantism. Johannes Gutenberg's printing press of 1450 allowed the Bible to become available to the masses in their own language. This greatly shifted power away from the dominant Catholic Church and empowered the individual Christian.

Many Christians could now directly relate to God through their own Bible and no longer believed that they needed to proceed through the Catholic Church. This also allowed the Bible to be individually interpreted and today has resulted in a multitude of doctrines, denominations, and sects that attempt to explain the Bible from a variety of perspectives.

Pursue the Kingdom of God and Live Simply

Luther proclaimed the idea that God calls us to specific tasks. He set forth the notion that in answering your calling, you are to work hard and dedicate yourself to it. All callings were of equal spiritual dignity and glory to God was given by succeeding at your work.

Luther believed that people should always fill their lives with useful and sober occupations suitable for their state of existence. Believers were sanctioned to choose the employment or vocation in which they were to be most serviceable to God, not merely to themselves and their own economic well-being.

Luther interpreted the scriptures as a call to live very simply and, as taught by the Catholic Church, to address only one's basic needs. Material goods were to be used and accumulated only to sustain life and serve the Kingdom of God. Wealth was seen primarily as an opportunity to share with those who might be less fortunate.

Luther was hardly a capitalist and believed that the charging of interest should be prohibited when money was loaned. Furthermore, he professed that a man should only sell his goods for a fair price, even if the market could command a much higher one.

The long-held theological belief endorsed by Luther and the Catholic Church was that man was to be dependent upon God for all things, including his essential material needs. It was a biblical principle (Luke 12:31 and Matthew 6:33) that God would continue to provide the basic necessities of life for those who pursued the Kingdom of God above all else.

Although Luther's message was spiritually compelling, it was difficult for the emancipated people of the Renaissance to embrace commercially. The Renaissance, which preceded and helped spark the Reformation, was an era of great cultural renewal during which art, literature, science, philosophy, and economics soared to new heights.

The Role of Profit in Salvation

It has been said that "when the student is ready the teacher will arrive." Likewise, when an economic environment changes substantially, new leaders with fresh ideas often will emerge to accommodate the transformation. During the material and technological progress of the Renaissance, it became increasingly difficult to reconcile a spirituality that was rooted in the poverty of the gospels. At that time, almost 16 centuries of theology became financially modernized.

John Calvin, a French lawyer, turned theology upside down by bringing the gospel into the newly transformed world of the Renaissance. Calvin was the first to promote a theological basis for materialism that was adopted by the masses. Whereas Luther taught that it was sinful to accumulate money beyond what was necessary for subsistence, Calvin helped sow the seeds of capitalism by proclaiming that profit was now to be seen as a grace from God.

Theologically, Calvin believed in predestination and thought that most would be damned; however, God saves those select few whom He has chosen. But how was one to know whether or not he or she was saved? The answer for Calvin was that although good works were useless as a means of attaining salvation, they were indispensable as a sign of election.

Calvinists used good works as evidence to persuade themselves and others that they were predestined for eternal life. Success at one's work or calling was proof that one was living a well-ordered, disciplined life and would be saved.

Under the influence of Calvin, there was a great commitment to earning, producing, and saving, rather than consuming. This belief greatly encouraged the accumulation of capital for investment and business expansion. Calvin had a liberal view of commerce and banking, and endorsed lending money with interest. Therefore, it was now permissible to develop business and commerce through debt without spiritual condemnation.

Calvinism had one major drawback—wealth was considered bad if used for personal enjoyment. Although you pursued material success as a sign of election, you could not enjoy the fruits of your labors—especially luxuries. You were to affably share some of your profits with the community and reinvest the remainder in your calling which, in turn, served to increase profitability.

As Max Weber stated in *The Protestant Ethic and The Spirit of Capitalism*—"To be idle, let alone relaxing, was to be sinful and guilty of sloth. Even the wealthy were not to eat without working. For although they did not need to labor to support their own needs, there was God's commandment that they, like the poor, must obey. For everyone had prepared a calling, which he should profess and in which he should labor. This calling was God's commandment to the individual to work for the divine glory."

Under Calvin "work" and one's "calling" expanded greatly and was primarily profit driven. No longer confined to God ordained occupations that fathers passed on to their sons, Calvin considered it appropriate to seek an occupation which would provide the greatest earnings possible. If that meant abandoning the family trade or profession, the change was not only allowed, but it was considered to be one's religious duty.

America's Religious Mindset

It was with this mindset that the Puritans, who were themselves Calvinists, set sail in the 1620s. While in England, they had hoped to "purify" the

Church of England of some of its Roman Catholic attributes, but they soon fled to the New World under persecution from King Charles.

The Puritans had been people of economic means and political influence while in England, and they soon became the most dynamic force in the American colonies affecting other Protestant beliefs. In due course, capitalism took hold with its private ownership, free markets, and incentive for profit. It flourished here especially because many Protestants believed they were called by God to use their unique gifts and talents in creative enterprise for the glory of God. Made in the image of their Creator, they envisioned themselves to be co-creators with a vocation to develop the New World.

When these spirit-filled colonists first set foot on the shores of the New World, they were full of hope. While profit should never have played a role in their salvation, their religious virtues, nevertheless, instilled in them the willingness to be productive, to graciously share their blessings, and to reinvest the fruits of their labors—to live each day planting seeds of spiritual capital.

In the course of time, however, Calvin's forbidden fruits turned into an insatiable appetite for consumption and material comfort. But as noted French philosopher Alexis de Tocqueville cautioned, "Materialism, among all nations is a dangerous disease of the human mind; but it is more especially dreaded among a democratic people…Democracy encourages a taste for physical gratification; and this taste, if it becomes excessive, soon disposes men to believe that all is matter only."

As the years passed in the New World, it became evident that the Protestant work ethic offered little protection against a material temptation that had beset humanity since the time of Adam and Eve.

CHAPTER QUESTIONS

1. Do you believe that you have a calling? If so, describe what it is. If you are not sure, what are some of your gifts and talents? What do you enjoy doing?

2. Is your vocation in line with your calling? How could they fit together if at all?

3. How should the "fruits of your labor" be treated? Something to be shared? Something to be enjoyed? Something to be reinvested? Something to feel guilty about?

When you discover your calling
you will have discovered your path to a rich life.

"Americans' chief business
is to secure for themselves a government
which allows them to acquire the things they
covet, and which will not debar them from the
peaceful enjoyment of those possessions which
they have already acquired."
—Alexis de Tocqueville

8

THE PRICE PAID FOR CAPITALISM

*"Tell the rich in the present age
not to be proud and not to rely on so uncertain a thing
as wealth but rather on God, who richly provides us
with all things for our enjoyment."*
—1 Timothy 6:17

Staying in good shape physically, much like maintaining spiritual fitness, is not something you gain or lose in a day. But as visits to the gym or quiet time for prayer and charitable endeavors become less frequent, there comes a time when we notice a distinct flabbiness.

We wonder how we let ourselves get out of shape because only now does the unsightliness of our present condition seem obvious. Likewise, the seduction of consumerism developed slowly in America, taking three steps forward then two back. Yet, as the years progressed, we became fat around the middle and lost sight of our foundational spiritual fitness.

The Stock Market Finds a Home on Wall Street

Before our first President, George Washington, voluntarily left office, he appointed Alexander Hamilton as Secretary of the Treasury. Hamilton's appointment was significant, because he transformed our country's credit system and gave Wall Street its start as a securities market.

In accordance with Hamilton's plan, we began trading bonds to refund the debt incurred during the Revolutionary War.

The securities markets eventually found a home on Wall Street in New York City, rather than the more financially established Philadelphia. This occurred primarily because of the rapid growth in commerce that came to New York as a result of the completion of the Erie Canal. New York quickly became the biggest boomtown of the then modern world. As the city expanded, Manhattan Island, which is only about two miles wide, became incredibly valuable real estate.

John Jacob Astor, who had amassed a fortune with the largest fur-trading business in America, sold his company and bought large tracts of Manhattan real estate with the proceeds. He purchased a particularly large portion of the desolate northern part of Manhattan, gambling that the growing city would eventually expand in that direction. His gamble paid off handsomely. He bought in acres and sold in lots, ultimately becoming Manhattan's largest landowner.

As the "Landlord of New York," he had the means to do much for society, but like a growing number of capitalists at that time, he was not charitably inclined. When he died in 1848, his estate was worth $20 million, making him the richest man in America. Nevertheless, his only real act of philanthropy was witnessed at his deathbed when he donated $400,000 to build the New York Public Library. The rest of his estate was left to his son, William.

Capitalism flourished on America's soil, and our limited democratic government did not hinder the pursuit of material wealth. French political thinker Alexis de Tocqueville observed in the late 1830s that "Americans' chief business is to secure for themselves a government which allows them to acquire the things they covet, and which will not debar them from the peaceful enjoyment of those possessions which they have already acquired."

The Civil War transformed America into the second most powerful securities market on the planet. Once again, the government was in need of funds to finance its war efforts. Some of the capital needed was raised when the government instituted income taxes and created the Internal Revenue Service. However, the vast majority of funds came from selling bonds on Wall Street. Investors snapped the bonds up once they realized that much of the money the government expended was going to profit companies like railroads and iron mills.

Wall Street grew dramatically as railroad expansion was financed through securities, and the telegraph—the Victorian "Internet"—made for instant communication. In 1878, the New York Stock Exchange (NYSE) consisted of only fifty-four companies—thirty-six railroad, five coal, four telegraph, four express, three mining, one steamship, and one land. When the Dow Industrials were first published in 1896, it consisted of just twelve stocks and closed the first day of trading at 40.94. Today, General Electric is the only remaining company from the original Dow list.

Railroads, not the industrials, were the blue-chip stocks of the day. This may sound farfetched until you consider that for 2,000 years, from Alexander the Great to George Washington, people, animals, wind, or water powered man's potential. It was through these four resources that the world's most powerful men assumed their wealth and position. With the advent of railroads, transportation radically changed.

The Industrial Revolution and Modern Day America

The marketplace changed dramatically when James Watt invented the steam engine. It set off the Industrial Revolution in 1760, and caused both technology and industrialization to advance significantly. Yet, the heart of America's capitalistic success was found in the creative capacity and resourcefulness of robust individuals. The period between 1890 and 1914 saw the invention of the telephone, camera, phonograph, automobile, airplane, and the electric light bulb—to name but a few.

The Protestant Work Ethic, a limited government that supported capitalism, and technological advancements all combined to increase America's productivity and prosperity. Be that as it may, economic growth was not a sure thing. Booms and busts were commonplace in America's emerging capital markets, and people in need generally received little or no governmental assistance. Instead, they learned to draw strength from their faith and inner reserves.

For example, in the still predominately agrarian economy of 1894, a severe drought devastated farmers resulting in one-fifth of the workforce being unemployed. Our government, nevertheless, was not willing to provide relief. As then President Grover Cleveland said, "Though the people support the government, the government should not support the people."

During this time, Americans were generally hardworking, resourceful, and rugged. Big business flourished. The new men of wealth became known as industrialists, and real power resided in the hands of only a few, like J.P. Morgan.

J.P. Morgan—*The Most Powerful Man on Wall Street*

Benjamin Franklin discovered electricity, and Thomas Edison harnessed its illuminating power. But it was J.P. Morgan who capitalized on its monetary value by bringing it to Wall Street as the great industrial, General Electric. Morgan, who grew up idolizing Napoleon, found that positional power became his mistress too.

He became the most powerful man on Wall Street and greatly influenced America's railroad and steel industries. Morgan became so powerful and influential that he was able to save America twice from impending financial disaster by acting as the de-facto Federal Reserve.

Morgan had become so powerful that Congress determined that too much of the country's financial well-being was concentrated in the hands of just one man. In response, the Federal Reserve was established, and the Sherman Antitrust Act was enacted to break up Morgan's behemoth trusts.

When he died, Morgan's estate (excluding his valuable art collection) was worth about $60 million, but none of it was left to charity. Upon learning the value of Morgan's estate, John D. Rockefeller smugly remarked, "Why, that was not enough to make him a rich man!"

The Gospel of Wealth and a Pope's Warning

The sacredness of private property, commercial competition, and accumulation of wealth became the divine law of economics, which directly influenced our spirituality. Psychologist Carl Jung noted that by the beginning of the twentieth century, "The good Christian was now the enterprising businessman, where worldly goods were the special rewards for his Christian behavior."

Not all, however, were pleased with the progress made under the Gospel of Wealth. A new form of property and labor termed "capital and wages" often showed no concern for sex, age, or family needs. In 1891, Pope Leo XIII voiced concern over the condition of workers during the Industrial Revolution. He urged people to come to the aid of the impoverished, because many were in a situation of misfortune and undeserved misery.

Pope Leo stated—"Every principle and every religious feeling has disappeared from the public institutions and so, little by little, isolated and defenseless workers have found themselves at the mercy of inhuman masters and victims of the cupidity of unbridled competition. To this must be added the concentration of industry and commerce in the hands of a few, so that it has become the province of a small number of the rich and opulent, who in this way impose an almost servile yoke in the infinite multitude of the proletariat."

While condemning Communism, the Pope, nonetheless, asked governments to intervene and establish a fair distribution of goods, working hours, weekly rest, and a minimum living wage. The Pope's request, however, fell on deaf ears. At about this same time, in another part of the world, Communist Karl Marx challenged workers everywhere to unite and overthrow the oppressions of capitalism.

Industrialization and Henry Ford's Model T

Industrialization began to fuel our economy, and Americans were convinced it would ensure that good times were here to stay. We became a nation entrenched in technology with the ability to mass-produce like no other. The greatest example of our technological savvy and ability to mass-produce was Henry Ford's Model T.

Ford came up with the innovative idea of the moving assembly line. His workers became so skilled at using it that they could produce a Model T in 93 minutes. This efficiency enabled Ford to drastically lower retail prices, with greater volume making up for lower profit margins. He became so successful at mass-producing cars that sales soared to over 15 million Model Ts. At the peak, Ford held 50 percent of the automotive market.

But life on Ford's assembly line was harsh. He found it necessary to hire 1,000 men just to keep 100 on the payroll. Henry Ford ran his assembly lines through fear and intimidation, and many workers felt that they had to give up their dignity to work for him.

When unions came into being and workers united to challenge the power held by big business, organized labor quickly made its way to Ford's factories. Ford fought against them vehemently, but begrudgingly relented when his wife threatened to leave him unless he recognized unions. He was never the same afterward. When he died, he left the bulk of his $1 billion estate to the Ford Foundation. Today, with assets in excess of $10 billion, the organization is one of the three largest private foundations in the world.

Unlike that of European nations during World War I, America's industrialization remained largely undeterred. America became the financial safe haven of the world. There was no fighting on U.S. soil, and manufacturing companies received enormous contracts during the war.

For example, Bethlehem Steel was awarded contracts that increased tenfold over normal activity. The Dupont Corporation experienced similar prosperity. It alone provided our allies with 40 percent of their munitions—making the Duponts America's wealthiest family. While other countries' economies were in shambles after the war, America emerged as the financial superstar of the world. President Calvin Coolidge summed up the spirit of those times best when he announced to the American people that "the business of America is business!"

Wall Street and Main Street Move in Opposite Directions

In 1925, the top income tax rate was lowered to 25 percent, and billions of dollars were invested in Wall Street as people began speculating on rising stocks. With greed at the helm, the speculative buying craze gained momentum. Many investors began to buy on margin or invested their life savings. They did not realize that insiders were using their positions to skim millions of dollars off the market. The little known reality was that Wall Street and Main Street were moving in opposite directions.

Gross National Product rose less than 50 percent during the 1920s while the Dow quadrupled. Between May 1928 and September 1929, the average stock price rose nearly 50 percent, despite what was going on in the rest of the economy. There were many bank failures, and important sectors like farming and construction were already depressed. The stock market, however, continued to fly first class on an airplane supplied with plenty of booze but not enough fuel.

Some on Wall Street began feeling very uneasy about the market's meteoric rise. Charles Merrill, the founder of today's Merrill Lynch & Co., believed that the financial skies were not clear. The resistance by investors to turning a very substantial profit into cash was an absolute mystery to him. So troubled was Merrill that he went to see a psychiatrist, stating, "Do you think I'm crazy... because I am beginning to think that I must be." The psychiatrist responded, "If you're crazy, then I must be too," and both began selling their holdings before the market crashed.

On September 3, 1929, the Dow Jones industrial average reached an all-time high of 381.17. Be that as it may, by Thursday, October 24, 1929, Wall Street's high-flying airplane finally ran out of fuel. And on Black Tuesday, October 29th, the market crashed. Ironically, that same Tuesday morning, *The New York Times* wrote, "The investor who purchases securities at this time, with the discrimination that as always is a condition of prudent investing, may do so with utmost confidence."

Thousands of investors, many of whom were ordinary working people, met with financial ruin and never recovered. Some could not cope with their financial loss and took a one-way trip through an open window in a downtown office building. But it was not just the individual that had fallen from grace. Many banks and businesses that had speculated with their customers' deposits and earnings were also wiped out, resulting in a nationwide run on the banking system.

As a result of the unbridled consumerism of the 1920s, many newly built mass-production facilities turned out goods to the point of over capacity resulting in diminished marginal returns. By the time the stock market crashed in 1929, there was a major glut of goods on the market, with factory inventories at three times their normal size.

Another Pope Warns as Calvin's Dreams Fade

In 1929, the richest one percent owned 40 percent of America's wealth. However, the growing number of our nation's poor began to hoard what little money they had. Another Pope, Pius XI, again admonished the rich. He believed that mankind was succumbing to human passions as economics began to divorce itself from moral law and religious virtues.

Pope Pius XI stated, "There has been not merely an accumulation of wealth, but a huge concentration of power and economic dictatorship in the hands of a few who for the most part are not the owners, but merely the trustees and administrators of invested property, handling such funds at their arbitrary pleasure... This irresponsible power is the natural fruit of unlimited free competition which leaves surviving only the most powerful, which often means the most violent and unscrupulous fighters."

Just how much our human passions were to blame for America's economic plight is debatable in view of the confluence of fiscal and monetary oversights that occurred during that time. Nevertheless, there was no debating that America had entered the Great Depression. The ease with which people spent money and amassed debt was quickly replaced by a hoarding mentality that comes when a nation is gripped by the fear of not being able to afford the basic necessities of life.

It was just a little over 400 years earlier that Calvin envisioned a devout society based on delayed gratification and production, solely for the glory of God. In contrast, Americans had indulged themselves with instant gratification and conspicuous consumption. Long gone were the simple days of working solely to provide for one's basic needs.

Consumerism, in more than a few cases had resulted in the instantaneous fulfillment of many of our temporal wants to the detriment of future economic needs. For many, the price paid for capitalism in the pursuit of a largely materialistic American Dream was much greater than anyone, including Calvin, could have foreseen.

It was during this economic calamity that most of today's Retirees were reared. This generation began to reevaluate and assess the essentials of the American Dream while attempting to cope with the economic and social realities of the time. As the country concerned itself with bread lines and finding work for the unemployed, the storm clouds of war collected across the ocean.

CHAPTER QUESTIONS

1. Is it wise to measure worldly goods as material blessings given for serving God? Why or why not?

2. What are the pros and cons of consumerism in our capitalistic society?

3. What responsibilities come with industrialization and modernization? Are we meeting these responsibilities both at home and abroad?

Living rich is finding contentment with what you have today, even as you work toward improving your circumstances for tomorrow.

*"The lessons of history,
confirmed by evidence immediately before me,
show conclusively that continued dependence
upon relief induces a spiritual and moral
disintegration fundamentally destructive
to the national fiber. To dole out relief
in this way is to administer a narcotic,
a subtle destroyer of the human spirit.
It is in violation of the traditions of America."
—President Franklin D. Roosevelt*

9

RETIREES EMBRACE INSTITUTIONS

*"Tell them to do good, to be rich in good works,
to be generous, ready to share,
thus accumulating as treasure a good foundation
for the future, so as to win the life that is true life."*
—1 Timothy 6:18–19

A few years ago, news anchor Tom Brokaw wrote *The Greatest Generation*, a book about today's Retirees. For the most part, they were born prior to 1946, and today number about 60 million. As the book pointed out, this generation was largely responsible for ensuring many of the freedoms and comforts that we enjoy today. These legions of now older Americans survived and overcame the challenges of the Great Depression and World War II. As such, many of today's Retirees were raised with selfless values, diminished expectations, a strong work ethic that stressed teamwork, and a penchant for frugality.

Perhaps more than any other characteristic that helped define their generation was that Retirees exhibited enormous trust in our conventional institutions. Many still yearn for the time when our faith will be renewed in these vital institutions and the revitalization of our earlier American spirit. Regarding the events of September 11th, Philip Meyer, consultant to *USA Today*, conveyed the sentiments of many Retirees when he wrote, "Maybe the analogies to Pearl Harbor are overblown. Or maybe not. Please allow me as one of the 12 percent of Americans old enough to remember December 7, 1941, to suggest what it could mean. The good news is that we would start trusting the government again!"

Retirees were reared in a time when people didn't plan to retire early and play golf, or even feel the burden to provide college educations for their children. They weren't as concerned about obtaining affluence as they were with securing peace and the basic necessities of life. Their generation became the steel that was forged through the fires of difficult times.

Hoover and the Fed Underestimate the Economic Downturn

At the beginning of the Depression, President Hoover believed that Americans just needed to bear down, work hard, and tough it out. He was unwilling to compromise on the need for fiscal discipline and a balanced budget even in the face of adversity. Adversity, after all, was part of the price to be paid for free markets to exist under capitalism.

Hoover preached that the market forces of supply and demand over time would restore order to the system. Under a protectionistic policy, he raised tariffs on imported goods to keep American workers employed. This backfired, however, as foreign nations retaliated by imposing higher tariffs and world trade collapsed. Additionally, the Federal Reserve, which had been battling inflation in a skyrocketing stock market, kept interest rates too high, too long. It failed to provide liquidity in a timely manner to an anemic economy.

Hoover had confidence that the American people and capitalism would be resilient. As an accommodation, he cut income taxes, but this offered little relief. Since the average income was only $750 a year, it amounted to only a $4 tax savings. Most people earned so little that they did not reach the level where they would have to pay income taxes.

In 1932, one-fourth of America was out of work, economic output had declined by 25 percent, and wholesale prices dropped nearly 40 percent. Charles M. Schwab, the head of Bethlehem Steel, said of the Depression, "I'm afraid, every man is afraid." Americans were not unaccustomed to dealing with tough times, but previous periods of adversity seemed, at least, to have an end in sight. During the Great Depression, there appeared to be little light at the end of the tunnel.

Hoover's Out and Roosevelt's "New Deal" Is In

Hoover soon discovered that the American people were not as patient as he thought. Prolonged economic anguish resulted in the election of Franklin Delano Roosevelt, with millions of Americans finding hope with his "New Deal" and its many relief programs. Roosevelt's government assistance programs, however, caused sizable deficits—the first time this had occurred during a period of peace.

In his 1935 State of the Union address, Roosevelt acknowledged traditional American policy regarding governmental assistance when he said, "The lessons of history, confirmed by evidence immediately before me, show conclusively that continued dependence upon relief induces a spiritual and moral disintegration fundamentally destructive to the national fiber. To dole out relief in this way is to administer a narcotic, a subtle destroyer of the human spirit. It is in violation of the traditions of America." Nevertheless, like a doctor who prescribes morphine to stop pain, Roosevelt soon found it necessary to increase government programs and budget deficits to finance them.

When faced with difficult times earlier in history, Americans had always looked to themselves, their extended families, or perhaps their neighbors to help meet immediate needs. Early Americans were not comfortable looking to their government for economic handouts.

In response to the first question ever asked by the Gallup Poll in 1935, "Is the government spending too much money for relief?", 60 percent of the respondents said yes, while fewer than 10 percent thought it was spending too little.

Roosevelt's New Deal alone did not end the anguish caused by the Great Depression. Many Americans routinely experienced the degradation of bread lines and soup kitchens. The foolish pride felt by many in the 1920s had turned into despair. The prosperity and promise found in F. Scott Fitzgerald's *The Great Gatsby*, written just a few year's earlier, had been engulfed by the bleakness of John Steinbeck's *The Grapes of Wrath*.

Those who had taken for granted the favorable economic conditions experienced in earlier times were left bewildered and economically devastated. Among them were a group of America's greatest businessmen and wealthiest individuals who had attended a business summit in 1923. The prominent list of attendees included Charles Schwab, head of the largest independent steel company, Bethlehem Steel; Samuel Insull, co-founder of the world's largest utility conglomerate, General Electric; Howard Hopson, head of the largest gas company, Associated Gas & Electric Company; Ivar Krueger, president of one of the world's largest companies at the time, the International Match Company; Leon Frazier, president of the Bank of International Settlements; Richard Whitney, president of the New York Stock Exchange; Arthur Cotton and Jesse Livermore, two of the biggest speculators on Wall Street; and Albert Fall, a member of President Harding's Cabinet.

Twenty-five years later, history books would recall their lives as follows: Schwab died penniless after living for five years on borrowed money. Insull died broke living in a foreign land. Krueger and Cotton also died insolvent. Hopson went insane. Whitney and Fall were imprisoned. Fraser and Livermore committed suicide. These men, like many others at the time, had put too much trust in a materialistic wealth that was fleeting.

Many people sought to escape the problems of the day, but there was little money for entertainment. Movies became popular with 60 million Americans on the average attending a movie each week. Captivating features like *King Kong, Snow White and the Seven Dwarfs*, and *The Wizard of Oz* cost only 15 cents for admission.

Those were also the days of the golden age of radio. Shows like *Amos 'n' Andy, Fibber McGee and Molly*, and *The Lone Ranger* filled the air waves as families huddled together in attentive silence. President Roosevelt used this medium skillfully as he administered hope during his fireside chats to a willing audience that eagerly took hold of his unfailing confidence.

Roosevelt's New Deal had given people hope and prevented the Depression from becoming more severe. In 1937, however, the economy again slipped into recession. The massive government programs created under the New Deal somehow lacked the economic strength needed to pry Americans free from the grip of the Depression. By 1939, the economy was still adrift and the unemployment rate was a staggering 17 percent.

In 1940 America, daily business and life in general were very different from today. More than 20 percent of Americans lived on farms and the majority of the workforce was still blue collar. Few workers had employer-paid health insurance or employer-financed pension plans. There were fewer than one-and-a-half million college students, and only about one in twenty citizens had a college degree.

The majority of Americans were renters, and more than half of all households had no refrigerator. Coal for stoves and furnaces was the main fuel, while most houses had no central heating or air conditioning. About one-third of all households lacked running water!

Most Retirees grew up without televisions, and only a few households had a telephone or labor-saving devices like an automatic washer or dryer. Travel was also very limited, because commercial air travel and the interstate highway system had yet to be developed.

The Depression Ends as America Enters WWII

The Great Depression finally ended when America entered World War II. Only after the United States had borrowed and spent an additional $1 billion to build its armed forces did America's manufacturing base recover. Few questioned why America was fighting Germany and Japan, as Americans responded readily to Uncle Sam's call, "I Want You!"

Once the war effort was in full swing, unemployment shrank below 2 percent. Although few Americans were buying new appliances, cars, or houses, they were back at work. Most people had ration books and received only a limited supply of gasoline, meat, tires, sugar, and coffee. Americans had become accustomed to doing without. Some 64 percent of the respondents said "no" when a Gallup Poll taken at the beginning of 1945 asked, "Have you had to make any real sacrifices for the war?"

As World War II ended, deficit spending ballooned resulting in a national debt that was 114 percent the size of the Gross Domestic Product. Taxes tripled and the top tax rate of 91 percent did not drop below 88 percent until 1963 when it was lowered to 70 percent.

During this same time, Wall Street went into a long hibernation. Although per capita disposable income was rising dramatically during the early 1940s, investors stayed away from Wall Street. They feared America could still lose the war, and many had been financially devastated during the speculative days leading up to the Great Depression.

The excesses and corruption that led to the market's dramatic rise resulted in the enactment of major reforms. The Securities and Exchange Commission (SEC) was created and headed up by Joseph P. Kennedy, Sr., the father of President John F. Kennedy. Joseph Kennedy was a Wall Street veteran, and quite likely he would never have become a millionaire had the SEC existed just 10 years earlier. Additionally, the Glass-Steagall Act separated banks from the securities business and made short selling by corporate officers illegal.

Instead of investing in the market, Americans saved an astounding one-third of what they made. Most put this money into safe, insured savings accounts and war bonds. They also paid down most of their consumer debt. The only bright spot for the markets came with the introduction of pension funds. These funds were designed to supplement Social Security and were demanded by the unions.

Institutional Trust and Mutual Interdependence

During the Great Depression and World War II, Americans became acutely aware of their own humanity and the hardships that life can bring. The daily struggles for survival in a severely depressed economy and the horrific destruction of war had a dramatic and profound impact upon the American populace. For a time, Americans looked away from consumption as the source of happiness and collectively turned to God and each other for support.

Mutual interdependence for day-to-day sustenance and fighting for world peace made those who lived during these critical days acutely aware of their need for one another. People from all walks of life exhibited tremendous faith in institutions during those trying times and willingly trusted their motives. Institutions like government, family, and religion were all very strong.

These institutions fostered virtues and instilled patriotic values for many who lived through many trying times. America became a community bonded together by a common cause where teamwork, and not the fulfillment of the individual, was essential.

Extended families often lived in the same community and sometimes under the same roof. Close relationships were formed during those hard times, and people willingly shared what little they had among family and friends. Married couples seldom divorced, not only because of their deep religious faith, but also because it was not an economic option.

Grandchildren often forged close relationships with their grandparents who passed on wisdom cultivated during a lifetime of overcoming difficulties. It was common to learn the craft of your father or grandfather. Families spent extended time together. Sundays found families worshipping in crowded churches and then off to visit grandparents for the afternoon. And when someone became ill, the family usually assumed the role of primary care-giver, while the words "nursing home" had little meaning.

Americans at that time lost something too. They were no longer masters of their economic domains. It was not the individual but massive government programs, deficit spending, and the war itself that finally freed many from economic bondage. It was the first time for many citizens to realize that individual will and inner reserve, alone, were not enough to enable them to recover financially. Unaware of the future consequences, Americans began to suckle from the government's bosom, empowering that institution to expand its role. Entitlement programs entered the picture in 1935 when Congress passed the Social Security Act.

For a brief moment, however, the problems future generations would face were far in the distance. The bleakness and desolation of the previous two decades had become a mere shadow of the past. America was at peace and economically sound. By the end of 1945, Americans had every reason to celebrate by starting new careers, raising families, building homes, and looking toward the promising future that beckoned.

CHAPTER QUESTIONS

1. Are Retirees the "greatest generation?" Why or why not?

2. What institutions can and should we put our trust in today?

3. In what ways can dependence upon institutions be a subtle destroyer of the human spirit?

*Selfless values, diminished expectations,
and a strong work ethic that stresses teamwork
are fit standards for creating Lasting Wealth.*

"Ask not what your country can do for you,
ask what you can do for your country."
—President John F. Kennedy

10

BABY BOOMERS QUESTION AUTHORITY

"Be careful that you do not forget the Lord your God,
failing to observe his commands, his law and decrees."
—Deuteronomy 8:11

If you grew up a Baby Boomer, you will probably recall your youth with fond memories. At the beginning of the era, big cities such as New York were still clean and safe. Most people left their doors unlocked 24 hours a day. Parents did not fear that their children's pictures might end up on milk cartons if they walked home late at night.

It was a period when most Americans raised their families in modest homes in the suburbs and pursued stable careers. Our institutions began this period with a renewed strength since they were empowered and needed to cope with the hardships surrounding the war and the Great Depression.

Baby Boomers are those who were born in the United States between 1946 and 1964. Today there are about 75 million Boomers, representing approximately 28 percent of the U.S. population. They are a major force in our society, as they determine a little over half of the nation's total consumer spending.

Unlike Retirees, Boomers grew up in relative peace and prosperity with heightened expectations of individual happiness in a world of renewed consumerism. As the decades have passed, many Boomers decidedly distanced themselves from conventional institutions.

Boomers Experience a Booming Economy

During the Baby Boom, the pent-up demand for products and services created by World War II turned into a dramatic buying binge—the biggest since the 1920s. By 1954, the United States represented less than 10 percent of the world's population, yet the American economy produced nearly half of the world's goods. Americans owned nearly 60 percent of the world's cars and telephones, and 45 percent of all radios.

Although the financial underpinnings necessary to propel the stock market higher had been in place for some time, Americans still lacked confidence in the market. Even so, Charles Merrill observed and acted upon a vast marketing opportunity. The dramatic increase in personal savings that occurred during World War II now enabled the average person to spend discretionary money. Merrill ingeniously capitalized on the opportunity by bringing Wall Street to Main Street.

Merrill Lynch became the first brokerage house advertising to the masses and providing thousands of public seminars throughout America. Investors experienced growing confidence that Wall Street was a good place to put their money. Beginning in 1954 this innovative wave of financial marketing helped thrust a new bull market past the old Dow record of 381.17 set in 1929.

Construction and manufacturing were also experiencing bull markets of their own. Before World War II, the average contractor was building five to six houses a year, and most U.S. families did not even own a home. But during the Baby Boom, a man named Bill Levitt believed that he could mass produce a modern-day American Dream. As a result of Levitt's vision, his companies built thirty houses a day in a Cape Cod style for a unit cost of about $7,000. By 1955, three out of every four new homes were built in Levitt fashion. Buyers were not that concerned their home looked just like their neighbors' so long as they owned a new home.

During the Baby Boom, the gap between the rich and the poor narrowed substantially, and seemingly overnight, many families were financially elevated to a new majority called the "middle class." The world became a much smaller place as jet airplanes made travel to distant locations a more common reality. Automobiles reached their critical mass among consumers who used them to traverse the thousands of miles of new highways linking major cities.

Three-quarters of the way through the Baby Boom early Boomers started becoming teenagers, and their spending power began flexing its muscle. A typical Boomer could earn about ten dollars a week; a tidy sum in those days. In the 1950s, Coonskin Caps, Hula-Hoops®, and a doll named Barbie® were a few of the products introduced to Boomers with ready money to spend.

The workplace also began to change as the percentage of white-collar employees surpassed blue-collar workers, and the business market started to move away from predominately manufacturing to a more service-oriented economy. For most of America's history, however, goods were purchased sparingly for one's needs and paid for with cash. Now, people bought what they desired and paid later with the introduction of credit cards in 1958.

Television Transforms Our World and Us Along With It

Television was the most influential technological development of the Baby Boom era. While fewer than 10 percent of Americans owned the device in 1950, the statistic rocketed to 90 percent of all households by 1962. Television held us spellbound, forever changing the way we experienced the world. Families were captive audiences as the world was brought right into their living rooms. Politics, civil rights, and the cruelty of war in distant lands were all presented in a new light, instantaneously, as things were happening.

By 1954, Americans began moving away from traditional sit-down family dinners and began eating "TV dinners" in front of the television. FCC (Federal Communications Commission) Chairman Newton Minow in 1961 declared that television, with only three major networks at that time, was a vast wasteland.

Family life was portrayed by shows such as *Ozzie and Harriett, Father Knows Best, Leave It to Beaver,* and *The Donna Reed Show.* They depicted a nurturing, stay-at-home mother and a well-meaning, career-minded father as the sole provider. Families stayed together and worked through their challenges without the aid of therapy. Life was never portrayed as too exciting but, then again, Americans had had enough excitement during the previous two decades.

Television soon became the world's most effective selling machine, and advertisers shrewdly used it to promote a material-based American Dream. The advertising industry targeted women and stressed the point that the female role was to oversee and organize the family. Corporations spent lavishly on advertising, hiring experts in psychology to resourcefully appeal to consumers. During this time, Vance Packard wrote the bestseller, *The Hidden Persuaders*, which discussed the various manipulative advertising techniques of the day.

Boomers Are Idealistic but Institutions Are Not Ideal

During the Baby Boom, America seemed to have everything going for it. With most of our material needs satisfied, there were more opportunities for focusing on personal ideals. Pediatrician Dr. Benjamin Spock wrote the world-famous book, *The Common Sense Book of Baby & Child Care*, asserting the need for idealistic children. In line with this thinking, many Boomers were raised to be idealistic, but unfortunately, America's institutions were not ideal.

While the Baby Boom continued, there was a growing disparity between what was being beamed into the living room and what was actually going on in real life. While Retirees were raised with a deep faith in institutions, like family, government, business, and religion, in contrast Baby Boomers started to question them and, in some cases, rebelled against them.

The "girl next door" who became the happy homemaker on TV confronted a reality that did not measure up to the fairy tale promised. In the real world, TV's girls next door, like Doris Day, Debbie Reynolds, and Dinah Shore, were unable to maintain solid family lives. Among these three television personalities, there were nine divorces as they searched for marital bliss.

Technology helped emancipate women during the Baby Boom era, and a growing number of women were no longer content to be housewives. In previous years, women were often physically spent from doing routine housework. Labor-saving appliances, once luxuries, became everyday household items during the Baby Boom. And the invention of antibiotics, like penicillin, drastically reduced the time mothers had to spend tending to their children's illnesses.

Like June Cleaver of *Leave It to Beaver*, intelligent women, dressed in pearls and high heels, waited for the daily return of their "all-powerful" husbands. But the scenario was not exactly fulfilling in real life. Many women began working in earnest outside the household. *The Feminine Mystique* by the late

Betty Friedan helped send a message to women that they could do unconventional things in a man's world. The book quickly became a must-read for those participating in the growing feminist movement.

Career-minded fathers were having problems securing ideal jobs in the real world. Many men latched onto the security of big corporations after experiencing the economic instability of the Depression and the daily quest for survival during World War II. As was depicted in the 1955 movie, *The Man in the Gray Flannel Suit*, men with family responsibilities were not willing to risk their economic stability by exploring more fulfilling career options.

Americans also soon discovered that what was good for big corporations, like General Motors, was not necessarily good for America. At times, companies placed profits ahead of consumers' best interests by turning out unsafe products, like GM's Corvair automobile.

Even the media that had captivated America's attention began to violate our trust. Television networks were busted for fixing game shows, like *Twenty-One*. The networks, along with their corporate sponsors who promoted a cheerful lifestyle that belonged only to suburban white families, were now being challenged by civil rights activists, like Dr. Martin Luther King.

The most important institution to come under attack, however, was the family. The idealized image of the happy American family started to come apart at the seams. In the real world, family life was often strained as people married too young—at an average age of 18 in 1955.

What was to have been blissful family life was, at times, scandalous and not unlike those indiscretions portrayed in Grace Metalious's *Peyton Place*. In the real world, families fought and couples were not always faithful. After conducting the most expansive sexual survey in history, Alfred Kinsey stunned Americans by claiming that 50 percent of married men and 25 percent of married women had been unfaithful.

Boomers Encounter the Sexual Revolution

Hugh Hefner started publishing *Playboy* in 1953. The magazine was promoted as one of style and charm that often appealed to educated readers. His first nude centerfold, Marilyn Monroe, became the most popular sex symbol the world has ever known.

Some Boomers freely took part in America's sexual revolution of the 1960s. A less-reproachful term, "premarital sex," quickly replaced its religious counterpart, "fornication." And the advent of rock and roll, with Elvis Presley leading the way, helped rouse the emotions of young adults and forever changed the course of music.

Aided by the invention of the birth control pill in 1960, Boomers were the first generation of young adults to experience "free love." Although the pill was designed to prevent unwanted pregnancies for married couples, unmarried woman could also have sex without the fear of pregnancy.

More Guns and Butter at the Same Time

At the start of the Baby Boom, America's government was committed to a balanced budget. A balanced budget, however, has not always been a reality in American fiscal policy. In fact, budget deficits often occurred during times of war and, to a lesser extent, through severe economic downturns such as the Depression.

Under President Truman, America balanced four of seven budgets from 1946 to 1952. President Eisenhower also saw a balanced budget as a necessary discipline. Eisenhower's message was simple: "…in good times, at the very least, we should pay our own way, and we should not have more government than the people are willing to pay for with taxes." In 1954, defense spending accounted for 70 percent of the federal budget, leading Eisenhower to warn that America could not have more guns and more butter at the same time.

In 1961, President Kennedy uttered his immortal inaugural words, "Ask not what your country can do for you. Ask what you can do for your country," challenging all Americans to do something for America. Nonetheless, Kennedy's administration helped provide Americans with ever-increasing public services.

People started to depend more on corporate pension plans and Social Security than on their individual savings. Likewise, healthcare shifted from individual responsibility to institutional responsibility. The majority of the coverage was either paid by the employer or funded through government insurance.

President Kennedy and his administration similarly introduced a new view of economics and budget deficits. Whereas deficit spending had been used only to prime the pump in times of war or severe economic hardship, it began being used to minimize sluggish periods during normal business cycles. No longer did deficits carry the moral stigma they once did. Deficits were now considered legitimate means to accomplish a worthwhile political end.

President Lyndon Johnson's administration helped push the deficit ceiling even higher by establishing more programs than our government could financially support. In 1964, President Johnson declared war on poverty, and America's "Great Society" came into full existence with the introduction of Medicare.

It was honorable to want to eradicate injustices by trying to improve the quality of life through the means of government. The trouble, however, was that the United States government was now taking on a much larger role than it could reasonably fulfill, a role that our Founding Fathers never intended.

The Fear of Communism Abounds

While Boomers questioned nearly all institutions, they openly challenged their government the most. And no issue was more provocative to Boomers than our government's use of military force to stop the spread of Communism.

During the Baby Boom generation, the fear of Communism abounded. We fought both the Korean War and the Cold War working to deter the spread of Communism. The fear of Communism was so entrenched that Senator Joseph McCarthy exploited it by accusing hundreds of State Department employees of being Communist Party members.

The Vietnam War began as an operation of containment against Communism. However, two days after President Kennedy's shocking assassination by an alleged Communist sympathizer, Lee Harvey Oswald, President Johnson stated, "It is the United States' goal to help the Saigon government to military victory."

As the war escalated, President Johnson believed that by applying greater amounts of pressure against the North Vietnamese, he could bring them to the negotiating table and achieve victory. Unfortunately, President Johnson mis-judged the mindset of those people who said through their leader Ho Chi Minh, "For every ten of us you kill, we kill one of you, and in the end we will win."

Before the Vietnam War ended, many Baby Boomers would do more than question their government and the establishment—they would openly protest against them. A chorus of Boomer voices began chanting, "Hell no, we won't go!" and "Hey, hey, LBJ, how many more did you kill today?"

The oldest and more outspoken Boomers protested on college campuses and burned draft cards. Some left America to avoid the draft by fleeing to Canada. Still others let their hair grow long, took drugs, participated in "love-ins," and were branded by the establishment as hippies.

The establishment fought back by jailing those who burned draft cards. It used military force at times to quash anti-war rallies. At Kent State University, four students died at the hands of National Guardsmen during a demonstration that got out of control. Even the self-proclaimed "greatest of all time," the newly-ordained Muslim, Mohammed Ali, was stripped of his World Boxing title when he refused to enter the military.

The Generation That Forgot God

During this time of civil unrest, America's religious institutions were not spared from criticism. Boomers argued that religion had become irrelevant and too distant. The "we" of community that had served Retirees well was starting to give way to the "I" of personal devotion. Toward the end of the Baby Boom generation, many people stopped turning to organized religion for meaning, reverting instead to self-reliance and New Age thinking.

Religious institutions found it necessary to redefine the expression of their message in order to adapt to a changing world. For example, Vatican II was held during the early 1960s in an effort to modernize the message of the Catholic Church and better meet the challenges of contemporary times.

Despite the positive changes that came out of Vatican II, there was a decline in Church attendance and baptisms with fewer men seeking to become priests. A reduced number of marriages were being performed in the Church as the practice of "living together" (out of wedlock) rose dramatically. Other denom-inations also experienced a decline in the participation of religious practices.

It was not only priests, rabbis, and pastors who suffered, many other figures of authority—teachers, police, and politicians—were now questioned by Boomers. But still, much of the falling away from God and organized religion that occurred at the end of the Baby Boom period remains a mystery.

Perhaps Beatle John Lennon offered the best explanation when, in 1966, he said, "Most young people are more interested in rock and roll than in religion... The Beatles are more popular than Jesus now." *Time* magazine captured the sentiment of the day in April 1966 by printing an issue titled "IS GOD DEAD?" Twenty-seven years later, an April 1993 cover of *Time* labeled Boomers "THE GENERATION THAT FORGOT GOD."

As the Baby Boom era came to an end, America had decisively moved away from traditional values, religious virtue, and the institutions that promoted them. During the mid-'60s, Harvey Cox Jr., Harvard theologian, made clear in his bestselling book, *The Secular City*, that mainstream institutions and religious beliefs were on the decline. Government, corporate, familial, and religious institutions were all considerably weakened, and we no longer placed blind trust in them.

The spiritual capital and patriotism produced in earlier times were on the wane. At some point during the Baby Boom, we lost sight of the moral underpinnings of our institutions and our nation. In the process of demythologizing our institutions, we also destabilized many of them. Into this unstable environment a new generation was born—Generation X.

CHAPTER QUESTIONS

1. Should we have high hopes and idealistic expectations, or is it better to be more pragmatic?

2. Is there a greater danger of placing too much trust or too little trust in our institutions? Why?

3. As a generation, did Boomers forget God or did religious institutions fail to adequately convey God's message given the times?

Lasting Wealth is found in letting go of idealistic expectations and in remembering that our institutions should in some way reflect our belief in a Supreme Being.

"No generation since the Depression
has been set up for failure like this.
Everything the dot-com boom delivered
has been taken away and then some."
—Forbes Magazine

11

GENERATION X GETS NO RESPECT

"Come to me, all you who are weary and burdened,
and I will give you rest. Take my yoke upon you
and learn from me, for I am meek and humble of heart,
and you will find rest for souls.
For my yoke is easy and my burden is light."
—Matthew 11:28–30

Generation X, much like the late comedian Rodney Dangerfield, "can't get no respect." These 46 million people born between 1965 and 1976, often came from fragile family units.

Economically, Xers witnessed the recessionary impact of double-digit inflation, a drastic stock market decline, the worst savings and loan crisis since the Depression, and a corporate America downsizing like no other time in history.

Xers were treated as a low priority when allocating benefits, yet the government demanded they pay a proportionately larger share in taxes. Spiritually, this generation was exposed far less to traditional religious institutions and more often to the unsteadiness of contemporary movements.

The Family Unit Begins to Break Down

While most Boomers as children enjoyed a relatively secure family life, Xers experienced the instability consistent with family breakdown and the abandonment of traditional values. During Generation X, birthrates dropped dramatically, and mothers throughout the 1970s aborted one out of every three pregnancies.

Many parents decisively moved away from the long-held traditional belief that they needed to stay together in order to properly raise their children. Xers were three times more likely to experience a parental breakup than were Boomers, with this translating into America's divorce rate doubling during their generation.

Demand for daycare facilities exploded and millions of Xers saw their mothers flock into the work force. During this generation, the proportion of preschoolers cared for by stay-at-home moms fell roughly by one-half.

With working mothers becoming more commonplace, many younger Xers reported that they shouldered considerable responsibility in raising themselves. As a generation, a lot of Xers found solace through television in an otherwise empty home. The typical 14-year-old watched three hours of television a day and did only one hour of homework.

Television shows like *The Courtship of Eddie's Father*, *The Brady Bunch*, and *The Partridge Family* made it clear that the nuclear family of the '50s and '60s had changed. Now children were merging together in the blended families of multiple marriages or living in single-parent households.

Corporate Downsizing, Inflation, and a Bear Market

Many Xers witnessed their parents looking for work because of a new process known as corporate downsizing. After World War II, big corporations implicitly promised their employees guaranteed paychecks and attractive benefits. But the favorable economic climate enjoyed during most of the Baby Boom changed. During Generation X, a plethora of corporations failed to make good on implied promises of employment security.

Big companies once took great pride in being able to make statements like IBM did in their company handbook titled, *About Your Company*, prepared in 1981—"In nearly 40 years, no person employed on a regular basis by IBM has lost as much as one hour of working time because of a layoff. When recessions come or there is a major product shift, some companies handle the work-force imbalances by letting people go. IBM hasn't done that and hopes it never has to do so. People are a treasured resource. It's hardly a surprise that one of the main reasons people like to work for IBM is the company's all-out effort to maintain full employment."

But many IBM employees were sorely surprised between 1986 and 1994 when the company cut its work force essentially in half. IBM was not alone as a host of other bellwether names, including the likes of General Motors, AT&T, Sears, Ford, Xerox, and Citicorp also implemented significant layoffs.

Downsizing became necessary because of the harsh economic conditions caused by the recessions of the 1970s and early 1980s. A loose credit system, deficit spending for bigger government, the Vietnam War, and higher oil prices all combined to produce runaway inflation that climbed to an all-time high of 13? percent in 1980.

For Generation X, inflation became a formidable adversary. President Nixon spent most of his presidency fighting the inflation caused by the "guns-and-butter" of the Vietnam War and the Great Society. Inflation continued to soar during the Carter Administration to levels not seen since the Civil War. When Ronald Reagan came into office, he and Federal Reserve Board Chairman Paul Volker took drastic measures to fight inflation as the prime rate soared to 20 percent, while unemployment rose to 10 percent.

Inflation also weighed heavily on Wall Street as the worst bear market since the Great Depression took hold. The Standard & Poors 500, on an inflation-adjusted basis, lost 50 percent of its value between late 1968 and late 1982. On top of the market's woes was the savings and loan crisis, which occurred during the late 1980s and early 1990s. Hundreds of savings and loans had to be rescued from insolvency at a cost of $500 billion.

The Government Offers Little Reassurance for Xers

As the government struggled to offer Xers fiscal and moral reassurance, the most famous modern-day political scandal in American history occurred in 1972. The Watergate break-in and cover-up unraveled a web of political spying, bribery, and the illegal use of campaign funds. The disclosure of these activities resulted in the indictments of some 40 government officials and the resignation of President Nixon. Years later, actress Meg Ryan spoke for many Xers when she said, "I think I have a deep distrust of authority. I'm a Watergate baby."

Xers also experienced the growing trend of our government investing less in the country's future, with inordinate federal resources going to support programs for generations born earlier. For example, Social Security and Medicare expenses grew exponentially during Generation X. And while many Retirees will collect Social Security benefits amounting to more than three times what they put in, Xers were told that Social Security could not be counted upon to meet their retirement needs.

Despite increasing amounts spent on entitlements, the United States has one of the highest rates of childhood poverty among all industrialized nations. Xers are much more likely to be below the poverty line than are Retirees.

Although Xers anticipate receiving far less of the benefits'-pie, the government expects them to pay proportionately more in current taxes. For example, in 1990, a Generation X couple with a baby and one parent earning $30,000 a year paid five times as much in taxes as the typical Retiree with a similar income from public and private pensions.

Deficits also rose dramatically during Generation X as the government spent heavily during the waning years of the Cold War. As our military was built up to out-muscle the Soviet Union, our national deficit swelled to $4 trillion. Annual interest payments, alone, were $200 billion. Many Xers felt that those in power had the luxury to ignore the swelling debt they were leaving to them.

America's infrastructure paid a heavy price to win the Cold War. From federal highways to public school systems, many government programs were scaled back. And some segments were more affected by the cutbacks than others. The timing could not have been worse for the U.S. Department of Education. The Agency warned in its published report titled, "A Nation at Risk," that there was a "rising tide of mediocrity" that was surfacing in our nation's schools.

Looking back, the risk of mediocrity was nothing compared to the risk that students and teachers actually faced during the spring of 1999 at Columbine High School. At that time, two high-school students made an all-out assault during the middle of the school day. Shooting guns and throwing bombs, the two seniors killed twelve students and one teacher, and injured many more. Before the mayhem ended, the two depraved seniors killed themselves.

Xers Are Not Easy to Find on Main Street

Individual differences, not what was shared in common, were highlighted during Generation X. Earlier generations experienced advertising and marketing that was intended for the masses, stressing what was collectively shared. During the Xer generation, however, advertisers and marketers continued to segment and subdivide America into smaller market fragments through *target marketing* and *niche advertising*. When polled, nine out of ten Xers agreed that earlier in our history people had more in common and shared more values than Americans do today.

Xers had no compelling cause to rally around and bring them together like preceding generations. Retirees and Boomers might look to movies like *Saving Private Ryan* or *Platoon* as defining moments. The short-lived war efforts of Operation Desert Storm, however, could not unite Xers in the same way—considering that during every 100 hours on American inner-city streets, three times more young people lost their lives in gunfire than were killed in the 100 hours of that war. And while joining the military may have been a safer alternative than street gangs, it was street gangs that seemed to offer many of America's disconnected youth a real chance to belong.

Unfortunately, most of today's young Americans know and care less about news and public affairs than do earlier generations. Many Xers today feel little connection to the broader issues of the world and are less inclined to identify with mainstream America.

As a whole, Xers are less likely to vote as compared with Boomers and Retirees. But when Xers do vote, they frequently do so as Independents often supporting candidates who, likewise, have disdain for the status quo. A candidate like ex-pro wrestler Jessie Ventura, Minnesota's former governor, was an overwhelming favorite among Minnesota Xers. During his governorship, many Xers proudly displayed bumper stickers on their cars that read, "My governor can beat up your governor!"

Religious Choices Without a Solid Spiritual Foundation

Traditional religious institutions also had minimal impact in shaping the values of many Xers. As the first Xers were born, Americans became noticeably distant from their conventional concept of God and religion.

While Xers' parents searched for their own faiths, Xers were exposed more to New Age movements. Xers valued the spiritual freedom to choose, however, many did not receive a solid spiritual foundation on which to make informed decisions.

In a culture where today's youth increasingly pierce, tattoo, or otherwise disfigure their bodies—once thought to be sacred temples—one might question if some of them have any spiritual convictions at all. Tom Beaudoin, the author of the book, *Virtual Faith*, notes that "Tattooing and piercing signify a need to be deeply marked." Moreover, he continues, "Young adults satisfy their spiritual hunger by using these piercings and tattoos as their own sacramentals, partly because they see that religious institutions are unable to provide for deeply marking, profoundly experiential encounters."

An article in *The Wall Street Journal* in the late 1990s reported, "Today's youth seek ancient rituals and mysticism as churches and synagogues compete with Eastern and New Age religion—as well as paganism, gangs, cults, and 12-step programs, which all offer the rituals that appeal to some young people."

Entire teen clothing lines became devoted to dark, mystical-looking "Goth" fashions. Perhaps there was more to worry about than just "Medieval" clothing. As the article also reported at the same time, an Episcopal Church in New York became bored with the same old Christmas pageant complaining that "it was always the one with the Virgin Mary." So, instead, they wrote a new version with characters from the cynical cartoon *South Park* to communicate the once holy message.

Not surprisingly, Generation Xers are the least likely adult group to have a religious affiliation or regularly attend a traditional place of worship. Professor Jeffrey Arnett of the University of Missouri-Columbia who has studied Generation X in detail, reports that only 15 to 20 percent attend conventional faith communities with any regularity. In tandem with these findings, religion ranked behind friends, home, school, music, and TV as factors Xers believed had the greatest influence on their generation, according to the George H. Gallup International Institute.

Is the "Golden Ladder" the Xers' Way Out?

Traditional values that our institutions helped impart to earlier generations had little opportunity to take root in Xers. Our weakened institutions had little genuine meaning for this vast group of Americans. Unable to depend on these institutions for support, many Xers made their own way.

With the launch of the personal computer in 1977, these innovative machines greatly shaped the lives of many Xers who decided to bet on themselves. *The Wall Street Journal* once stated of Xers, "This generation is more willing to gamble their careers than earlier generations," as many had started their own small businesses. What a difference a few decades made; forty years earlier only a select few wished to take on the risk of being self-employed.

But the economic prosperity that occurred for numerous others during the 1980s and 1990s seems like a pipe-dream to many Xers today. In October 2002, *Fortune* magazine had this to say of Xers—"No generation since the Depression has been set up for failure like this. Everything the dot-com boom delivered has been taken away and then some. Real wages are falling, wealth continues to shift from younger to older, and education costs are surging. Worse yet, for some Gen Xers, their peak earning years are behind them. Buried in college and credit card debt, a lot of them won't be able to catch up…."

Xers were born much too late to embrace the words of President Franklin D. Roosevelt: "The very objectives of young people have changed, away from the dream of the golden ladder, [which is] each individual for himself, and toward a broad highway on which thousands of your fellow men and women are advancing."

On the contrary, our institutional base did not provide a promising future for Xers' collective advancement. As other generations advanced their economic positions, scores of Xers came to believe that the golden ladder may be the only thing left of the American Dream that provides a way out.

According to *Roper College Track,* "Three quarters of American college seniors during Generation X said that it will be harder for their generation to achieve the American Dream than it was for the last generation." It comes as little surprise that a 1989 Gallup Poll found that nearly 80 percent of adults thought young people were more selfish and materialistic than they were 20 years earlier.

Before the implosion of the NASDAQ in March of 2000, an online trading commercial captured the sentiment of numerous Xers—"We're not relying on the government; we're not relying on the company; we're not relying on some big fat inheritance; we're relying on ourselves. We plan to retire rich!" Unfortunately, Xers could not even rely on online trading for prosperity. Comparatively speaking, Rodney Dangerfield seemed to have received a lot more respect.

No generation can write the history of its own time. There are simply too many social, political, and economic factors in the near and distant future that will ultimately define the perception of this and other generations.

Xers have been institutionally disadvantaged concerning matters of foundational values. This vast group of Americans must strive to overcome the handicap they have inherited. In the aggregate, however, all living generations today are facing the challenges of a rapidly changing post-modern culture, where unsteady values are undermining the foundation of the state of our Union.

CHAPTER QUESTIONS

1. Are certain generations really more materialistic than other generations? Why or why not?

2. If our institutions are weak or stress a secular agenda alone, then how will meaningful values and virtues be imparted?

3. How can we best ensure that each generation has a solid spiritual foundation from which to choose?

If you are nurturing your soul away from the Golden Ladder then you are living rich.

"Yes, we did produce a near-perfect republic,
but will they keep it?
Or will they, in their enjoyment of plenty,
lose the memory of freedom?"
—President Thomas Jefferson

12

THE STATE OF OUR UNION

"See, I lay a stone in Zion, a tested stone,
a precious cornerstone for a sure foundation;
the one who trusts will never be dismayed."
—Isaiah 28:16

Nine days after September 11th, President George W. Bush, speaking from the floor of the House of Representatives, addressed a joint session of Congress and said—"My fellow citizens, for the last nine days, the entire world has seen for itself the state of our union, and it is strong!"

Thunderous applause and a roaring ovation broke out from the House floor in response. It was a defining moment of President Bush's presidency as the country rallied behind the President and pulled together with a determined will that rose above the adversity at hand.

Hardship had once again summoned virtue and determination with Americans readily responding. However, as the immediate crisis passed, the foundation of our Union returned to a wary state. Skepticism, in time, replaced trust. Even Saddam Hussein's removal from power would not be enough to silence nagging questions regarding the missing weapons of mass destruction.

The current state of the Union has notably changed from its former image and is now driven more by distrust than trust. Consider that in the 1950s about 70 percent of Americans said they trusted the federal government to do the right thing most of the time. Today, only about 30 percent express such trust.

The strength of our Union is also in doubt today. A USA TODAY/CNN/Gallup Poll taken the week before President Bush's 2006 state of the Union address found most Americans pessimistic about the economy, divided on the war and doubtful that Bush has the best plan to address the issues that matter most to them—among them health care and corruption. By more than 2-to-1, those surveyed said "things have gotten worse in the United States over the past five years."

A Wavering Public Sector

In recent times, it is all too often polls, not sound principles, that have dictated our leaders' actions and our perceptions of national figures. In our volatile environment, leaders frequently yield to current public sentiment in order to protect their positions in office. Our republic, however, desperately needs principled leaders of conviction, whom we entrust to make tough decisions.

The Founding Fathers began with a healthy Constitutional distance, found in the safeguards between electing those who would decide and what was ultimately decided. Imagine how our country might look like today if our nation's greatest leaders, like Washington, Lincoln, and Roosevelt, had made their magnanimous decisions based on opinion polls or some focus group's recommendation.

Character must be the most important factor by which we judge those who hold our highest political offices. Yet, prior to 9/11 in the 1990s, it became glaringly apparent that we were willing to overlook suspect character in our elected officials as long as the economy was in good shape.

When we vote in favor of our pocketbooks at the expense of our principles, we weaken the foundation of the state of our Union. To a large degree, we are still living off the intangible assets that were entrusted to us with the immortal words inscribed on the Iwo Jima memorial: "When uncommon valor was a common virtue."

Over time there has been a gradual decay in our commitment to patriotic principles. Many of us have become desensitized to conduct that used to offend our moral heritage. Today, a cultural tolerance is becoming preferable to seeking moral truth. In the light of changing values, we are in danger of losing our spiritual conviction and marginalizing our morality. Actions that may have been considered reprehensible in the past may no longer incite us in the present to do the right thing.

Deficit of Decency

The lead-in segment to a recent ABC's *Monday Night Football* game featured an attractive middle-aged woman from the hit TV show *Desperate Housewives*, seducing one of the game's best players in a locker room before the game. Dressed only in a bath towel, she beckons the star player not to take the game. "I've got a game that we can play," she seductively suggests and then discards the towel. In response to the blatant use of sex to boost ratings, the NFL issued the following statement, "While ABC may have gained attention for one of its other shows, the NFL and its fans lost."

But it is the halftime show at the 2004 Super Bowl that will go down as the granddaddy of all wake-up calls. While the VonTrapp Family Singers from *The Sound of Music* may not stir up an audience today, it is sad commentary to note that burlesque-like rock performances are increasingly becoming the norm. The halftime-spectacle featured Kid Rock, who dressed in a poncho of the American Flag; the pop-rap singer Nelly, who grabbed his crotch more than the microphone; and Janet Jackson and Justin Timberlake, who bumped and grinded their way into a rather revealing ending.

Shortly afterwards, Senator Zell Miller spoke from the Senate floor about the decline of moral values in America. He said, "So, if I am asked why— with all of the pressing problems this nation faces today—why I am pushing these social issues and taking the Senate's valuable time, I will answer: Because it is of the highest importance. Yes, there is a deficit to be concerned about in this country—a deficit of decency."

More and more, progressive judges are legislating against our moral heritage, instead of adjudicating to protect it. The Supreme Court in contemporary times (at least prior to Justices Roberts and Alito joining the Court) has increasingly established itself as an oligarchy, ignoring the will of the people and their views on the Constitution. For example, the Supreme Court recently shocked the majority of private citizens by ruling that local governments may now seize their homes and businesses in order to make way for private commercial development.

Similarly, state courts are likewise legislating down a slippery slope, as four members of the Massachusetts Supreme Judicial Court not long ago mandated same-sex marriage, undermining the views of the majority who reside in the state. As a result, eleven states recently secured constitutional amendments to prohibit same-sex marriages.

Even with this decisive action, is the will of the people now starting to wane? 60% of Americans now consider gambling, cohabitation, and sexual fantasizing as "morally acceptable" according to Barna Research Group. Nearly half of those surveyed felt it was morally acceptable for a person to have an abortion or to have sex with someone other than his or her own spouse. And about a third said that they had no real problem with pornography, profanity, homosexual activity, or drunkenness.

The freedom of democracy is great, but the responsibility to uphold freedom and promote the common good is even greater. Before his death, Pope John Paul II issued a chilling warning: "History demonstrates, a democracy without values easily turns into open or thinly disguised totalitarianism."

Before he died in 1975, historian Arnold Toynbee, who wrote the much-admired *A Study of History*, believed that of the 22 civilizations that have appeared in history, 19 of them collapsed when they reached the moral state America is in today. Toynbee affirmed that a culture that loses touch with its roots becomes a cut-flower civilization—while it looks beautiful for a while, the beauty will eventually wither.

The Private Sector and Our Misplaced Trust

In this post-Enron environment, many have painfully experienced the grim consequences of misplaced trust. While we surely lack trust in our government, we may trust those who run corporate America even less. A recent article from *USA Today* reported, "More than seven in ten Americans say they distrust CEOs of large corporations, as nearly eight in ten believe that top executives of large companies will take improper actions to help themselves at the expense of their companies."

The list of those who betrayed investor confidence in recent times is long. Consider the following exploitations:

1.   Many Wall Street analysts gave us tainted research crafted in "workshops full of conflicts of interest." Prominent brokerage houses often publicly

pumped up stocks that they privately scorned in order to acquire investment banking business.

2. Investment banking firms played both sides of the fence. In Enron's case, those firms were not only some of the main investment bankers, but also some of the largest investors who profited the most from Enron's questionable partnerships.

3. Historical guardians of financial information, like Arthur Anderson, had a hard time objectively carrying out their audits on large conglomerates. Tax consulting fees industry-wide often brought in three times the amount of revenue as compared to that brought in by auditing fees.

4. Dishonest CEOs in a few cases pillaged the very companies they were entrusted to manage and protect. The leaders of WorldCom, Tyco International, and Adelphia were all convicted with looting their respective companies. Even home-decorating diva Martha Stewart was found guilty of four counts of obstructing justice and one count of lying to investigators.

5. Boardroom conflicts of interest were widespread. Although boards of directors are supposed to represent stockholders independently, the reality on Wall Street revealed that many directors were handpicked by the respective CEOs, and that CEOs and Chairmen of the Boards were usually the same people.

6. Mutual funds, the stronghold of small investors, were rocked with trading abuses by Wall Street brokerage firms. Although violations may have amounted to just a few pennies for each individual investor, in the aggregate, they cost small investors billions of dollars annually.

7. Substantial insurance companies in some cases conducted a practice known as "contingent commissions," where there were insurer payments to brokers who would in exchange steer business back to the insurer by rigging bids and fixing prices.

Laws Cannot Impose Business Ethics

Self-regulation in our free market economic system failed miserably in recent times. Without state securities regulators, like New York Attorney General Eliot Spitzer, it is unlikely that any consequential action would have been taken against unprincipled investment banking conduct.

The 1990s were another "boom" period in America's economic history when business ethics were carelessly cast aside in the chase for material gain. We were once again reminded that laws can only persuade proper conduct; they cannot instill integrity, personal responsibility, or business ethics.

There is nothing innately moral about free markets or democracy. They are only as good as the morality of the self-governing individuals who participate. And worthy business ethics are nothing more than commendable personal ethics in the aggregate. Therefore, when personal ethics become divorced from morality and religious principles, more often than not, they become relative and impotent.

It is important to note that America's businesses are not inherently corrupt. Many honorable and faith-filled citizens are at the helm of these vital institutions. Much of the problem stems from the fact that the majority of businesses are fixated upon the short-term bottom line.

Wall Street offers little consolation for those companies who may have taken current charges against profitability in order to build for the longer term. Financial capital and executive compensation are both clearly tied to their immediate bottom lines.

In total, contemporary business executives may receive hundreds of millions of dollars in annual compensation based primarily on their companies' performance—even though conflicting with healthier long-term fiscal decisions for the company. Bonuses, stock options, and extravagant perks are generously offered as carrots to attract managerial talent.

But should we squabble with effective executives who are paid well when athletes, pop stars, and other entertainers often command outrageous sums in the marketplace? On the contrary, valuable executives who create jobs and other forms of wealth should be monetarily rewarded for their industrious efforts. However, rewarding senior executives for performance generated by self-serving manipulation of the bottom line is immoral if not criminal.

With tremendous pressure to perform and intense global competition, some companies have stopped making prudent longer-term investments in their most precious resource—their people. As jobs are increasingly outsourced to save costs in the short-run, too little attention is being paid to effectively balancing the bottom line with employee development. Over the long-term this may curtail productivity since it is precisely people who are the real engine behind economic development; they are the ultimate resource in the marketplace.

Perhaps former Federal Reserve Chairman Alan Greenspan expressed it best when he said, "People today aren't greedier than people in the past, it is just that the avenues to express greed are so vast." As with so many things in life, investing is an act of faith requiring trust. Without faith and confidence that a company's financials reflect reality, our capital markets simply cannot function properly.

Increasing shareholder wealth requires the public's trust, with this trust resting upon ethical business practices. If you remove the non-economic asset of integrity from the marketplace, the constructive interplay regarding all other economic assets comes to a grinding halt. More importantly, in order to receive "true riches," we must be trustworthy with worldly wealth.

Ethical values ultimately affect all facets of society—not just business practices on Wall Street. Syndicated columnist Chuck Colson put it this way: "Societies are tragically vulnerable when the men and women who compose them lack character. A nation or culture cannot endure for long unless it is under-girded by common values such as valor, public-spiritedness, and respect for others and for the law; it cannot stand unless it is populated by people who will act on motives superior to their own immediate interests."

Families Have Their Own Challenges

Former Senator Patrick Moynihan of New York said the biggest change he had seen in his 40-year political career was that the family structure had come apart all over North America. There is plenty of evidence to back Moynihan's claim.

Since 1960, the divorce rate has more than doubled; out-of-wedlock births have gone from one in twenty to one in three, and the percentage of single-parent families has more than tripled. And yet, even in light of these dramatic statistics, the most important institution charged with forming moral character is the family. In his book, *The Broken Hearth,* William J. Bennett states, "The family has suffered a blow that has no historical precedent—and one that has enormous ramifications for American society."

The technological advancements of recent years have failed to provide greater opportunities for parents to spend extended quality time with their children. More and more working couples and single parents are discovering that nannies and daycare centers are ill-equipped to impart meaningful values to today's youth.

"Family values," so casually paraded around during political campaigns, nonetheless, are vital to our nation's well-being and our sense of morality. Apart from racy sit-coms like *Sex in the City* and *Desperate Housewives*, we also need engaging TV shows that revere the nuclear family, uphold moral values and support committed relationships.

Many children and young adults are spending more time watching television, using the Internet, or playing computer-driven games than personally interacting with their peers. In our quest for technological advancement, we unknowingly may be creating an environment where our children are becoming more comfortable with things than they are with one another.

By the time our children become teenagers, on average, they have already spent three years in front of televisions, some of it watching programs on MTV or VH-1 which often border on soft porn. And a favorite video game among our youth today, which has won numerous "Game of the Year" awards, is a trip to the party capital of America called "Grand Theft Auto Vice City™," where players can interact with hookers, gangsters, and corrupt politicians.

Sadly, almost half of U.S. high school students feel unsafe in their schools, according to a recently released survey based on responses from students at 87 high schools in 19 states. "Even the best of families are in danger of falling victim to a *Home Invasion*," commented noted author Rebecca Hagelin— "not by a pack of criminals who brazenly and forcefully assault us in order to rob us of our possessions, but by a culture that has slyly slithered into our senses in order to rob us of our souls."

Television, in many cases, only serves to heighten consumer expectations and appetites. As religious historian Robert Bellah commented, "That happiness is to be attained through limitless acquisition is denied by every religion and philosophy known to mankind, but is preached incessantly by every American television set."

In our neighborhoods, we are experiencing far less face-to-face contact than we did 50 years ago, which has led to a decline in our sense of community and need for one another. Weekly trips to Wal-Mart, Home Depot, and Blockbuster do not satisfy the need for community-building events. As corporations increased in size to gain competitive advantage, Americans began losing touch with the mom and pop shops that helped create a sense of community and common identity.

The vibrancy of American civil society has noticeably declined over the past several decades. Individuals are now more isolated and our social capital ("connections among individuals") has likewise diminished. In order to build up individual associations, institutions, communities and social capital itself, it may take another "great awakening," according to Harvard Sociologist Robert Putnam, whose influential work on social capital found that religion and spiritual capital are by far the greatest determiners of social capital in the United States.

A Threat Greater than Terrorism

Every day we receive new reports on the threat of terrorism. FOX News routinely flashes "TERROR ALERT: ELEVATED" across the bottom of the TV screen as many of us view the day's news. While those unnerving reports pose some serious concerns, is there a greater threat to our quality of life that until recently has managed to escape detection on the radar screen?

This foe is not found in Baghdad. Rather, this enemy is located in our homeland and is made up of unrestrained government spending and a swelling debt, both private and public. Yet, it is an adversary that threatens our very foundation and an essential part of the American Dream. In 1816, Thomas Jefferson spoke of this enemy when he warned, "I place the economy among the first and most important of republic virtues, and public debt as the greatest of dangers to be feared."

In more recent times, President George W. Bush informed the American people that "to win the war, protect the homeland, and revitalize our economy—our budget will run a deficit that will be small and short term so long as Congress restrains spending and acts in a fiscally responsible manner." The facts were, however, that the deficit proved to be quite large and long term, where a fiscally irresponsible Congress failed to contain spending.

A projected 10-year budget surplus of $5.6 trillion at the beginning of the Bush Administration quickly became a projected deficit of $3 trillion over the next decade. To be fair, the combined effect of the stock market bubble, an inherited recession, 9/11, and the ongoing War on Terror went a long way in dramatically reversing budget projections.

Be that as it may, Republicans and Democrats did little to defend our country's need for fiscal restraint. Excluding the growth in entitlement spending, not a single member of the 108th Congress had a net voting record that would have reduced government spending. Likewise, President Bush overlooked pork barrel projects and did not veto a single bill during the same period.

Federal spending has skyrocketed in recent times—up over 33% since 2001. Now well in excess of $22,000 per household, federal spending is at its highest levels since World War II. There have been massive increases in defense, farm subsidies, education, and Medicare—where the Prescription Drug Program became the first major entitlement bill enacted without any taxes to pay for it.

President Ronald Reagan used to remark, "It is not that people are taxed too little; it is that government spends too much." Reagan's words were right on the mark, but little has been done to stem the tide of fiscal irresponsibility. In just twenty-five short years, America shamefully went from being the largest creditor nation in the world to being the largest debtor nation.

Red ink has become commonplace as the numbers keep mounting. But budgets are more than just a set of black and red numbers. They are moral and cultural statements about our priorities in allocating limited resources. Budgets demand wisdom and discipline when being crafted and carried out, where promoting the common good must take precedence over special interests.

In growing numbers, politicians often place their own interests first and their respective party's interests second, while the needs of the American people (particularly young Americans) remain a distant third. Rather than responsibly pairing interim tax cuts with permanent spending cuts, permanent tax cuts are being sought along with hefty spending increases.

Just the same, "spending cuts" are openly touted in Washington when there are no spending cuts, only minor adjustments that slow spending growth. For example, the White House recently proposed to "cut" Medicare by about $36 billion over the next five years. But this "cut" only represents 1.5% of Medicare's outlays and merely slows the growth of Medicare from 70% to 66% over the next five years.

We live in a time where tax cuts and spending increases are popular and painless, while tax increases and spending cuts are demanding and discarded. Yet, this reckless combination has all the makings of becoming a serious bombshell where the fallout will be severe. The federal debt has already increased from about $6 trillion in early 2002 to nearly $9 trillion by the end of 2007. Without major spending cuts, tax increases, or both, the national debt is projected to grow by more than $3 trillion through 2010 to $11.2 trillion.

Warren Buffet recently commented on the current political and financial debacle by stating, "Today, too many of our country's key economic decisions are being made with an eye toward the next election rather than to the next generation."

Hundreds of billions of dollars are being projected as annual budget deficits through the end of the decade. More disturbing is the fact that non-defense related items have represented the biggest bulk of the spending increase since 9/11. In fact, half of all new spending in the past two years is from areas unrelated to defense and homeland security.

America's trade deficit poses a real problem too. Americans are now buying foreign goods with the money foreigners lend to finance our trade debt (in excess of $725 billion for 2005). In essence, we are using borrowed dollars to buy goods we do not produce. Should foreigners ever lose their appetite for dollar denominated assets and the dollar loses it coveted status as the world's reserve currency, America's economy would be at serious risk.

In contemporary times, America's longstanding commitment to fiscal restraint has been missing in action. Since 2002 we no longer have budget rules that require a future increase in benefit payments or cuts in taxes to be paid for by cutting spending in other areas or increasing taxes. The fervor for permanent tax cuts has replaced the restraint of a pay-as-you-go system.

Will we dispense with the lessons of history which make evident that tax cuts without offsetting spending cuts inevitably causes government deficits to swell, and subsequently, undercut national savings and the ability to grow the economy? While liberal "tax and spend" policies correspond with those of a spendthrift, it is hard to support conservative "borrow and spend" courses of conduct.

Will we continue to go down the undisciplined path of having more government than we are willing to pay for with taxes? After all, it is the level of federal spending that determines the level of taxation; not the other way around. The primary problem in Washington is spending, not how it is financed.

Be that as it may, we seem to be acting like a nation convinced that it can have "guns" and "butter" together. In fighting the War on Terror we were not asked to pay higher taxes for it; instead, we were given four considerable tax cuts. We were not even asked to endure shortages, conserve oil, or reduce our dependence on it. On the contrary, we were advised that it was our patriotic due to live normally and to keep up our economic consumption, where for too long we have consumed far more than we have produced as a nation.

Although many would like to believe that we will simply "grow our way out" of any economic plight without tax increases and accompanying benefit reductions, the unsettling truth is that we would be better off putting our faith in the benevolence of the Easter Bunny.

Many, however, seem unconcerned with deficits in this debt-based economy, where debt has become tantamount to an inalienable right. How can this be when our national savings rate is practically zero (the lowest savings rate in the developed world), and where consumer debt along with personal bankruptcies are at an all time high?

Part of the problem is that the size of the federal debt—now about $8 trillion—relative to the overall economy and GDP is perceived as manageable. But federal debt, due mainly to swelling entitlements, should be growing much faster than GDP in the years to come. In a few decades or less the federal debt will plainly be too large a percentage of GDP to ignore.

As a whole, people are not preparing for what is likely to come. Instead too many of us are sleepwalking through our window of preparation. Tens of millions of Americans are seriously under prepared to meet the financial demands they will face in retirement. Only 15% of working age Americans have an IRA and only 22% contribute to a 401(k) plan, according to Employee Benefit Research Institute (EBRI). EBRI forecasts that retirees will have $45 billion less in retirement income in 2030 then they will need to cover basic expenses.

It used to be said, "What was good for General Motors was good for America." Today, what has become reality for General Motors is becoming reality for America. Just as General Motors overextended itself, so too, will our government and other corporate conglomerates continue to ratchet back on benefits and other financial promises earlier made.

The dispiriting truth is that the vast majority of pension plans face massive cash shortfalls. Of the 369 Standard & Poors companies that offer pension plans, 311 do not have enough money to cover their obligations. Most likely the Pension Benefit Guaranty Corporation may need a substantial taxpayer bailout by the end of the decade. The majority of public employee pension plans are not well managed either and in the aggregate they are hundreds of billions of dollars under funded.

We live in a world that simply ignores the Bible's admonition to "Let no debt remain outstanding, except the continuing debt to love one another" (Romans 13:8) and to be aware that "The wicked borrow and do not repay, but the righteous give generously" (Psalm 37:21).

Are we willing to heed the latest warnings of the economic bombshell to come? As former Fed Chief Greenspan warned shortly before leaving his post, huge fiscal strains pose "significant economic risks" and the government should seek to "close the fiscal gap primarily, if no wholly, from the outlay (spending) side." Clearly, deficits are the symptoms, but spending is the disease.

In this regard, entitlements are the "Mother of all monetary time-bombs" and will surely cripple America unless reformed soon. Already, entitlements and interest on the national debt account for nearly two-thirds of federal spending today. Without present reform, the current pay-as-you-go entitlement system will become unsustainable in future decades as payroll taxes on a shrinking workforce will not provide the promised benefits for an expanding elderly base.

Alarmingly, there is a gigantic imbalance of around $46 trillion in unfunded obligations in our entitlement system. To put this number in perspective, consider that if a person lived for 70 years, he or she would have to spend $39,138,943 every day for 70 years to equal just one trillion dollars. Our nation's unfunded liability number is a staggering large sum of money.

It is interesting to note that under Sarbanes-Oxley corporate America is required to disclose its future obligations for retirement and medical benefits.

This has an immediate negative impact on profitability. The government, on the other hand, has no such mandate. If the government were required to follow the same set of rules of transparency, however, then America would be nearing "bankruptcy" because its' entire net worth is only about $50 trillion. This sum marginally exceeds the previously mentioned unfunded liability number of $46 trillion.

The fiscal battlefield will become even uglier when Baby Boomers begin retiring near the end of the decade, and Medicare will quickly doubles in size. At that time, the cash-flow surplus from Social Security will no longer be able to be used to pay for Medicare's swelling deficits and escalating costs.

Lest we forget, our recent efforts at Social Security reform flatly failed and there is not a political prescription in sight to even attempt Medicare reform. The harsh reality is that entitlement programs have now become akin to massive "Ponzi schemes."

Will Baby Boomers, who put the word "shop-a-holic" into our lexicon, be counted on to press for fiscal restraint when they retire? Or will our lack of fiscal discipline continue and ultimately succeed in taking down America and the Dream in a way that the terrorists could not?

America's chief financial architect, Alexander Hamilton, once said, "A *well-funded* debt would be a national blessing that would protect American prosperity." But today's debt is not well-funded; it has become a national curse that threatens the very core of America's continued prosperity.

In reality, Hamilton was adamantly against having the type of perpetual public debt that exists today. He strongly believed that "the creation of debt should always be accompanied with the means of extinguishment." As the first Secretary of the Treasury (1789–1795), Hamilton issued a grave warning when he said *"the progressive accumulation of debt is perhaps the NATURAL DISEASE of all Governments. And it is not easy to conceive anything more likely than this to lead to great and convulsive revolutions of Empire."*

Around the same time as Hamilton's admonition, Professor Alexander Tyler similarly forewarned: "A democracy will continue to exist up until the time that voters discover that they can vote themselves generous gifts from the public treasury. From that moment on, the majority always votes for the candidates who promise the most benefits from the public treasury, *with the result that every democracy will finally collapse due to loose fiscal policy..."*

America is in serious danger of becoming a welfare state. In a protracted war on terrorism that is sure to be fought in the words of President Bush, "for years and decades, not weeks and months," getting a firm grip on how best to apportion our already burdened economic resources is critical. In that regard, Will Rogers offered sage advice, "If you find yourself in a hole, the first thing to do is to quit digging."

"Great Necessities Call Out Our Great Virtues"

If Retirees are the greatest generation, it may well be that the calamitous circumstances they faced demanded greatness from them. Great necessities call out our great virtues.

Within each generation, however, there are those who are largely self-seeking and materialistic, as well as those who are often unselfish and spiritually minded. Espousing generational superiority and reminiscing about the "good old days" can present a rather limited view of our world. Additionally, many people belonging to the "greatest generation," who supported government policies focused on the future, now seem content to live off government policies that support the moment at the expense of the future.

It is a natural tendency to believe that in the present we are on some slippery slope, with the past nostalgically viewed as an ascent toward a noble ambition. Yet, there has never been a time when the Founding Fathers would have found the state of our Union in complete harmony with their virtuous desires.

Patrick Henry was deeply concerned about the decline of morality after the Revolutionary War. Likewise, Abraham Lincoln warned that the indispensable virtues that the Revolutionary War taught were being leveled by the silent artilleries of time. And the Roaring 20s did not bring America to a moral high ground. Still, religious principles and patriotic values were much more a part of the moral fabric of our society in years past than they are today.

As an increasingly materialistic American Dream has been passed down from Retirees to Boomers to Xers, there has been a distancing from traditional religious virtues and patriotic values. The community reserve of available spiritual capital has noticeably declined with some people questioning whether younger generations will have the moral fortitude to deal with difficult times ahead.

The greatest impact may be felt by Generation Y (1977–2002), which is more than 70 million strong and still defining itself. From daycare to day camp, this is the most structured generation in history. They are a generation with very high expectations of themselves and others, and they can be high maintenance.

But there are reasons for optimism. Many Xers have fought courageously in the War on Terror. Recent reports published by the *City Journal* suggest that Generation "X" has begun the process of self-correcting from nontraditional values as the number of married-coupled families increased during the 1990s. In addition, Xers tend to spend more quality time with their children as compared to Boomers.

Early indications are that violence, drug use, and teen sex have started to decline among today's youth. And this may well lead to more team-oriented and civic-minded young Americans over the next twenty years as suggested by noted generational authors Neil Howe and William Strauss.

At this critical juncture in our nation's history, however, we are by no means out of the woods. As the unifying effect of September 11th fades, coming together as "One Nation under God" will not be easy. A recent USATODAY/CNN/Gallup Poll "found that 65% of Americans say the country is 'greatly divided' about the most important values, and 72% say people are more deeply split on major issues than at any time in recent years." Finding common ground and shared moral values will surely demand our best effort and our willingness to have faith, not only in ourselves, but in God's grace.

There is an immense need for more high-caliber leaders. We especially need ordinary heroes from everyday life—those who will help pave America's way to a promising future.

Retirees, as elders and counselors, perhaps may have a special part to play in shaping America's future. Traditional roles and values, so essential to our nation's beginning, have fallen into obscurity. To a large degree, our world reveres those who are young and successful, often ignoring the wisdom of those who have prevailed in facing the challenges of the past.

It feels good to hear the President say that the state of our Union has never been stronger. The foundation of our Union and the American Dream, however, are only as strong as our moral values, our fiscal responsibility, and our faith in God.

Present-day military might and material abundance in comparison to the rest of the globe are a testament to the greatness our Union. But they can only carry our republic so far. As was the case for so much of our history, America's wellbeing very much depends upon the guiding hand of divine Providence and the moral character of a free people.

If we lose sight of these truths, we will surely lose the heart and soul of a great nation. Thomas Jefferson put it this way, "Yes, we did produce a near-perfect republic, but will they keep it? Or will they, in their enjoyment of plenty, lose the memory of freedom? Material abundance without character is the path of destruction."

In his 2005 State of the Union speech, President Bush properly observed, "Now, as we see a little gray in the mirror, or a lot of gray, and we watch our children moving into adulthood, we ask the question: What will be the state of their Union?" The President's answer was that first, we must be "good stewards of the economy;" and second, we must "honor and pass along values that sustain a free society."

Whether we are able to meet the challenges of providing a proper state of the Union for our children will in no small way depend upon our ability to reconnect with the unwavering principles found in the city of God.

CHAPTER QUESTIONS

1. Which deficit is of greater concern—a deficit of decency or of economics? Why?

2. What things can you do to insure that your personal ethics will bolster business ethics?

3. Can great virtue be formed in the absence of great adversity? Why or why not?

Lasting Wealth depends upon a foundation of moral values and an allegiance to virtue.

"I believe that George Washington knew
that the City of Man cannot survive
without the City of God, that the Visible City
will perish without the Invisible City."
—President Ronald Reagan

13

RETURN TO THE CITY OF GOD

*"If my people who are called by my name
will humble themselves and pray and seek my face
and turn from their wicked ways, then will I hear from
heaven and will forgive their sin and will heal their land."*
—2 Chronicles 7:14

In his classic, *City of God*, St. Augustine says there are two kinds of cities. The earthly city, or City of Man, sets forth the notion that life on Earth is temporal. In this city, obtaining power, acquiring possessions, and building vast empires are the goal. The American Dream for the City of Man revolves around the domain of the state, political authority, and what people possess.

The City of God, on the other hand, accepts following God's will as the highest purpose, all people as brothers and sisters, and eternal life as the primary goal. How gifts and talents are used to transform the temporal world in order to build God's kingdom, above all, describes this city and, accordingly, defines the American Dream.

As Rome was perishing in the early fifth century, Augustine's work describing these two cities made it clear that as man's world passes away there is another more enduring world, which is more essential. Few literary works have had a greater impact on the development of Western civilization.

These two cities naturally have very different understandings of the purpose of life, the role of God, and the necessity of virtues. Unfortunately, our culture today more closely resembles a City of Man, even though America began as an attempt to found a City of God.

Despite theological differences, the early settlers were devoted to their religious faiths and virtuous conduct. Although religion and our federal legislature were to be separated, our limited government was designed so its people and their Creator would stay united.

Our Creator and Our Inalienable Rights

The Declaration of Independence, principally drafted by Thomas Jefferson, was greatly influenced by the principles of the Enlightenment, where self-interest was balanced against the common good in accordance with human reason. But America rejected the Enlightenment's hostility to faith.

The Declaration of Independence refers to our Creator, directly and indirectly, four different times, and clearly states—"All Men are created equal, that they are endowed by their Creator with certain inalienable Rights, that among these are Life, Liberty, and the pursuit of Happiness. That to secure these rights, Governments are instituted among men...." These rights, as given to us by our Creator, were the very truths that the Founding Fathers held to be self-evident.

It was never the framers' position that individuals had inalienable rights in and of themselves, or that the government possessed its power to govern independently of our Creator. The Declaration of Independence affirmed the notion that God alone gave us our inalienable rights, and that the primary purpose of government was to secure those God-given rights. The Constitution does not grant us any rights; it simply guarantees them.

The notion that our inalienable rights are a gift from God, and not from the state, has been repeatedly underscored throughout our nation's history. In his *Notes on the State of Virginia* (1781), Thomas Jefferson wrote: "God who gave us life gave us liberty. And can the liberties of a nation be thought secure when we have removed their only basis, a conviction in the minds of people that these liberties are a gift from God?"

Likewise, Ben Franklin in his *Maxims and Morals* stated: "Freedom is not a gift bestowed upon us by other men, but a right that belongs to us by the laws of God." Even John F. Kennedy in his Inaugural Address in 1961 held that, "The rights of man come not from the generosity of the state, but from the hand of God."

America's government was unique because it was established with the understanding that God does not choose select groups or certain families to rule. Our newly established republic decisively rejected the Divine Right which many monarchies had used for centuries to justify their rule. The Divine Right of kings and queens long held that their power came to them directly from God, which they used in governing the people.

Our limited form of government, in contrast to Divine Right, adopted the Transmission Theory, whereby God's authority is not transmitted directly to those who rule, but indirectly to the rulers through the people. Under this theory, power came unswervingly from God to the people who, in turn, loaned it to the government. The government, therefore, should reflect godly principles.

Today, regrettably, many of us see little or no connection between our God and our country's future. We have outlawed any meaningful expression of the Creator, prayer, and many religious traditions and customs in our public institutions.

School children can apparently feel good about showing off their latest toys during "Show and Tell" sessions, but must hide their faith as if it's something embarrassing. Even academically they are rarely learning about each other's faiths. Unfortunately, this precludes children from respecting differences and celebrating common interests.

Our youth need to be receiving an ample amount of information regarding our Christian heritage through school history, but this instruction is generally prohibited. In the past, textbooks like *The New England Primer* and, thereafter, *The McGuffey Readers*, although not "politically correct" because they espoused only a Protestant-Christian perspective, nevertheless imparted an education rich in convictions, principles, and moral excellence for well over 200 years.

Similarly, many of the first colleges and universities like Harvard, Yale, and Princeton were founded for the purpose of teaching students about the Creator and all of creation. Today, not one of America's 50 top colleges and universities even requires students to study American history. The history of the United States has essentially been ignored and the important role of religion forgotten.

A 1999 survey of seniors at fifty-five top colleges revealed the following: "More than a third did not know the Constitution established the division of power in government. Forty percent could not say within half a century when the Civil War was fought. More students named the Civil War general, Ulysses S. Grant over George Washington as the man who defeated the British at Yorktown. And only twenty-two percent could identify the Gettysburg address as the source of the phrase "government of the people, by the people, for the people."

For the majority of our nation's history, school teachers have played an important role as character educators. During the 1960s and 1970s, however, they became "facilitators" as students were encouraged to clarify their own values. This mindset has continued unaltered today as student values are radically influenced by television, hit movies, the Internet, and pop music.

For example, Eminem, a foul-mouthed rap artist, is a very powerful name in music and exerts a tremendous influence on today's youth. Far from being a healthy role model, Eminem's lyrics are often racist, sexist, and otherwise offensive. President George W. Bush once referred to him as "the most dangerous threat to American children since polio."

In school systems across America, sex education is mandatory while religious education is frowned upon. But, as distinguished theologian and social policy commentator Michael Novak pointed out, "Americans are starved for good conversations about important matters of the human spirit. In Victorian England, religious devotion was not a forbidden topic of conversation; sex was. In America today, the inhibitions are reversed."

Freedom From Religion as Church and State Separate

The framers of our Constitution plainly wanted to safeguard our federal government from adopting a national religion that would give preferential treatment to particular religious sects or denominations. They envisioned healthy competition among religion in a free and open society. Like Adam Smith, they believed that religion would prosper in a free marketplace. In our concern over "separating church from state," however, we have extended preferential treatment to those who would prevent the practicing of religion at the expense of free religious expression.

Consider the *Annals of Congress* where James Madison initially proposed the following religion clause regarding the First Amendment—"The civil rights of none shall be abridged on account of religious belief or worship, nor shall any national religion be established, nor shall the full and equal rights of conscience be in any manner, or on any pretext, infringed."

Madison believed people feared that one or more Christian sects might obtain preeminence, or join together to establish a national religion. Madison ultimately withdrew the word "national," because others objected that the Constitution created only a limited federal government, not a national government. The First Amendment embodied a simple yet profound notion: you cannot establish a national religion or disestablish matters of religion within the states.

Our country's founders merely wanted to prevent the type of religious persecution that had occurred in parts of Europe from happening in America. Americans, however, were always supposed to have the religious freedom to openly pursue God in their state and local communities. Religious freedom of expression, as opposed to religious abstinence, was seen as necessary for the proper functioning of society.

At the time our Constitution was created, relationships between religion and civil governments were defined in most state constitutions and local charters. In fact, if you read through the preambles to each state's constitution today you will most likely find a reference to God.

Our Constitution essentially provided enumerated powers to a limited federal government, and religion was not one of the powers given to Congress. For this reason the original Constitution reveals little regarding religion.

The Library of Congress's highly acclaimed exhibit on "Religion and the Founding of the American Republic" by Dr. James H. Hutson (found at www.loc.gov/exhibits/religion/), makes this point regarding the Constitution's relative silence on religion—"That religion was not otherwise addressed in the Constitution did not make it an 'irreligious' document any more than the Articles of Confederation was an irreligious document. The Constitution dealt with the church precisely as the Articles had, thereby maintaining, at the national level, the religious status quo. In neither document did the people yield any explicit power to act in the field of religion. But the absence of expressed powers did not prevent either the Continental-Confederation

Congress or the Congress under the Constitution from sponsoring a program to support general, nonsectarian religion."

The Constitution was not meant to replace existing state constitutions; it was created primarily to establish limits on the powers of a new federal government. The First Amendment of The Bill of Rights clearly reflects this since only "Congress shall make no law respecting an establishment of religion or prohibiting the free exercise thereof." State governments had no such restrictions. More importantly, they would not have ratified the Constitution and The Bill of Rights if they had understood that this would dismantle religious expression in public institutions within each state.

The Constitution simply deferred to the states on matters of religion. This did not mean that the people of all religious faiths within any state were treated equally. Rather, some states like Massachusetts and Virginia adopted state religions. When state constitutions adopted a bill of rights that promised religious freedom to individuals, most "religious freedom" was tied to professing only some form of Christianity.

In this regard, the efforts of Thomas Jefferson and James Madison were instrumental in establishing religious freedom in their own state of Virginia—a standard other states soon began to endorse. Virginia, like other states at the time, was supporting religion through a general religious tax. Taxpayers earmarked which church they wanted to support. Yet, this resulted in only Christian churches being supported with already-established churches benefiting the most. Madison's *Memorial and Remonstrance Against Religious Assessments* and Jefferson's *Statute for Religious Freedom*, thwarted state aid to religion in Virginia and established religious liberty.

Noticeably, there were no Moslems, Hindus, or any other non-Christian faiths sufficiently represented in our nation's founding documents. Deists like Benjamin Franklin and Thomas Jefferson were in the minority of this highly Christian group of men. Just the same, all people in America are entitled to an appropriate expression of their religious beliefs.

The demand for freedom cannot ignore the duty to the free exercise of religion in society. The right to religious freedom has its foundation in the dignity of the human person. Governments should take into account the religious life of its citizenry and safeguard the religious freedom of all of its citizens.

Politics and morality are inseparable; every piece of legislation has somebody's morality attached to it. It is not a matter of whether religion should be in government; rather, it is a question of whose religion, secular or otherwise, will serve as a basis for the morality underlying our government. Sadly, and in the name of offending no one, we have established the religion of secular humanism.

Religion, however, provides worthwhile principles by which to govern and maintain moral order. Historian Will Durant put it this way, "There is no significant example in history, before our time, of a society successfully maintaining moral order without the aid of religion."

Our government needs to accommodate the active participation of people from all faiths. In our pluralistic society today, republican virtue rests on more than the free exercise of any one religion. Still, the principles of our Judeo/Christian heritage represent a tried and true foundation upon which to build.

In no event should there be an "impenetrable wall" separating church and state because this type of barrier prevents sensible and limited expressions of religion in our public institutions. It also abandons vital customs and traditions that are part of our moral heritage. Even Jefferson and Madison, during their presidencies, encouraged and attended the largest Protestant church services in America, which were held at the Capitol beginning in 1800 and continued there over the next 50 years.

Staying connected to our Creator, regrettably, has little place left in our public domain. This is true despite the fact that, according to a recent *Newsweek* poll, most Americans believe it is acceptable for the government to promote religious expression, as long as no specific religion is mentioned.

Although Congress still has no law respecting the establishment of religion, our laws often publicly prohibit free expression. A donated monument regarding the Ten Commandments displayed in an Alabama courthouse rotunda was declared unconstitutional and removed. A simple monument that memorializes our religious heritage and also serves as the basis for many of our laws today was alarmingly seen as rising to an "establishment of a religion."

Instead of freedom of religion, we more often have freedom *from* religion. Church and State are distinct, but they are also interrelated. While the State should never impose a religion, it should seek to guarantee religious freedom.

Government should always protect orderly and privately initiated religious expressions and activities from government interference and discrimination. Any efforts to separate church from State should not separate God from the citizens of the State.

Are We Still "One Nation Under God"?

Around the start of the Baby Boom, the Supreme Court in *Everson v. Board of Education* (1947) essentially rewrote the First Amendment to say "Congress [and all States] shall make no law regarding the establishment of religion..." The Court's decision in that case made a *de facto* amendment to our Constitution, something which Congress was never able to accomplish.

The rationale for the Court's decision in *Everson* was to link the First Amendment and Fourteenth Amendment together, but this was not the intent of the authors of the First and Fourteenth Amendments. The First Amendment, along with the other nine Amendments to the Constitution that comprise The Bill of Rights, was originally intended as a limitation on the federal government's action against the citizens of individual states. However, during the twentieth century, the Supreme Court began using the Fourteenth Amendment (adopted in 1868), which was initially enacted to extend civil rights to freed slaves, and also limit the actions of state and local governments.

In *Everson* the Court in making its unprecedented ruling, reflected the spirit of religious atrocities that had been committed against minorities both here and abroad. As such, the Court began ignoring the religious sentiment of the majority of Americans. For the first time in the Court's 150-year history, it began finding that the Establishment Clause of the First Amendment was intended to erect a "wall of separation" between church and state.

During the Baby Boom and Generation X, the Court built the wall higher and made it more impenetrable. States were no longer permitted to have nonobligatory, nondenominational prayers recited in public schools, nor could they set aside one minute of the day for silent voluntary prayer. Schools were generally prohibited from having the Ten Commandments posted in public classrooms.

Recently, the U.S. Supreme Court failed to decide whether the words "under God," as recited by teacher-led school children in the Pledge of

Allegiance, were unconstitutional. Ironically, pledging allegiance to our nation's flag "under God" may one day become illegal in our public school systems under the First Amendment. Yet, burning the flag as an act of insurrection receives Constitutional protection under the same amendment as "freedom of speech."

There is simply no consistently applied judicial principle regarding freedom of religious cases—each ruling must be done on a case by case basis. This has led to results that are mixed and often inconsistent. Consider that in recent rulings the Ten Commandments were allowed to be displayed outside a Texas State Capital but not inside a Kentucky courthouse.

The dispiriting truth, however, is that we are no longer free to publicly pursue God in our local communities as our Founding Fathers originally intended and practiced for over 150 years. C.S. Lewis noted that "the modern world insists that religion be a purely private affair, then shrinks the area of privacy to the vanishing point. When the state moves in, separation means forcing the church to move out. And the state keeps moving into new domains that it claims as its own."

America, however, was founded upon godly principles, and religious faith played an important role in our nation's history. It is a matter of historical record that all of the colonies were founded on the religious precepts of Christianity. Moreover, all of the colonial constitutions acknowledged that God had a hand in their founding and expansion. For more evidence consider the following:

The Continental Confederation of Congress

The Continental Confederation of Congress governed the United States from 1774 to 1789 with many members in disagreement due to differing state interests and various religious backgrounds. At their first meeting, there was rumor of an impending war with Britain which had the most powerful army and largest navy in the world. What was the new Congress's first official act? Members requested a session of prayer.

Some initially objected because differing religious perspectives (Episcopalians, Quakers, Anabaptists, Presbyterians, Deists, and Congregationalists) would not allow them to join in the same act of prayer. Yet, they quickly put their differences aside and found common ground in piety, virtue, and patriotism as they read a Jewish prayer, Psalm 35, in *The Book of Common Prayer.*

John Adams who attended the meeting, wrote his wife Abigail, "I never saw a greater effect upon an audience. It seemed as if heaven had ordained that Psalm be read on that morning. It was enough to melt a stone. I saw tears gush into the eyes of the old Quakers of Philadelphia. I must beg you, Abigail, to read that Psalm."

The Articles of Confederation did not officially authorize its members to become involved in religious affairs. Nevertheless, Congress appointed Congressional chaplains, sponsored the publication of the Bible, and proclaimed national days of thanksgiving, humiliation, fasting, and prayer at least twice a year throughout the war—beseeching God to establish "the independence of these United States upon the basis of religion and virtue."

George Washington

George Washington believed in the importance of religious principles for the new republican government. As Commander-in-Chief, Washington had his troops begin each day in public prayer. His first official act after being sworn in as President was to join with all the members of the House and Senate in a two-hour worship service. At the end of his public service in office, George Washington warned all in his Farewell Address:

"Of all the dispositions and habits which lead to political prosperity, religion and morality are indispensable supports.... And let us with caution indulge the supposition that morality can be maintained without religion. Whatever may be conceded to the influence of refined education on minds of peculiar structure, reason and experience both forbid us to expect that national morality can prevail in exclusion of religious principle."

Benjamin Franklin

Though widely known as a deist, Benjamin Franklin acknowledged the need for prayer within government during the Continental Convention on June 28, 1787. At 81, he addressed George Washington, the Convention's

President, as follows: "In the beginning of the contest with Great Britain when we were sensible to danger, we had daily prayers in this room for Divine protection.

"Our prayers, Sir, were heard and they were graciously answered…. I have lived, Sir, a long time and the longer I live, the more convincing proofs I see of this truth that—God governs in the affairs of men. And, if a sparrow cannot fall to the ground without His notice, is it probable that an empire can rise without His aide?

"We have been assured, Sir, in the Sacred Writings that, 'except the Lord build the house, they labor in vain that build it.' … I firmly believe this; and I also believe that without His concurring aid, we shall succeed in this political building no better than the Builders of Babel… I therefore beg leave to move that henceforth, prayers imploring the assistance of Heaven and its blessing on our deliberation be held in this Assembly every morning before we proceed to business, and that one or more of the Clergy of this City be requested to officiate in that Service."

John Adams

For many years our nation's second President, John Adams, made it a practice to annually read through the entire Bible, and routinely stressed the importance of biblically based principles in government. On October 11, 1798, he addressed the military as follows: "We have no government armed with power capable of contending with human passions unbridled by morality and religion. Avarice, ambition, revenge, or gallantry would break the strongest cords of our Constitution as a whale goes through a net. Our Constitution was made only for a moral and religious people. It is wholly inadequate to the government of any other."

And in a letter to Benjamin Rush, dated August 28, 1811, Adams noted that "religion and virtue are the only foundations, not only of republicanism and of all free government, but of social felicity under all governments and in all the combinations of human society."

Alexis de Tocqueville

This French philosopher wrote the acclaimed, *Democracy in America*, a two-volume study of the American people and their political institutions.

In his writings, de Tocqueville notes that, "I sought the key to the greatness of America.... Not until I went into the churches of America and heard her pulpits flame with righteousness did I understand the secret of her genius and power. America is great because America is good, and if America ever ceases to be good, America will cease to be great....

"Religion in America takes no direct part in their government of society, but it must be regarded as the first of their political institutions. I do not know whether all Americans have a sincere faith in their religion—for who can search the human heart? But I am certain that they hold it [religion] to be indispensable to the maintenance of republic institutions."

James Madison

The father of our Constitution proclaimed: "We have staked the whole future of American Civilization, not upon the power of government... We have staked the future upon the capacity of each and all of us to govern ourselves, according to the Ten Commandments of God. If this freedom be abused it is an offense against God, not against man."

Gouverneur Morris

A signatory to the Constitution, Gouverneur Morris spoke more than any other member from the floor of the Constitutional Convention. He was also head of the committee responsible for the final wording of the Constitution. In a letter to Lord George Gordon on June 28, 1792, Morris said, "I believe that religion is the only solid base of morals and that morals are the only possible support of free governments."

Abraham Lincoln

Abraham Lincoln, the sixteenth President of the United States, demonstrated great courage by risking the nation for the sake of liberty. When he gave

The Gettysburg Address he expressed his hope, "...that this nation under God shall have a new birth of freedom, and that government of the people, by the people, for the people shall not perish from the earth."

Also noteworthy is the little known fact that in a Presidential proclamation made on March 30, 1863, Lincoln established a National Fast Day. He stated, "We have grown in numbers, wealth, and power as no other nation has ever grown. But we have forgotten God. We have forgotten the gracious hand which preserves us in peace, and multiplied and enriched and strengthened us; as we have vainly imagined, in the deceitfulness of our hearts, that all these blessings were produced by some superior wisdom and virtue of our own.

"Intoxicated with unbroken success we have become too self-sufficient to feel the necessity of redeeming and preserving grace; too proud to pray to the God that made us. It behooves us then to humble ourselves before the offended power to confess our national sins and to pray for clemency and forgiveness."

"In God We Trust"—The Foundation of Our Nation's Strength

Our nation's motto, "In God We Trust," was originally placed on United States' coins beginning in 1864, largely because of the increased religious sentiment that existed during the Civil War. At that time, the Secretary of the Treasury received many appeals from people throughout the country urging that the government recognize the Deity on U.S. coins. It was believed that no reasonable citizen could object to "In God We Trust" since we openly claimed "divine protection."

American People are a Religious People

In the Case of Church of Holy Trinity v. United States (1892), the Supreme Court decision emphatically declared that history clearly demonstrated that we are a Christian nation and the American people are a religious people. This was shown by the religious objects described by the original grants and charters of the colonies, and the recognition of religion in the most solemn acts of their history. It was also displayed in the constitutions of the states and that of the nation.

Since the middle of the last century, however, our courts, in many cases, have been legislating against a reasonable accommodation of religious expression. Today, almost all references to God and religion are prohibited in our public institutions. Civil laws, particularly those regulating marriage, are no longer reflective of biblical morality as so often has been the case throughout American law.

Ironically, there is now more religious correctness under the guise of "ceremonial deism" allowed in our federal institutions than in our state institutions. For example, both houses of Congress begin each day with prayer by clergy appointed by official chaplains and paid from the Treasury of the United States. Similarly, the Supreme Court opens each session with an invocation for Divine protection—"God save the United States and the Honorable Court." Public schools, on the other hand, are forbidden to have even one minute devoted to non-mandatory silent prayer.

The Ten Commandments appear as part of a mural on the wall of the Supreme Court where Justices hear oral arguments, while public schools are routinely forbidden to even inconspicuously post a copy of the Commandments on a bulletin board in a classroom. Every President of the United States has placed his hand on the Bible and asked for God's protection upon taking office, whereas the Bible is not called upon in many of our public institutions.

America's heritage is interwoven with God and religious convictions but this part of history is no longer found in our textbooks. The state and our institutions, rather than adopting formal religion, need only to embrace the virtues of religion and the principles of a loving God.

The Supreme Court in Zorach v. Clauson (1952) said, "We are a religious people and our institutions presuppose a Supreme Being." Today, it is evident that America is not an irreligious nation but a multi-faith nation of religious beliefs. The survival of our moral heritage, to some extent, depends upon our institutions being allowed to reflect our belief in that Supreme Being.

The Wall between Church and State needs to be Porous

America need not abandon the significant contributions of Jefferson and Madison in establishing religious liberty for all people. It is obvious that having close ties between church and state has proven to be a flawed model for government in America as well as in Christendom. Jesus was careful to point out that there is a demarcation between rendering what belongs to Caesar and what belongs to God.

Abandoning all sensible ties between church and state, like prohibiting faith-based initiatives, a noncompulsory pledge of allegiance, consideration of the intelligent design theory, or a moment of silence to permit non-mandatory school prayer, goes too far. The wall of separation between church and state needs to be porous allowing reasonable accommodation between the two.

The voices of the countless religious sects in America should not be drowned out. They should be allowed to be heard above the noise and flourish in a free market system for the good of the public order. As French philosopher Voltaire put it, "With one church you have tyranny; with two, civil war; but with a hundred, peace."

It should also be noted that Americans by and large want more religion—not less. Former Speaker of the House and historian, Newt Gingrich, recently opined, "By better than a 9-to-1 ratio, Americans want the words, 'Under God' to remain a part of the Pledge of Allegiance. Almost 8-in-10 Americans believe that children should be allowed to pray in school. Better than 7-in-10 Americans want the government to help faith-based initiatives help the poor. And by an almost 3-to-1 ratio, Americans believe that the Constitution promises freedom of religion, not freedom from religion."

Sponsors of a 2000 poll on religion in *American Life* concluded that "Americans strongly equate religion with personal ethics and behavior, considering it an antidote to the moral decline that they perceive in our nation today. Crime, greed, uncaring parents, materialism—Americans believe that all of the problems would be mitigated if people were more religious."

After the 2000 election, 69 percent of Americans said that "more religion is the best way to strengthen family values and moral behavior in America, and 70 percent said they wanted the influence in America to increase." In a recent poll by Time magazine, nearly 80% of those polled agreed with the statement that "we are a religious nation, and religious values should serve as a guide to what our political leaders do in office."

Organized religion, however, does not represent a cure-all remedy. Being an institution maintained by human beings, it suffers from the same imperfections that come with our human condition. As our spirited nation began, for example, religion was used to condone and institutionalize horrendous practices like slavery, which received constitutional protection under the "three-fifths" compromise—five slaves were counted as three free men toward representation. State supported religion also helped foster divisiveness and discrimination against those residents who held contrary views.

For thousands of years, all around the world, wars have been fought in the name of religion. Today, escalating tensions between Jews and Muslims are rooted in religious differences. Some even argue that since the 9/11 terrorist attacks, people are becoming more leery of religion because we were attacked in the name of "the God of Abraham." It remains important to note that religious confrontations are most often fought over religious supremacy, not over religious virtues.

Religious virtues, regardless of one's particular faith or values, need to advance the common good and each person's human dignity. Despite the shortcomings of organized religion, religious faith is a tremendous teacher of virtues, with the Golden Rule being the most recognized admonition throughout all major religions. Religion as an institution helps us distinguish right from wrong, and provides a viable platform to commune with our Creator in realizing the fullness of the American Dream.

Is Acknowledging our Christian Past Politically Incorrect?

I was scheduled to appear on CNN the Friday before July 4th, 2004, to offer some perspectives on the significance of our Independence Day and Iraqi independence. It was an interesting time in history that found us celebrating our nation's independence just as Iraq was beginning theirs in a post-Saddam government.

The segment was to focus on several aspects of this momentous occasion: What advice would the Founding Fathers give for winning the War on Terror? Would democracy continue to flourish in America and would it take hold in Iraq? And what was it about today's culture war that was unifying people in a way that had not occurred since our nation's founding or at anytime since?

As part of the standard protocol for "Live TV" on CNN, I shared some of my thoughts on these topics with someone from the network the morning before I was to appear. In part, I talked about how the Founding Fathers had paid a price in securing freedom at Bunker Hill and how there was an ongoing price to be paid in preserving freedom in Iraq. I then opined that terrorism, in time, would decline if the principles of democracy and a free marketplace system were exploited in Iraq to raise the quality of life for all Iraqis. The issue that seemed to be politically sensitive, however, was the "culture war" going on in America today.

I related that America began as a nation composed of predominately Christian people who were often theologically divided. I went on to say that divisiveness is part of our religious heritage as a nation. When John F. Kennedy, a Catholic, ran for president, he had to convincingly make his case to the American people that his allegiance was to America's national interest first and not to the Catholic Church.

In objective fashion, I went on to share that there are currently controversial issues, such as stem cell research, same sex marriage, abortion, and our status as "One nation under God" causing many in various faiths to look past their theological differences and unite against a growing secular world view.

The person from CNN then remarked that my sentiments were "too Christian" and that I should try and be "more ecumenical" when doing the program live. Although I said I would be mindful of the request, I thought to myself, "Too Christian—you've got to be kidding. Would the same be said to a person of another faith in the context of a similar discussion? Does history need to be secularized, rewritten, or forgotten in order to be politically correct today?"

In the evening of the same day, I received a call from a producer at CNN who said that my segment for the next morning had been cancelled. They "decided to go in a different direction" with their two hour show.

Obviously, CNN has the journalistic right and responsibility to make any changes to its programs it deems proper. But it does raise an important issue in general. Liberty, the independence we celebrate every 4th of July, and our nation's religious heritage may begin to erode under circumstances where there is media censorship.

For a country whose population still polls at around 80% Christian, it is sad to see "political correctness" progressively superceding the call for Christian values. Instead of undergirding the principles of the Christian faith, activist groups like the American Civil Liberties Union (ACLU) and "fictional" bestsellers like Dan Brown's *Da Vinci Code* undermine the core of our Christian tradition.

Secularizing society is on the rise as America increasingly follows Europe's long waged assault against religion. Strict separation between Church and State is now standard in Europe. European leaders recently rejected any mention of the role of Christianity in its new Constitution for the 25 European Countries.

We should take note, however, that every major religion is declining in Western Europe except for Islam. Pope Benedict XVI recently lamented on the weakening on churches in Europe "There's no longer a need for God, even less of Christ." In Europe traditional Church's are dying.

Christmas, a once revered national holiday openly celebrating the birth of Jesus Christ, is being more and more curtailed under the secular banner of "happy holidays." Becoming just another seasonal holiday to celebrate in America, Jesus in many cases can no longer be the reason for the season.

It should not be forgotten, however, that the American Dream was born out of the noble principles of our Judeo/Christian heritage. Over the course of American history, waves of diverse immigrants became citizens by adopting those very principles. Still today, it is difficult to find our national identity without an allegiance to that faithful heritage.

Values Are Not the Same as Virtues

Today, we have come to expect differences in values as expressed in the contemporary phrase, "You have your values and I have mine." Values are usually personal and relative, and may have nothing to do with the notion of advancing an objective good.

For example, since Roe v. Wade was decided by the Supreme Court in 1973, we legally protect a woman's right to choose whether or not to have an abortion. In some cases, nonprofit agencies, like Planned Parenthood, which receives millions of dollars in government funds, assist women in making or carrying out the decision to abort. The bitter political fight over abortion divides our nation because people have different opinions and values regarding this controversial issue.

If values are simply a matter of personal preference, with none being objectively superior, then stealing, cheating, and lying are presumably as good as any other conduct. And for a nation whose citizens are still predominantly Christian, abortion presents some disheartening commentary.

The leading cause of death in America each year is not heart disease, cancer, or stroke; the leading cause of death is the killing of innocent human life with over 1 million abortions performed annually. What can we say in response to Mother Teresa's admonishment, "It is a very great poverty to decide that a child must die that you might live as you wish?"

Clearly, not all values are on equal footing. It stands to reason that if there were no values worthy of becoming virtues, we would have no standards by which to make wise choices. Only values which advance an objective good can serve as the basis for virtuous conduct. Only values that are consistent with the City of God can develop into virtues for our lives.

Virtues, unlike many values, withstand the test of time. They are habitual and result in a firm disposition to do an objective good. Although there is liberty in our changing values, there is unity in steadfast virtues. Our Founding Fathers, regardless of their particular religious beliefs, agreed that virtues were indispensable for the maintenance of the republic.

Virtues, as we have come to understand them today, were first espoused by Socrates, Plato, and perhaps most importantly, Aristotle. Aristotle divided all virtues into those that were moral and affected character, and those that were intellectual and concerned one's thoughts.

Aristotle taught that virtue is a sensible midpoint between two extremes. For example, the virtue of courage is that midpoint between the coward who runs from danger and the reckless individual who blindly rushes ahead into harm's way. A courageous person boldly faces up to those appropriate dangers when he or she must. Similarly, while fear causes excessive clinging to the sidelines, and greed rushes in with an "all eggs in one basket" mentality, the virtue of prudence provides that an investor take reasonable risks by properly diversifying.

Christian theologian St. Thomas Aquinas grouped four key virtues together as the cardinal virtues: prudence (wisdom), justice (fairness), fortitude (moral courage), and temperance (moderation). Faith, hope, and charity subsequently became known as the theological virtues for Christians, with the greatest of these being charity.

Benjamin Franklin believed that there were thirteen virtues necessary for true success: temperance, silence, order, resolution, frugality, industry, sincerity, justice, moderation, cleanliness, tranquility, chastity, and humility.

Several years ago, in *The Book of Virtues*, William J. Bennett promoted ten virtues: self-discipline, compassion, responsibility, friendship, work, courage, perseverance, honesty, loyalty, and faith.

As we clarify our own core values, we need to do so within the context of religious virtues. But virtues should not be imposed simply because they are on a restrictive list. There is nothing virtuous in unquestioned obedience. Sincere and mature faith should drive us to reflect on and even question what is virtuous and why is it so. In the final analysis, virtuous conduct needs to be discerned in accordance with the dictates of one's informed conscience to the degree that it helps advance an objective good.

If we are to responsibly move forward as a nation and realize the fullness of the American Dream, we need to look earnestly to our Creator to help us recast our country into a City of God. In doing so, the City of God will depend in no small way upon faith, unseen realities and experiencing the world more with our souls than with our senses.

This does not mean that are free to evade our earthly responsibilities in the City of Man. On the contrary, we are citizens of both cities and must perform our duties faithfully in the sprit of the Gospel. But the City of God must take precedence.

President Ronald Reagan underscored this point when he said, "I believe that George Washington knew the City of Man cannot survive without the City of God, that the Visible City will perish without the Invisible City."

CHAPTER QUESTIONS

1. Can morality over the long term be maintained in the absence of religion? If so, where will we get our moral basis from which to choose?

2. What values are most important to you? Do they represent virtues in your life?

3. What can you do to help ensure that America resembles the City of God?

Lasting Wealth can only be created
when we are living in a manner where we see that liberty
and freedom are gifts from God, and not from the state.

"Many have pain-stakingly climbed the ladder of success rung by rung —the diploma, the late nights, the promotions—only to discover as they reached the top, that their ladder of success was leaning against the wrong wall."
—Dr. Stephen Covey

14

COMMIT TO CLIMBING
GOD'S LADDER FIRST

"So we fix our eyes not on what is seen,
but on what is unseen.
For what is seen is temporary,
but what is unseen is eternal."
—*2 Corinthians 4:18*

We make many choices every day. Ultimately, our decisions dictate the ladders we spend our precious life's energy trying to climb. It is rare to write down goals. But it is rarer still to think them through in terms of their overall contribution toward our mission to love God and one another. Many of us go through life letting the media, advertisers, and others' opinions determine what we should value and how we ought to behave.

There are times when we demonstrate our goodness and love for our neighbors. The problem is, however, that loving God and our neighbors is frequently no longer our primary focus. We are more likely to value possessions and accomplishments over prayer and people. Many have replaced love-centered values with secular ones, spiritual capital with financial capital.

Be that as it may, we are designed primarily to be nurtured by immortal love—not just for the temporary gratification that the material world offers. St. Augustine astutely said, "You have made us for Yourself, Lord, and our hearts are restless until they rest in you."

We may often cry out for God's love to fill us up, but fail to notice we are already filled with worldly concerns. It is ironic how job titles, money, and other earthly achievements lack the vigor to keep us fulfilled for long. It is all too common to place more meaning on temporal affairs than on eternal matters.

Seek Spiritual Development—*God Hasn't Changed*

Several years ago while riding on a tour bus during a vacation in Greece, I was awed by what humanity had been able to accomplish over the centuries. From the architectural genius of the Acropolis in Athens to the scholarly writings of men like Aristotle and Plato—it was all quite impressive.

It made me wonder whether humanity has really progressed much over the past few thousand years. We now do business globally on the information superhighway, but what about our personal and spiritual development? We may have better means but not better ends.

Our tour guide had been rambling on for quite a while, pointing out one Greek structure after another. Just about the time I was ready to tune her out, she said something that spoke straight to my heart. She said, "It's funny that the ancient Greeks dedicated their entire lives in service to the gods. They lived life knowing they would only play a small part in the building of a structure which honored a being greater than themselves. Today, we have lost that ancient spirit."

Looking back with the advantage of hindsight, we can see that our expectations and understanding of God have, in some cases, changed. For nearly 1,900 years, Christians called upon God predominantly to assist them in their walk toward salvation. Beginning in 1952, however, the groundbreaking international bestseller, *The Power of Positive Thinking* by Dr. Norman Vincent Peale, urged the masses to call upon God to help us achieve personal happiness and success. The idea was that God should be our partner in business, as well as in all other aspects of our lives.

Is it right to call upon our Creator to be our partner in business, as well as in all other aspects of our lives? Yes! We stand more of a chance of being successful in business where it matters and in living the American Dream when God is a part of everything we do.

Divine inclusion enables us to better live out the dreams our Maker has planted in our hearts. It also enables us to more readily treat others in a compassionate, encouraging, and giving manner. The calamities at Tyco, Enron, and WorldCom would not have happened had the key people truly had been acting with God as their business partner.

Proclaiming that God is our business partner does not necessarily make it so. Kenneth Lay, former CEO of Enron once said: "I grew up a son of a Baptist minister. From this background, I was fully exposed not only to legal behavior but to moral and ethical behavior and what it means from the standpoint of leading organizations and people. I was, and am, a strong believer that one of the most satisfying things in life is to create a highly moral and ethical environment in which every individual is allowed and encouraged to realize their God-given potential."

Likewise, Bernie Ebbers, former CEO of WorldCom said in an interview with *Fortune* magazine: "I can't take credit for the Lord's leadership. There is a plan for our lives and for our participation in the world. How could one company be so dang lucky? I mean it's pretty hard to explain, isn't it?"

Regardless of self-professed proclamations and the best of intentions, business leaders, like the rest of us, cannot be persons of good character in the absence of virtue. This points to the fact that the natural human condition is not one that easily embraces virtue.

St. Augustine once prayed, "Lord, make me chaste, but not yet." And Paul writes in Romans 3:10, "There is not one righteous, not even one." In Romans 7:19–20, Paul shares his own pretense: "The willing is ready at hand, but doing good is not. For I do not do the good I want, but I do the evil I do not want. Now if I do not do what I want, it is no longer I, but sin that dwells within me."

There is a fine line between seeking God's assistance in becoming all that we can be in accordance with our Creator's plan and seeking to change it to conform to our own material desires. In some cases, we may be too busy soliciting God about our will to be able to discern *God's* will for our lives.

It is easy to make the modern mistake of existentialism as health and wealth gospels distort the actual blessings from our Creator. In truth, material blessings and abundance are not generally given as payment for pre-scribed behavior. God is not a cosmic gumball machine. Rather, living a rich life involves accepting and acting on God's abundant graces so that we can be generous with others and give thanksgiving to God (2 Corinthians

9:6–11). God is and has always been the CEO of the universe and the blessings of divine Providence consist of many intangibles far greater than just financial profits.

Let Material Success Be Evidence That You Have Given

Is it wrong to be successful and have nice things? There is nothing wrong with worldly success and the material goods that often come along with prosperity. We need to feel good about and be grateful for our accomplishments and the possessions we have. Our accomplishments and acquisitions may provide credible evidence that we have been of service to others—and to God.

But we also need to ask, "Why were we created? Was it just to be successful in worldly matters? Or do we need to focus on using our desires, gifts, and talents to spread God's message of love and salvation?" If eternity truly is our reference point, then we must focus on the unseen realities which are no less real.

When Mother Teresa was visiting the United States, a Senator asked her, "In India, where there are so many problems, can you ever be successful at what you do—isn't it hopeless to try?" She replied, "Well, Senator, we're not called to always be successful in the eyes of the world, but we are called to be faithful."

Take Notice of Where You Have Placed Your Ladders

We expend our life's energy climbing ladders in pursuit of our goals. But as author Dr. Stephen Covey points out in his book, *First Things First*, "Many have painstakingly climbed the ladder of success rung by rung—the diploma, the late nights, the promotions—only to discover as they reached the top, that their ladder of success was leaning against the wrong wall." Many of us would do well to inspect, from time to time, which walls our ladders are resting against, because being successful in something that does not really matter is not being successful after all.

The material-capital worldview tells us that our accomplishments and possessions determine how we should measure our intrinsic worth. In contrast a spiritual-capital mindset reveals that how well we have served others is the final word on how successfully we have each answered our life's call.

Culturally, many of us continue to move away from traditional religious institutions as we search for the truth. Some members of religious establishments believe that going to worship service is all that they need to do to be faithful to God's calling. But spending one day a week, waiting for our one-hour obligation to be over, does not make us any more spiritual than attending Major League baseball games makes us professional ballplayers. Being spectators alone does not get us into the game.

Faith is not just a weekend obligation; it is a pervasive reality to be practiced every day in homes, offices, factories, schools, and businesses across our nation. Followers must seek to avoid the tragic separation between faith and everyday life.

Perhaps a better indication of our faithfulness may be found when we periodically review our checkbooks, daily planners, or personal digital assistants (PDAs). Ask yourself this: "If I lost my checkbook, daily planner, and PDA, and a stranger picked them up, would that individual be able to see evidence of the person I believe myself to be?" We write the biography of our lives one day at a time though our checkbooks, daily planners, and PDAs. It is these things that show us where our hearts truly lie.

Success Comes in Reaching for another Rung

We continue to fall short, time and time again, in our efforts to love and serve God, no matter how faithful we endeavor to become. Many of us will still spend most of our days straddling ladders between God's wall and the material-world's wall. Our personal success, however, should not necessarily be measured by how far up God's ladder we climb. It is best found in the *courage* by which we reach for another rung. We are successful when we are making worthy efforts—not when we are ultimately recognized for those efforts. As C.S. Lewis wrote, "Virtue—even attempted virtue—brings light; indulgence brings fog."

It is a challenge putting Godly principles first, while living in a world where we need to make money. But it has always been a challenge, even for those who are looked upon as saints. The vast majority of us are not called to be a St. Francis or a Mother Teresa in the sense that we must live in a state of poverty in order to serve God foremost. We should not be taking a vow of poverty so much as we should be taking a vow of stewardship.

It is reasonable to wonder, at times, whether we should be withdrawing from the workplace in order to serve God. But perhaps our bigger challenge is to serve God faithfully while staying in the midst of the marketplace. After all, most of us have been entrusted with the responsibility of feeding our families and putting roofs over their heads. Be that as it may, all of us are called to pursue godliness in the world, to live a life not dominated by material things, and to bring justice in the workplace.

Poverty Itself Is Not a Virtue—*Even Jesus Received Financial Aid*

Material wealth is not a bad thing. We should be careful against making rash judgments that canonize poverty and condemn riches. There is nothing holy about debt, or not being able to pay your bills, or an economy that has run out of money. In many ways, we can financially serve the poor better by not allowing ourselves to join their ranks. Humanity is better served by helping to alleviate tangible poverty rather than contributing to it.

There is nothing virtuous about material poverty itself. It alone has no intrinsic goodness. Only the motive behind becoming impoverished may be virtuous if the desire is to help remove the obstacles which stand in the way of working toward spiritual perfection. Ironically, it is through weeding out our attachment to things that we discover another type of poverty—spiritual poverty—where becoming "poor in spirit" allows us to become rich in God.

But material wealth can support a quite holy effort—depending on how it is accumulated and used. Jesus did not condemn the possession of worldly goods or even great wealth. Some of His friends were financially well-off. In fact, in Luke 8:1–3, several Galilean women who followed Jesus aided Him considerably in His ministry with their financial resources. These women, who had little standing in society, helped sustain Jesus and His twelve disciples with their monetary contributions. Jesus, however, continually warned about the dangers of being *attached* to riches. For Jesus, having money in your hand was not the problem; it was having money in your heart.

The reason why it is easier for a camel to go through the eye of a needle than for a rich man to enter the kingdom of God, is not because a man is materially rich. Rather, it is because the rich may find themselves to be more attached to material wealth than to God (Mark 10:25).

Possessing possessions is all right as long as those possessions are not in the end possessing us. In life's balance sheet, when we become attached to property and possessions, they cease to be assets and instead become liabilities. When we get attached and hold on too tightly, money is just another piece of paper.

The challenge is not that money itself prevents us from climbing God's ladder first. Money is not wealth. It simply stands for the things we attribute to wealth—nothing more than a medium of exchange that is morally neutral. The greater concern is that many of us do not suspect that we are spending the majority of our time climbing ladders that rest on walls belonging only to the material world.

When we put our faith first, we may actually help produce economic success by giving us the courage to take on sensible risk. In the book, *The Millionaire Mind* by Thomas J. Stanley, Ph.D., nearly four in ten millionaires surveyed reported that "having strong religious faith" was a key source in helping them eliminate or reduce the fears and worries associated with placing financial related assets on the line.

Confidence, action and religious faith are oftentimes connected. The late Tom Landry, the Dallas Cowboys coach of 29 years who led America's team to five Super Bowls, put his faith first before winning. In coaching, where value is often determined by your last season's record, Landry was frequently asked, "What would you do if you had a couple of bad seasons and you lost your job?" In response, Landry would confidently smile and say, "If I lost my job tomorrow, I'm confident that God still has a plan for me as part of His team today."

At the end of the day, we should use our material wealth in ways that bring us closer to God and not away from our Creator. A barometer of gauging our progress is to note that if our attachment to material wealth or worldly matters becomes more important than our desire for God, then we can be sure that our ladders are leaning against the wrong wall.

In the larger picture of life, the decline of many great civilizations began not so much by their failure to choose "the better walls," but in their indifference as to which walls would lead to better places. Jacob's "ladder" which reached from earth to heaven in his dream as described in the Book of Genesis (28:11–19) can only reach the heavens in our day when we have it resting against the right wall.

CHAPTER QUESTIONS

1. What can you do to insure that your ladders are leaning against worthwhile walls?

2. Do you believe in divine Providence directing your life? If so, how does this occur? If not, why not?

3. In what ways are possessions leading you closer to or away from God? What do you value the most? What do you hate to lose?

Living rich is using material wealth
in a way that brings you closer to God.

"The Soviet Union is suffering
from a spiritual decline. We were among the
last to understand that in the age of
information technology the most valuable
asset is knowledge, which springs from
individual imagination and creativity.
We will pay for our mistakes
for many years to come."
—Mikhail Gorbachev

15

PURSUE GODLY DEPENDENCE BEFORE FINANCIAL INDEPENDENCE

"So do not worry, saying, 'What shall we eat?'
Or 'What shall we drink?' Or 'What shall we wear'...
But seek first his kingdom and his righteousness,
and all of these things will be given to you as well."
—Matthew 6: 31–33

It is human nature to want independence. As babies, we first struggle to crawl, then walk. We fall many times in the process, but in our efforts to stand on our own two feet, we remain undaunted. Later on as adolescents and young adults, we strive to become independent of our parents and our surroundings, as we continue to nurture our own sense of autonomy. Innately, we yearn to have no masters over us.

America is increasingly emphasizing the development of the individual, which may come at the expense of the community. Self-determination, self-fulfillment, and self-sufficiency are often valued more today than teamwork, fidelity, and altruism.

Our contemporary culture is in part driven by the allure of financial independence. This can be a noble pursuit, provided we put our Creator first in the process.

Our Latest Expression of the Desire for Freedom

The August 1999 edition of *The Wall Street Journal* magazine, *Smart Money*, featured a cover which boldly stated: "RETIRE TEN YEARS EARLY—It's America's newest obsession!" A gentleman from New York responded in a follow-up letter to the editor, "What's next? How to retire in your senior year of high school? I would like to see one—just one—article on money management for people who would like to continue to contribute, in addition to remaining active and mentally alert."

There are obviously many ways to contribute and build wealth. Depending upon what we wish to accomplish, financial independence can provide the time and money to pursue higher purposes more fully. On balance, it's easier to focus on helping our neighbors when we are in a position to pay our monthly bills.

While most of today's Retirees in their youth may have given little thought to one day achieving financial independence, younger generations are pursuing this newest obsession with great fervor. At the end of the previous millennium, a survey of college juniors and seniors revealed that most thought they would retire between the ages of 40 and 50. Financial independence is becoming the latest expression of our yearning to be free.

In many cases, it is a freedom born out of responsible planning and discipline. Financial independence can also be a wonderful blessing if it fosters the development of our talents and the pursuit of worthy causes. However, it is only beneficial when it leads us toward our Creator and inspires growth in true riches. As we pursue financial independence, however, we should not forsake our dependence upon God.

In the New Testament, Jesus instructed the apostles to go forth and continue His mission. He further commanded them to take nothing for the journey—no food, no sack, and no money in their belts. His instructions seem so contrary to how we live life today. Jesus was not overly concerned that His followers might incur physical inconveniences during their journeys. He wanted them to always be conscious of their dependence on God for everything. Although we may think and act in a different way today, discipleship is still a dependent process.

Do we acknowledge and thank our Creator for whatever prosperity has been entrusted to us? Are we humble about it, or do we have the attitude that we did it all on our own? Do we label ourselves "self-made" when we are really "Creator-made?"

As we seek to answer these questions, we should recognize that our economic world today is vastly different from what it was when the *Bible* was written, or even when the American Dream came into being. We no longer live in an agrarian society when small communities were relatively self-contained, and people worked the land together to provide for life's basic needs. Today, our needs are met through a global marketplace. Many household products can now be conveniently delivered to our homes by the simple click of a mouse. As our world has advanced, there are many positive financial benefits passed on to others when we pursue our self-interests under capitalism.

Be Rich by Being Resourceful

After America declared its independence from Britain, political economist and philosopher Adam Smith, author of *The Wealth of Nations*, promoted the idea that government needs to let the market operate freely with little or no regulation. He described how the unfettered pursuit by individuals of their own self-interests led directly to the increased well-being of the larger society. Smith observed that an "invisible hand" guided the unintended actions of individuals toward increased societal wealth.

In his book *God Wants You to Be Rich*, Paul Zane Pilzer builds upon Smith's observations by telling us that God wants all of us to increase our individual wealth, because this usually results in a larger increase for societal wealth. Capitalism, in no small way, is built on common interest where one's profit can occur without the expense of another.

Traditionally, economists defined wealth as being limited to those well-to-do individuals who stockpiled as much of a given natural resource as possible. They depended exclusively on the natural resources that God deposited on the earth, consuming or amassing what they found, then moving on to find more. The thinking of the day suggested that the more resources one puts aside, the wealthier that person becomes since there was less available for others.

In modern times, the synergism of technology can expand the natural resources that currently exist. Consider the American farmer for a moment.

In 1930, there were 30 million farmers barely producing enough to feed 100 million people. By 1980, however, there were 3 million farmers producing enough to feed over 300 million people.

The major part of today's economy is involved in producing innovative products and services that did not exist when the twentieth century began. Still, the most precious resources available to us are not found in the earth or on the Internet. They are found in our minds that conceive of innovative ways to do things and in our hearts that give us the will to carry them out.

Pope John Paul II commented on the importance of our resourcefulness as follows: "Whereas at one time the decisive factor of production was the land, today the decisive factor is increasingly man himself, that is, his knowledge, especially his scientific knowledge, his capacity for interrelated and compact originations, as well as his ability to perceive the needs of others and to satisfy them."

Every man and woman has been created in the image of the Creator, and each of us helps co-create the future of the world. Each person is endowed with an inalienable responsibility to create with reverence for human dignity.

Let Desire Be a Positive Motivator

Human beings desire far more than they need. People, unlike other creatures, do not stop wanting when their primary needs have been met. Although our basic needs are few, our desires are never ending.

This has motivated many to employ their gifts and talents to create, resourcefully benefiting others as well as themselves. In many ways, it is because of our capitalistic economy and an ever-increasing consumer demand that we have the incentive to invent new and better ways of doing things. No matter how much we may earn or possess most continue to want more and to purchase more.

Socialism and the community of goods concept failed because there was no economic incentive to develop one's gifts and talents. Without private ownership and the ability to make a profit, creative innovation within the Soviet Union remained suppressed. Former Soviet Union leader Mikhail Gorbachev wisely recognized this when he said: "The Soviet Union is suffering from a spiritual decline. We were among the last to understand that, in the age of information technology, the most valuable asset is knowledge, which springs from individual imagination and creativity. We will pay for our mistakes for many years to come."

The pursuit of the American Dream through capitalism, on the other hand, continues to spur the improvement and modernization of our goods and services. Our vigorous consumer demand is the primary reason that there is more than one of the same type of product in our households today. Consider that 50 years ago most families had only one television, car, and phone. But now most homes have at least two or more of each.

We keep demanding better quality and more features for the same product. For example, we traded in our small black-and-white televisions for color ones, small color televisions for consoles, and consoles for big-screen TVs. Big-screen televisions of today are being exchanged for even bigger screens that have clearer, high definition pictures.

The point is that as long as technology keeps advancing, the demand for greater quality will never be satisfied, and the list of what constitutes "necessities" will keep growing. As John Kenneth Galbraith noted in 1958 in his book, *The Affluent Society*, "No sharp distinction can be made between luxuries and necessities as societal wealth increases."

Our current preoccupation with private property and acquiring more, however, can blur our ability to recognize our true needs and responsibilities. The right to private property does not do away with the universal destination of goods and call to help others in need.

Not all of our capitalistic desires are good. In our material world, our desire for prosperity often competes with our need for spiritual sustenance. C.S. Lewis, who diverted most of his royalties to charitable and individual needs, put it this way, "Prosperity knits a man to the world. He feels that he is 'finding his place in it' while really it is finding its place in him."

Much has been written about the dangers and right uses of riches. There are over 2300 verses devoted to money, economics, and possessions in the Bible. A lot more is said about those things than either faith or prayer. Consider that three of the Ten Commandments warn against materialism. Additionally, more than 25% (11 of 39) of Jesus' parables recorded in the New Testament deal with money, possessions, and proper spiritual conduct in economic life. In fact, Jesus said more about the right use of money and possessions than any other single subject.

If we are to love God completely, there can be no room for a competing love. 1 Timothy 6:6–9, clearly warns that the driving desire to get rich and possess more takes us from faith into temptations and traps. Therefore, the desire for material wealth needs to be kept in check; it cannot outweigh our desire to be good stewards first.

Money Is a Tool—*Not a Magic Elixir*

Financial independence if often pursued as if it were a way of obtaining lifelong emotional security or some type of immunization against the problems of life. But economic freedom is only one component of human freedom. It is our attachment to money that causes us to feel insecure no matter the level of income and affluence we reach. We may reach financial independence but still may not be financially free if we are attached to material and monetary drivers. Many people find that the more wealth they accumulate, the more they fret about losing it.

When we equate happiness with material gain, we never seem to achieve enough to keep us happy for long. Benjamin Franklin wrote, "Money never made man happy, nor will it. There is nothing in its nature to produce happiness. The more a man has, the more he wants. Instead of filling a vacuum, it makes one."

Likewise, Ecclesiastes 5:10–11 warns: "Whoever loves money never has money enough; whoever loves wealth is never satisfied with his income... As goods increase so do those who consume them. And what benefit are they to the owner except to feast his eyes on them?" Our happiness should not be based upon some false illusion regarding worldly attachments—true happiness will never be found in earthly riches, power, prestige or any human achievement, but in God alone, the source of every good and of all love.

Any "happiness" surrounding money is relative and not absolute; it is temporary, not lasting. In his comprehensive work *The Psychology of Happiness*, Oxford University psychologist Michael Argyle observed, "There is very little difference in the levels of reported happiness found in rich and very poor countries. Although the upper classes in any society are somewhat more satisfied with their lives than the lower classes are, the upper classes of rich countries are no more satisfied than the upper classes of much poorer countries. The conditions of life which really make a difference to happiness are those covered by three sources—social relations, work, and leisure. The establishment of a satisfying state of affairs in these spheres does not depend upon money, either absolute or relative."

The tenth century ruler of Cordova, Abd-Al-Rahman, had this to say: "I have now reigned above 50 years in victory or peace, beloved by my subjects, dreaded by my enemies, respected by my allies. Riches and honors, power and pleasure, have awaited my call; nor does any earthly blessing seem to have been wanting.... I have diligently numbered the days of pure and genuine happiness that have fallen to my lot; they amount to fourteen."

In one sense, if we have enough money to pay our bills and take care of most of our needs, then we have as much security from money as it can give. To be sure, there is real satisfaction in knowing that we can pay our own way, or handle life's little financial emergencies. However, having greater amounts of money or mountains of possessions does not proportionately increase our levels of self-satisfaction.

It is oftentimes true that with greater financial resources, we are better positioned to share and affect positive change for the betterment of the world. Unless these resources are prudently shared, however, financial prosperity may serve only to further distance us from the needs of the people we are called to help.

Security gates and alarm systems can create an environment where it is difficult to see that the sick, poor, and society's so-called undesirables are our brothers and sisters too. And meaningful change can occur without ever possessing significant financial capital. Notable figures like Dorothy Day, Susan B. Anthony, Gandhi, and Mother Teresa brought about considerable change for humanity, yet did so primarily by expending spiritual capital through acts of love and service.

We live in a society of instant credit, where things seem to come so freely. It is easy to forget our need for God and each other. Should we face a sudden crisis or need, we quickly can go from being a self-sufficient adult with little need for God or anyone else, to a needy "newborn." Sayings like, "There will always be prayer in school as long as there are tests," and "There are no atheists in fox holes," help illustrate this point. Perhaps that is why many theologians believe that the greatest purpose for human suffering is to cause us to turn to our Creator.

We would do well to listen to the wisdom of Douglas Copeland, a Generation X writer, who stated: "Now here is my secret: I tell it to you with an openness of heart that I doubt I shall ever achieve again, so I pray that you are near in a quiet room as you hear these words. My secret is that I need God—that I am sick and can no longer make it alone. I need God to help me give, because I no longer seem to be capable of giving; to help me be kind, as I no longer seem capable of kindness; to help me love, as I seem beyond being able to love."

CHAPTER QUESTIONS

1. How can you exploit your desire for more in ways that are worthwhile? At what point does your "desire for more" begin to become problematic?

2. The spiritual decline of the former Soviet Union stemmed from what? What can we do to prevent this from happening in America today?

3. If economic freedom is just one of the human freedoms, then why, in many cases, does it seem so all important?

If we are prosperous in worthy endeavors
then we are living rich.

"Life is no brief candle to me;
it is sort of a splendid torch I have a hold of
for the moment, and I want to make it burn
as brightly as possible before
handing it on to future generations."
—George Bernard Shaw

16

USE YOUR GIFTS AND TALENTS
OR LOSE THEM

"I have fought the good fight, I have finished the race,
I have kept the faith."
—2 Timothy 4:7

There is a story about a preacher who was driving by an immaculate farm. The fields were beautifully cultivated and abundant well-cared-for crops. The fences, house, and barn were neat, clean, and freshly painted. A row of fine trees led from the road to the house where there were shaded lawns and flower beds. It was a beautiful sight to behold.

When the farmer working in the field got to the end of the row near the road, the preacher stopped his car and called to him. "God sure blessed you with a beautiful farm." The farmer stopped, thought for a moment, and replied: "Yes, He has, and I am grateful. But you should have seen this place when He had it all to Himself."

God Is the Creator—*You Are Only One of His Junior Partners*

Each one of us has been entrusted with a plot of ground. How we tend our portions of land through our words and deeds has a significant impact on whether our plots will become beautiful farms or barren wastelands. The Creator did not design our world complete; God has graciously chosen us to help finish the job.

When we find ourselves taking all the credit for the bounty and blessings of life, we need to be mindful that none of us created our own existence, our innate abilities, or the many exceptional people who helped us along the way. Owners and mangers in the marketplace have not created capital on their own. They have benefited from the work of many others and from the local communities that support their endeavors. At best, each of us is only a junior co-creator, but never the Creator alone.

All the blessings the farmer had—his ability to reason, to conceive of the possibilities for the farm, to move his limbs and work the land, and to receive the assistance provided by others—were created and conferred on him by God. Like the farmer, we can nurture and manage our abilities and talents, but the truth is that God originally gave them to us. All that we bring to work is a gift from God.

All that we call our own, God has entrusted to us in some manner. "The earth is the Lord's, and everything in it" (1 Corinthians 10:26). We do not even own ourselves since we were bought at a price (1 Corinthians 6:19–20). Because God owns everything, we are our Creator's trustees and money managers.

Even though titles to financial accounts and other property may be in our names for the time being, we still owe a fiduciary duty to the Maker of the Universe. Whether we are spending money for our daily bread, or making investments for our future wellbeing, at the end of the day, we must be mindful of who really owns it all.

It is not unusual to have the feeling that God blesses unevenly, especially in terms of material wealth. Some say this divinely occurs so that those who receive more can share with those who have less. Although divine Providence certainly affects our lot in life, it seems unlikely that God deliberately distributes tangible material wealth to some while intentionally withholding it from others. Instead, it is more likely, from the gifts and talents entrusted to us by God, that we can create and realize material wealth in an inequitable manner. As such, those with more material wealth owe a special duty to help those who have less.

No matter how much we may have done in helping to write our own life's story, we are not the author of life. In his commencement address at Yale University in 2001, President George W. Bush remarked: "When I left here, I didn't have much in the way of a life plan. I knew some people who thought they did. But it turned out that we were all in for ups and downs, most of them unexpected. Life takes its own turns, makes its own demands, writes its own story. And along the way, we start to realize we are not the author."

Products Receive a Special Blessing

In one of the more serene moments of Mel Gibson's movie, *The Passion of the Christ*, Jesus presides over a Passover meal with his twelve closet friends. On the table, in accordance with Jewish tradition, would have been wine, lamb, matzos (unleavened bread), bitter herbs, greens, water, and salt among other things.

As Jesus finishes his last meal with his dear companions, He decides to offer up a special and final blessing. Jesus had a number of items at His disposal and could have blessed whatever He wanted. But instead of choosing the lamb, bitter herbs, greens, water, salt, or even the apostles themselves, Jesus specifically chooses to bless the bread and wine alone.

Now the lamb, bitter herbs, greens, water, and salt were all raw materials that came directly from God. Although they may not have been in their natural state, mankind did nothing to change or alter their essential composition. However, humankind clearly altered the fundamental makeup of both wheat and grapes for the bread and wine that were on the table.

In each case, God's raw materials were transformed by human hands into a new creation. The significance of this final blessing is that Jesus not only honors God in doing so, but also recognizes God's greatest creation, humanity, and the creative capacity of mankind.

While there is nothing holy about products in and of themselves, they are representational of the blessings of creation. Production in countless forms presents us with occasions for giving glory and honor to God, provided our products are crafted for good ends.

Become Part of a Virtuous Circle

Recently, I attended an annual meeting of a large financial institution. During the course of the meeting, the President of the company spoke of a "virtuous circle" in the marketplace. The concept fascinated me, and I was very eager to hear what he had to say. As he went on to define the components of the circle, however, I became quite dismayed.

As it was explained, the circle (Diagram A) started with producers engaged in a lot of productive activity. How the producers amassed a large volume of production in the first place was never explained. Nevertheless, these big producers would naturally attract the largest financial carriers, who wanted to increase the sale of their goods and services through these producers.

Subsequently, sizable financial carriers would make available considerable economic resources, increasing market opportunities that would then be exploited by these producers leading to even greater production, as the cycle would begin anew.

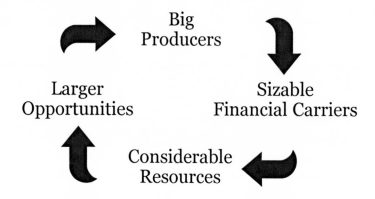

The executive coolly laid out what is often the reality in the marketplace: "bigger is better." Many of us can surely relate to the special treatment, enlarged resources, and increased opportunities available to those who excel at production and performance. Exceed production quotas and performance standards, and you become a star who is in demand. But if you fail to meet expectations, watch out; you drop from the ranks of the "in crowd."

To some degree there is no quarrel with the logic of the corporate official. A free market system does simultaneously reward production and punish those who fail to produce. I do take issue, however, with the notion of it being a "virtuous circle." Bigger is no more virtuous than smaller, and it may well be less. When it comes to virtue, size matters little. But there is a "virtuous circle" in the marketplace.

In this model (Diagram B), virtue also begins with producers, but without regard to a stated level of production. In order for producers to thrive, however, they must first enjoy liberty—the freedom to choose their own way. And although liberty is not a virtue by itself, it is always an integral part and pre-condition for virtue to exist.

We must be free from coercive State regulation, excessive taxation, and socialistic oppression in order to allow free markets to properly function. Consequently, a primary role of the State should be to encourage global trade in unburdened markets, and to secure, protect, and enforce the rights of individuals in order to maximize their creative capacities for the common good.

It is creative enterprise that is at the very core of capitalism. Every day we create something that did not exist the day before. Whether an act or an attitude, we are continually creating something new with each moment of our life's energy.

Admittedly, some are more proficient than others in their creative endeavors and the marketplace regularly compensates them for it. It is no accident, for example, that the "Millionaire Next Door" is often an innovative person of good character, who began without much in the way of financial resources, but learned how to capitalize on market opportunities that were frequently overlooked.

All of us are producers in one way or another with unique callings as expressed in our particular God-given gifts, talents, dreams, and desires. And when these distinctive attributes intersect with human wants and needs in the marketplace, there are an abundance of business opportunities.

Conceiving of new and better ways of doing things, with the mindset of being of real service to others, should be what capitalism is all about. In fact, our democratic and capitalistic country is designed to be of service to our neighbor. Democracy depends upon capitalism, and capitalism depends upon creative enterprise and the civility of the human spirit. The workplace not only represents an opportunity for personal economic initiative; it also serves as a means for building virtue and goodwill in association with others.

Simply put, the market and world of commerce should be nothing more than people bringing their gifts and talents to the service of others through exchange. Prosperity occurs precisely because we serve our neighbor well when we provide worthy goods and services to them around the globe.

As worthy goods and services are increased through consumer purchases, producers are financially rewarded and the virtuous circle not only continues on but is strengthened. In reality then, a virtuous circle does not begin with big production; in due course it helps creates it.

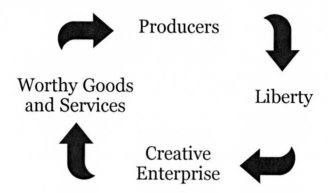

Share Your Talents and You Will Have Success

Many of us are familiar with the parable in the New Testament where a man who was going on a journey called in his servants to entrust his possessions to them. To one he gave five talents; to another, two; to a third, one—to each according to his ability. Then he went away. The servants who received the most talents used them wisely, each doubling what he had received. But the man who received only one talent was so fearful of losing it that he buried it in the ground.

Eventually, the master returned and settled his accounts. He congratulated the two who had doubled their talents and invited them to share in his joy. He also gave both greater responsibilities since they had been faithful in small matters. The man who had received just one talent, however, was chastised for his laziness and fear. He was labeled as a useless servant. His talent was taken from him and given to the servant who had the most.

Many of us today are like the last servant. Out of fear, we bury our gifts in darkness, rarely allowing them to be exposed to God's illuminating love. The fear of rejection is at times all too real.

But it is only by faithfully using our talents and gift of faith that we will experience a much fuller participation in the Kingdom; lazy inactivity will mean something much less. It should not be assumed, however, because our gifts and talents are faithfully shared that we will necessarily receive an abundance of material success as some would have us believe—pointing to the second and thirds servant's financial windfall.

On the contrary, Jesus makes known that, "Foxes have dens and birds of the sky have nests, but the Son of Man has no place to rest his head (Luke 9:58). Likewise, St. Paul's faithful journey finds that he labored greatly, often without sleep; that he was hungry, thirsty and often starving; that he was cold and without clothes (2 Cor.II:26–28).

While the Old Testament considers wealth and material goods as signs of God's favor, the same cannot be said of the New Testament. Wealth and material goods are not seen as signs of God's grace and salvation. In fact, Jesus rejects them utterly as a claim to enter the Kingdom. Because wealth generates a false security, Jesus makes clear that God's favor and salvation is beyond human capability and depends solely on the goodness of God who offers it as a gift (Mark 10:23–27).

As we strive for success, we will fail along the way without ever becoming a failure in life. These so-called failures are simply opportunities to learn and grow. Consider the failure that George Bailey believed himself to be in the heartwarming Christmas movie, *It's a Wonderful Life*. He dreamed of traveling the world and becoming a famous architect. Yet life had different plans for George Bailey, and he never left the surroundings of his quaint hometown of Bedford Falls. Nor did he have a job other than working at the modest Bailey Building and Loan.

George Bailey felt that he had also failed his family as a provider. Consumed by his own shortcomings, he believed life was no longer worth living. It took an angel-in-training to show him that, despite having fallen far short of his dreams, George had been given a wonderful gift and had used it wisely.

Throughout his life, George Bailey had unselfishly given of himself and demonstrated a willingness to help his neighbor. It was his selflessness in everyday occurrences that had touched many and made a difference in their lives. As the movie ends, George finds himself surrounded by the generative love of his family and friends, who have now come to support George. It is at that precise moment, that George realizes firsthand the meaning of a rich life, as his younger brother, Harry, says, "A toast to my big brother, George: The richest man in town."

Life Presents Winning Hands to Those Who Keep Playing

President Clinton once remarked, "The American Dream that we were all raised on is a simple but powerful one—if you work hard and play by the rules, you should be given a chance to go as far as your God-given abilities will take you." But using our gifts and talents does not necessarily mean we are going to achieve extraordinary worldly success. The vast majority of us will never receive a multi-million dollar endorsement contract like 18-year-old basketball sensation LeBron James or 16-year-old golf superstar Michelle Wie did. Furthermore, there are only an exceptional few who have a legitimate chance of becoming the next *American Idol.*

The rest of us, like George Bailey, need to have faith. We need to believe that by unselfishly sharing our gifts and talents in the ordinary affairs of everyday life, we will touch others in countless small ways. Each of us can have a wonderful life and achieve success where it counts the most. Life will continue to deal unfair cards, but it will also present us with winning hands as long as we selflessly stay in the game. Periods of desolation and consolation are a part of the natural ebb and flow of life.

In today's culture, many of us are not content with our God-given talents. We long for those certain qualities that will make us exceptional so we can stand out. We want good looks, athletic and artistic ability, and enough enterprising talents to ensure worldly success. We often lose touch with those God-given abilities that enable us to fulfill aspirations that may have nothing to do with the material world. Yet, getting in touch with these innate talents in many cases allows us to explore our true callings and passions.

Each of us has been given gifts by our God, although not everyone receives the same gifts, nor are they distributed in equal amounts. Each of us has been entrusted with certain God-given desires or talents when it comes to artistic, social, or enterprising endeavors. For that reason, some of us are more inclined to become engineers or businesspeople, for example, instead of artists or counselors.

The challenge today is that much in our culture pulls us away from our inner callings and passions. Society often encourages career paths that seem to provide the best opportunities for material success alone. Yet, living the American Dream requires getting in touch with our true God-given abilities and desires. Our creative energies need to be used in ways that contribute to society and make a positive difference in the world.

Expand Your Definition of Work

Many of us spend much of our life's energy at a place of work trying to increase our standard of living and keeping up with the Joneses in an effort to impress others. Historically, as we moved from agriculture to industrialization the socialization of work hours increased dramatically. Standards were created that labeled a person as lazy if he or she did not work full-time in a 40-hour workweek.

The notion that everyone should have a job began with the Industrial Revolution, and full employment has only been a goal of our government since the Depression. Although our average standard of living has risen dramatically in the last 100 years, we continue to work harder to keep advancing the standard.

Work today is seen as something we do only for money. Money, in fact, appears to be the primary tangible evidence that we have worked. It has become a stored medium of exchange for which we trade our precious time and valuable life energy. And yet, learning is work, raising our children is work, community service is work, and sharing our faith and pursuing our callings and passions is work. In essence, work is any activity by human beings, whether manual or intellectual.

The most profound motive for our work, however, is sharing in God's creation. Man was placed in the Garden of Eden "to work it and take care of it" (Genesis 2:15). God created us to work a lifetime, and the real objective of work is ministry, not money. Work ends only when life does, and with an eternal perspective there is no such thing as retirement from work.

Work type and job title are very important contributors to our sense of self-worth. The most popular question after "What is your name?" is "What do you do for a living?" But if work is who we are, then how do we define ourselves when we are no longer working? When the job is done and has gone away, from where will we derive our self-worth and self-esteem?

Consider the sentiments of a wealthy inheritor who had no need to work for a living, as described in *Inheritors and Work—The Search for Purpose*, by Barbara Blouin and Katherine Gibson. The inheritor shares her story of how she found self-esteem while performing community service on a trip to India. During the trip, she visited some of Mother Teresa's missions. She recalls her experience: "I'd walk into a hospital, and a sister would hand me a mop or ask me to bathe a patient. The sisters just let us be a part of their work, and I felt they were working at a deep spiritual level that had much more to do with a contemplative presence than it had to do with fixing up the world. It was for me a process of moving from being special to being ordinary, and coming into that everyday, ordinary kind of process and work.

"The main spiritual question for me has had to do with the sense of separation I have felt between myself and God, and between myself and other people. I knew I needed to heal that estrangement, that sense of separation, and come into wholeness. And work has helped me do that.

"I have had to work through a lot of guilt and shame before I could see the advantages of wealth. Now I'm beginning to feel grateful in ways I couldn't have felt before. Money has given me dream time—time to develop my inner spiritual life. I can have quiet time in the morning or evening. I can take walks. The challenge for me, however, is to bring that inner world into the outer world. You could set me down on a rock and I'd be content forever, but to move out into a relationship with the world—with people and with work—that is the challenge."

More important than enabling us to pay our bills, work allows us to connect with our Creator and our communities. It gives us viable forums to share our unique gifts and talents in association with others. Work is not just a means of providing only for our needs and those of our families. Work also makes resources available to others in our communities, in our nation, and around the globe.

Listen to the Divine Voice within You

It has become so common to pay attention to the many outer voices of the world that many of us are having difficulty recognizing the Divine voice within. Yet, our inner voice is probably the most direct and personal communication we can experience with God.

Discerning our God-given desires can be difficult. It requires much careful thought. For some it may mean striking out on their own in pursuit of their passions, taking the road less traveled without a well-defined map. For others it may require making numerous changes as they discover the most appropriate path.

For a great number of us, however, it means doing exactly what we have been doing, but with a renewed sense of purpose. The road to holiness for most of us lies in our secular vocations. In Colossians 3:23 we are advised that "whatever we do, work at it with all of your heart as working for the Lord, not for men." Regardless of our place of employ, we are all called to give love, the most precious gift entrusted to us.

Become Used Up—*Not Burned Out*

Many of us feel so burned out these days that we have little left over to give others. The burnout generally is not from giving too much of ourselves—but rather from not being in touch with our dreams and our higher purpose. We too often try to give from an empty place.

It is great to give of yourself but greater still to let God give through you. In this regard, prayer is a prerequisite for providing the wherewithal to give without burning out.

George Bernard Shaw said, "This is the true joy in life of…being used for a purpose recognized by yourself as a mighty one…being a force of nature instead of a feverish, selfish little clod of ailments and grievances complaining that the world will not devote itself to making you happy." Shaw added, "I am of the opinion that my life belongs to the whole community, and as long as I live, it is my privilege to do for it whatever I can. I want to be thoroughly used up when I die. For the harder I work, the more I live. I rejoice in life for its own sake. Life is no brief candle to me; it is a sort of splendid torch which I have got a hold of for the moment, and I want to make it burn as brightly as possible before handing it on to future generations."

As we prepare to pass the torch from our generation to the next, how many of us are living lives that belong to our communities? Will we be thoroughly used up when we die? Have too many of us let age become our excuse?

Age was not an excuse for people like Senator Claude Pepper, Mahatma Gandhi, and Mother Teresa, who all began making their most significant contributions in the same age range as many of today's Retirees.

Consider the career of Albert Schweitzer. He began his adult years as a renowned musician. He then switched tracks and became an acclaimed theologian, philosopher, and writer. At 30, he attended medical school, and by 38 he established a hospital in West Africa, taking care of the needy. After World War I, he discovered that his hospital was in ruins and all that he had worked for had collapsed.

At nearly 50, however, Schweitzer rebuilt the hospital and ran it until his death at 90. He drew his life's energy from selfless giving. As Schweitzer wrote: "You must give some time to your fellow man. Even if it is a little thing, do something for those who have a need of help, something for which you can get no pay but the privilege of doing it. For remember, you don't live in a world all of your own. Your brothers are here too."

Have you withdrawn from being an active participant in making a meaningful difference in life? A man quoted in Dr. Stephen Covey's book *First Things First* answers the question this way: "As I began to think about what matters the most to me, I suddenly realized that over the past years, that feeling, that sense of purpose, has somehow gotten lost. I've been lulled by a sense of security. I haven't made a difference. I've basically been watching life go by through the hedges of my country club."

We should never be retreating from an active life where we quit at the three-quarter pole in terms of making a difference. Since we are to work for a lifetime, we should not be in a hurry to retire. Instead, we should be focusing on finishing well. Like the Apostle Paul, we need to be fighting the good fight, keeping the faith, and finishing the race (II Timothy 4:7).

Don't Discard God-Given Dreams—Believe in Them

Any muscle in your body if not exercised regularly, begins to waste away. Likewise, the gift of spiritual capital may be enlarged with exercise or shrunken by neglect. Realizing the purpose for which spiritual capital was created requires us to cultivate it on a consistent basis.

If dreams and desires are not generously shared and used, their effectiveness for giving life and co-creating will inevitably degenerate. Unfortunately, we often take to our graves a host of dreams and desires that were like fine china locked in the cabinet and seldom used.

Whether the cultivation of your dreams allows you to experience success as others have achieved does not really matter. What matters is that we use our God-given desires and abilities with love—in a way that allows each of us to better realize the potential of what the Creator designed us to become. What we are is a gift from God, and what we become is our gift back to Him.

At times this may mean stretching ourselves to pursue a sizeable goal or ambition that, out of fear, we might have been avoiding. Doubt often holds us back. That little voice of doubt often whispers in our ear, "Who are you to do something so grand? You're just an ordinary person."

But ordinary people, every day, in every walk of life, are able to accomplish extraordinary things by trusting in a power greater than themselves. As Dr. Robert H. Schuller, bestselling author and founder of The Crystal Cathedral Ministries, says, "Make your goals big enough for God to fit into them." If you think you can accomplish your dream without God's help, you need to have a bigger dream.

Set faith goals even though the means of accomplishment may not be evident and your present resources may be lacking. But be assured that, "Faith is the assurance of things hoped for, the conviction of things unseen" (Hebrews 11:1).

Whatever your dream is, if it is worth having, then it is worth believing in. In fact, belief is essential to reaching your dreams. You may not know how or when you are going to reach your dreams, but faith in the outcome is essential. In Mark 6:4, we discover that the greatest miracle worker whoever lived was unable to perform any miracles in his hometown, except to heal a few who were sick, because the people who lived there lacked faith and belief. By steadfastly believing in your dreams, you remain open, and release the strength of spiritual capital.

Failure is not an option for those who are committed to their dreams. During the Apollo 13 flight, Gene Krantz, who received the Presidential Medal of Freedom, guided the astronauts of a surely doomed spaceship safely back to earth. Success was made possible because Krantz steadfastly believed, and instilled the belief in his team at Houston's ground control that failure was not an option. Like many of us, they had no clear-cut plan of how to do it, but through determination, figured it out along the way. More important than how to do something is having a big enough why to do something.

Part of living the dream is sharing it and helping others achieve it. The more we achieve, the more we need to share. And no matter how big or small the deed may be, we need to do it with love. As Mother Teresa said, "It is not how much we do, but how much love we put in the doing. It is not how much we give, but how much love we put in the giving."

In the final analysis, God will not measure how much we did in comparison to what others have done. The foolish pride within us does that. As long as we look for frequent opportunities to cultivate spiritual capital and create lasting wealth, we will have lived lives deserving of the words, "Well done, my good and faithful servant!"

CHAPTER QUESTIONS

1. What are your unique gifts, talents, dreams, and desires?

2. What things are holding you back in life from being the person that the Creator intended you to be?

3. What is your definition of work, when does it end, and when you meet God will you hear the words, "Well done, my good and faithful servant?

Lasting Wealth is found in sharing your gifts
and talents in a way that allows you
to become used up without burning out.

"Pride gets no pleasure
out of having something,
only having more of it than the next man...
It is a spiritual cancer."
—C.S. Lewis

17

PRIDE, NOT MONEY,
IS THE ROOT OF OUR EVILS

"Keep your lives free from the love of money
and be content with what you have,
because God has said,
'Never will I leave you; never will I forsake you.'"
—Hebrews 13:5

During the bull market of the 1990s, Newsweek ran a story, "The Whine of '99, Everyone Is Getting Rich, But Me." It related the sentiments of a 31-year-old electrical engineer at General Motors earning $60,000 a year. He said, "If I didn't know any better, I'd be perfectly happy with what I am doing. But it gets to me to see my peers, people I relate to, people my own age, doing better than I am. You start to feel discontent." He was not alone. Many of us were envious of those investors who appeared to be getting rich from the venture capital boom of the Internet.

The pursuit of money, as an end in itself, can become an addiction. Many people believe the amount of money they have makes a statement about themselves—the more they have the better they are, and the less they possess the more inferior they must be. Most Americans have *so much* in comparison with the rest of the world, yet we often display an attitude that life and God have conspired against us.

Most of us get more upset at the thought of the relatively few wealthy people in our society than by the millions of poor in the world. It is all too easy to overlook the more than 40 million people in America who live at or below the poverty line, while worldwide over one billion live in abject poverty.

Americans are continually reminded to be discontented with what we have. The typical U.S. consumer is bombarded by thousands of advertisements daily and is constantly urged by popular culture to demand more. Will Rogers spoke wisely when he said, "Too many of us spend money we don't have, to buy things we don't need, to impress people we don't like."

Choose Contentment over the Comparison Trap

In John:21, Peter, who earlier denied knowing Jesus three times, reconfirms his love for Him three times by promising to feed His sheep. Jesus then forewarns Peter that in following Him Peter would one day suffer a cruel death of his own. Peter, in turn, responds by asking a most reasonable question about John, who is also standing nearby. Peter asks: "What about him?" Jesus essentially answers: "What concern is he of yours; your business is to follow me."

How often do we take our eyes off God and to look to others and their lot in life? It is only natural to compare our circumstances with those of others to determine our own position and standing. Capitalism and contentment do not exactly go hand in hand. But as Peter discovered, that is not what we are called to do, nor will it in many cases bring about fairness in accordance with our designs.

It is common to fall into the trap of comparing ourselves, especially comparing our possessions to those of others and what they appear to possess. If we seem to have more than our peers, we feel superior—we believe we are ahead in the game of life. If they appear to have more than we do, we are envious as the feeling rises of being behind.

God has given the gift of life for us to love others, but in many cases, we have used our precious energy to love things and envy those we should love. The only comparison we need to make is how much our love for God and others has grown over time. Have we become more loving over the years, or have continual comparison and envy led to our discontentment?

High school and other reunions help illustrate our need for exterior comparison. Rather than looking forward to seeing some familiar faces and reminiscing about the good old days, attendees often become anxious about how they look, and about the status of their relationships and careers.

The need to compare and evaluate one's standing is at the center of our pride. It is our ego's most treasured resource. As C.S. Lewis said of pride: "It gets no pleasure out of having something, only having more of it than the next man. It is the comparison that makes you proud; the pleasure of being above the rest. It is a spiritual cancer: it eats up the very possibility of love, or contentment, or even common sense."

Our inevitable comparison to others would be much healthier if we looked to the rest of the world instead of only to our little Western corner of it. The truth is that most of us have hit the jackpot without ever knowing it. Of the nearly 6.5 billion people on the planet, only around 300 million people (5%) live in the United States, and they control over half of the world's wealth.

However, if one could shrink the Earth's population to a small village with all existing human ratios remaining the same, it would reveal the following: the majority of the villagers would live in substandard housing; most would be unable to read; many would suffer from malnutrition; and relatively few would have a college education or a computer.

The painful truth is that nearly half of the world's population is poor. Despite increasing global prosperity, more than 1 billion people still survive on less than $1 a day; 10.7 million children will die before their fifth birthday; and 115 million are not in school altogether.

A few centuries ago the vast majority of people on the planet were poor, but the Industrial Revolution helped change all of that. Since then some western countries, most notably the United States, have seen there GDP rise 25-fold.

But not everyone has participated, especially Africa where almost half of population lives in extreme poverty. Even in America roughly 8 million people die each year because they are too poor to survive.

We need to be more content with what we have. Contentment is mentioned seven times in the Bible, and in six of those cases, it has to do with money and material things. The secret of being content in whatever situation we may find ourselves, however, is found in believing that we can do everything through God who will give us strength and provide for our needs.

Like St. Paul, we must learn how to get along with humble means and how to live in prosperity so that we can be filled whether rejoicing in abundance or suffering in need.

Despite our relative economic good fortune, there is much restlessness in America today. Many expect the journey to begin with the end in sight. Often we fail to notice that much of the journey is beyond our control, and that what is really needed for a successful trip is profound gratitude to God for the many blessings we have received. We need to set goals and diligently pursue them, but we need to do so without becoming consumed by those aspirations. We can control much of the input but not the ultimate result.

St. Ignatius urged us to pray like it depends on God, and work like it depends on you. Give it everything you have, while mentally preparing for the possibility that you might not get what you set out to achieve. Trust that God can see in ways that we cannot.

We need to be careful not to blame money, or the lack thereof, for many of our difficulties. Money represents many things to many people: power, freedom, the root of all evil, or the blossom of all blessings. But money always has been, is, and will remain an inanimate, neutral object. It is nothing more than a store of value and a medium of exchange. In reality, money and possessions by themselves offer very little, although Western culture would have us believe otherwise. It is simply our attitude toward wealth and material prosperity that determines how we react.

Imagine you could live anywhere in the world and have anything you wanted except love and people with whom to share it. How many of us would honestly choose that situation? The thought of being like Macaulay Culkin's character in *Home Alone*, with all the toys to ourselves, may appear to be enticing at first glance. But on further reflection, the things of this world have little to offer us in terms of lasting wealth.

Some argue that money is the root of all evil. They naively believe that the *Bible* supports their claim. The New Testament, however, reveals: "The love of money is a root of evil; and to let our lives be free from the love of money and to be content with what you have." Further, we are instructed to remember that: "…it is the *covetous* man who is never satisfied with money and the *lover* of wealth who reaps no fruit from it."

We have been endeavoring to get a handle on pride, some of us more successfully than others, since Adam and Eve were in the garden. Why did Adam and Eve partake of the forbidden fruit? They ate the fruit because they naively believed they would become god-like. They were told by the serpent that the moment they ate the fruit, they would be like gods who know what is good and what is evil. Mankind's first sin was one of pride, and today pride is still leading us astray.

Be Careful—*Your Thoughts Are Spiritual Currency*

Sigmund Freud believed that our behavior is best explained by the way we handle our basic instincts and thoughts regarding sex and aggression. If Freud is right we may not be able to control most of what pops into our heads, or the goodness of our thoughts. But we do have something to say about the amount of time we spend entertaining less than worthwhile ambitions.

How many times do we answer the knock on the door of our imaginations to find greed or envy outside, and then willingly welcome them in? Too often we mentally entertain these prideful intruders long after they should have worn out their welcome. And the more time they are given, the more likely they are to take up residence and obtain our souls' consent.

We flirt with danger by allowing unwholesome thoughts to become habitual. Sooner or later, detrimental thoughts that have long been entertained find their way into our actions. In fact, most actions, good or bad, are born out of a prior thought. Therefore, in a real sense, our thoughts are a type of spiritual currency.

As in the "Parable of the Sower," we hear the call to love God and others, but then worldly anxiety and the lure of riches choke our efforts, allowing them to bear little fruit. Pride often gets the best of us when we forget we are here to love and make a difference in the world—not just to compete for secular glory. When we reject our duty to love, we lose our way.

Humility Heals the Unseen Wounds of Pride

St. Augustine once compared pride and humility and said: "It is better to do an evil deed with humility than to do a good deed with pride." Humility is the antidote to the poison of pride. Humility heals pride's unseen wounds.

Selflessness eradicates unhealthy competition, because our focus shifts to a purpose greater than ourselves and our own desires. Where there is true humility, there is no need to judge and compare. Humble people understand that the world is bigger than they are individually, and they were never meant to be on center stage for very long.

Perhaps humility is best viewed as envisioning God as a loving artist painting a portrait of our lives as part of the mural of creation. In one sense, we are a little paintbrush and need to trust that the Artist alone has the skill for realizing every precise detail. But at the same time, we need to use our God-given abilities and desires. This helps to bring out the defining lines of meaningful character through right thought and action.

Being humble does not mean thinking of ourselves as deficient and lowly. In fact, a poor self-image may hamper our efforts at humility just as much as a prideful self-image. In both cases, the focus is too much on us and not enough on God and others. We should think a lot of ourselves, but at the same time, a lot less often about ourselves. In no case does being humble require a poor self-image or lack of self-respect.

As noted author Marianne Williamson stated, "Our deepest fear is not that we are inadequate…It is our light, not our darkness, that most frightens us. We ask ourselves, who am I to be brilliant, gorgeous, talented, and fabulous? Actually, who are you not to be? You are a child of God. Your playing small doesn't serve the world…We were born to manifest the glory of God within us." When we get past our narcissistic self—our self-centered nature—our true radiance shines. After all, we are the most brilliant color seen in all creation.

Add Prayer First—and *You'll Start to Find Humility*

Humility is best acquired by a gradual change in one's heart that often begins with faithful prayer and focusing on God's grace. Still, many of us seek God through prayer only when we experience sickness, loss, and other difficulties.

Somehow it is all too easy to feel that God is distant or inattentive to our daily concerns. But could it be that we are the ones who are not paying attention to God? Perhaps we fail to receive grace because we may not realize we need it, or we have not sought it with firm faith. Prayer brings

God into our lives, not necessarily according to our desires, but according to God's loving will. As Jesus made clear in the Garden of Gethsemane, the purpose of prayer is about conforming our will to God's and not the other way around.

Mother Teresa once said, "I do not think there is anyone who needs God's help and grace as much as I do. Sometimes I feel so helpless and weak. Because I cannot depend upon my own strength, I rely on Him 24 hours a day." Mother Teresa's secret was very simple: she prayed constantly and believed that all of us need to cling to God through prayer.

More important than the formalities of prayer is the frequency and faithfulness of it. Real prayer is more than what we say to God. Perhaps the greatest blessing of sincere, earnest prayer is that we are quiet long enough to hear what God is saying.

Faithful prayer will frequently help change you or your circumstances with the sequence of change mattering very little. A vivid example of this for me occurred when I was continually praying for God's direction as to where to live and what to do with my life. During this particular period, I was traveling in Europe and journaling much of the time.

At some point in my journey, I found myself praying at the Sistine Chapel for heavenly guidance. During the night, I had a vivid dream where a woman I greatly respected and once worked for urged me to move to San Diego. I awoke immediately after the dream to a bright morning sun beaming in through the window.

I recorded my joyful, excited feelings in the journal never thinking that this could be God's divine finger. I was already planning on visiting San Diego when I left Europe and simply passed off the dream as future anticipation.

I did visit San Diego and moved there shortly thereafter without a job and without really knowing anyone. I soon found employment in a law office where one of the founding partners had recently passed away. Coincidentally, I ended up in the deceased partner's office and often wondered what he must have been like. I eventually learned that he was a man of great faith, which I found very comforting.

Several years later, I received a call from the deceased partner's wife who requested some papers from his estate file. When I went into the file, I noticed the date of his death which triggered something in my mind.

That evening at home I looked through my journal entries and suddenly discovered that the day the partner died was the same day that I had that dream. While some would write this off to coincidence, I feel that God was using me in some way to help fill a vacant post.

Prayer is our most sincere way of asking for the wisdom of God's love to guide our lives. When we feel lonely, unworthy, sick, and forgotten, we are still precious to God. The act of praying combats the pride of trusting in only ourselves. More than a responsibility to be dutifully discharged, prayer presents and opportunity to engage the Creator of us all.

With each new day God gives us a gift of another 86,400 seconds. Surely we can use a few of them to reconnect with our Maker. But prayer alone is not enough to do away with pride. That requires actively caring for others.

CHAPTER QUESTIONS

1. Whom do you fall into the comparison trap with most often? Can you experience contentment when you are comparing yourself to others?

2. Are you content with what you have? Why or why not? If you had more would you be content then? How much is really enough?

3. How consistent is your prayer life? Do you ever pray for humility—where you ask to become poor in spirit so that God may become rich in you?

The road to a rich life begins with faithful prayer.

"Only through loving and giving
can we leave the prison cells of our aloneness.
We must make someone else's needs
as important as our own."
—Eric Fromm

18

SERVING OTHERS SERVES GOD

...Amen, I say to you, whatever you did
for one of these least brothers of mine,
you did for me."
—Matthew: 25–40

When feeling worried or overwhelmed, most of us, at some point with various degrees of success, have tried to let go of our concerns and give them to God. As many of us have experienced, the notion of "letting go and letting God" is easier said than done. Why? The ego's pride likes to maintain control.

The Ego's Grasp on the Nets We Carry

When we are truly able to quiet the ego and trust God, there is often an undeniable sense of relief. It is as if a burdensome weight has been lifted from our shoulders. God, however, doesn't necessarily take away our trials simply as a result of our prayers and earnest desire to let go. Something more is frequently required. Many times, we need to loosen the grip we have on the trials we face and selflessly stretch out our hands in service to others before Divine Providence intervenes.

The movie, *The Mission*, helps illustrates this point. In the beginning scenes, a ruthless captain tracks down island natives to be used as slave labor for a king. After one such successful conquest, the captain returns to town and discovers his girlfriend in bed with his brother. Blinded by pride and anger, the captain kills his brother. Thereafter, the captain is overcome by intense feelings of guilt and remorse. He suffers great emotional agony and a missionary priest tries to help the broken captain in his anguish. The priest asks the captain to fulfill a painstakingly difficult penance to cleanse him of his sin and release him from his torment.

His penance is to follow a group of missionaries up a steep waterfall, while carrying his cumbersome weapons and armor in a net behind him—the outward evidence of all that he has become. The ascent is extremely strenuous and the captain falls hard many times in the process, but is unwilling to accept any assistance from others. During the climb, a missionary priest in the group pleads for the captain's penance to come to an end, convinced that he has suffered long enough. Yet the priest who issued the penance disagrees and tells his contemporary, "The captain doesn't feel it is yet time. Only he will know when his penance is done, when it is time to finally let go."

As the missionaries reach a crest, they encounter several natives from a tribe that the captain had formerly hunted down. Bloodied and near collapse, the captain finally reaches the group and is immediately face to face with a native who has drawn his knife. But instead of wielding the knife upon the captain in revenge, the native mercifully cuts the captain's weighty net. It is only then that the captain is released from his tremendous burden, his penance finally completed. The captain commits his life to God and spends the rest of his days in service to the mission and the natives who live there.

The captain was finally free of his torment but, in a sense, the priest who issued the penance had been wrong. It was not that the penance issued was wrong, but that the captain did not know when his penance was done—when it was time for him to let go. Without the native's merciful act of love, the prideful captain would have continued to carry his heavy burden until he collapsed. Many of us are like the captain. We fail to realize that it takes faith in God and acts of service, both to and from others, to help us truly let go.

Letting Go Takes More Than One Step

In everyday life letting go is perhaps best illustrated by the millions of alcoholics who have found solace through the distinguished 12-step program of Alcoholics Anonymous. In the book *Alcoholics Anonymous*, the essence of many alcoholics' undoing is revealed: "Selfishness and self-centeredness! That, we think, is the root of our troubles. What usually happens in the alcoholic's life is that the show doesn't come off very well. He becomes, on the next occasion, still more demanding or gracious, as the case may be. Still the play doesn't suit him. Admitting he may be somewhat at fault, he is sure that other people are more to blame. He becomes angry, indignant, and self-pitying. Therefore, and above everything else, we alcoholics must be free of this selfishness. We must or it kills us!"

Many of the alcoholics who gave their personal testimonies in that book possessed exceptional credentials. Curiously, not one of them was able to break the addiction through using willpower. All turned to a higher power for help in overcoming the addiction. But if admitting you are an alcoholic, powerless, and willing to surrender your life to a higher power, were enough to cure you of your dependency on alcohol there would be only three steps to the program, not twelve.

Alcoholics also need to take a fearless moral inventory, make a list of those they have harmed, and seek to make amends with those people. In addition, recovering alcoholics need to carry their personal message of spiritual awakening and serve other alcoholics.

We may not have a debilitating addiction like alcoholism, but for many of us, antidepressants and professional counselors are in great demand. The number of Americans treated for depression nearly tripled in the 1990s. While confiding in a trained therapist may be helpful, the potential drawback of most therapy is that the spotlight remains brightly fixed on the patient. People can spend years and vast amounts of money in therapy dealing with the same issues because they stay fixated on themselves.

Much like when we focus on the throb of a toothache, continual self-examination of our difficulties may only serve to intensify the pain. While there is need for professional counseling, many of us would be healthier emotionally if we worked through our difficulties, while lovingly turning our attention toward helping others. Service and giving of self can cause an amazing catharsis and healing.

How to Cultivate Spiritual Capital

The ways to cultivate spiritual capital will be limited only by our failure to think creatively. Consider the following short list as a starter on how to grow and cultivate spiritual capital:

- If appropriate, buy a meal for and spend some time with a homeless person, or at least send that person your silent blessing when your paths cross.
- Volunteer to do someone else's chores around the house.
- Make it a priority to pay three people a sincere compliment before the day ends.
- Take the money that you were going to spend at happy hour and start a charitable piggy bank with your kids.
- Take a few kids on the little-league team out for ice cream when they lose. Praise their hard work and have fun. It is just a game.
- Pay the bill at the drive-through window or a highway toll for the person behind you.
- Before having dinner tonight, pray with your family and share one thing that each of you was grateful for during the day.
- Forward a personal note of congratulations to someone who has had a recent success.
- Spend ten minutes alone in nature with the Creator, giving thanks for all that you have.

We need to do our best to give, at least in some small way, to all those whom we meet every day. When we seek to sincerely acknowledge and understand those around us, we cannot fail to love them.

Pay It Forward—*Pass on to Three Others the Good Deed That Was Done for You*

A few years ago, the movie *Pay It Forward* provided a compelling look at a model for producing spiritual capital. The general theme was that our world would be a much better place if each of us did a good deed for three other people. The movie encouraged viewers to pass on the good deed that was done for us without expectations and for no particular reason other than kindness. Upon receiving the favors, these three people would then be asked, in turn, to "pay it forward" to another three people, thereby creating an exponential growth of spiritual capital.

Following a sermon on stewardship a church in California literally "paid it forward", when Denny Bellesi stunned his congregation by distributing $10,000 among one hundred volunteers and sent them on a "God assignment." Each person was given $100 on three conditions: First, that they understood the money belonged to God; second, that they invested the money in God's work; and third, that they reported the results in ninety days.

What happened thereafter won national media attention (including Oprah) and influenced hundreds of thousands of lives across the community and around the world. According to published reports, the original $10,000 increased to $150,000 through the creative efforts of the recipients and the generosity of others.

Another example of paying it forward with spiritual capital occurred during the Kosovo crisis at the end of the 1990s. Some friends in Los Angeles had learned from a server at dinner of a local refugee family in need. For several months, they generously welcomed the immigrants as part of their own family. My friends began by buying a few simple things for the family like food and clothes.

As they opened up to other possibilities of giving, my friends also provided costly dental care for the family members and looked for ways to make it possible for the family to have a place of their own. My friends did not take a charitable tax deduction for the time and money spent in assisting the refugees, but their unselfish acts of love were their own reward.

Adding to the societal treasury of spiritual capital need not be as elaborate and involved as helping a refugee family. It can be as simple as giving a smile to those who cross our paths every day. Recently, I read a sign at a car rental agency counter, which extolled the value of a smile. It read something like this:

> *SMILE! It costs nothing to give, but creates much. It not only enriches those who receive it, but also those who give it. None of us are so rich that we can get along without it. It creates happiness in a home and fosters goodwill in a business. And it is something that is no good until it is given away.*

Some altruistic acts, even one simple deed, can benefit the integrity of an institution. Baseball, a sport recently marred by rumors of extensive steroid abuse by its players, received a much-needed shot in the arm when a young man named Tim Forneris scooped up Mark McGwire's 62nd homerun ball—the hit that broke Roger Maris's long-standing record.

Before the homerun was hit, prognosticators everywhere talked about how much the prized ball would bring to the lucky person who retrieved it. It was also rumored that the IRS would assess a gift tax on the transfer of the ball if it were sold for less than its fair market value.

But all pundits were fittingly silenced when the young St. Louis groundskeeper simply returned the ball so it could be given back to McGwire, saying, "It's not mine to begin with. McGwire just lost it, and I brought it home. I'm a regular Joe."

Two seasons later that selfless example of the young groundskeeper was completely ignored by two grown men. They squabbled in court for well over a year-and-a-half regarding who rightfully owned Barry Bonds' record-setting 73rd homerun ball.

Like a must-have toy that two siblings fuss over, that ball brought nothing but disagreement. In the end, the judge ruled that the prized ball be sold and the proceeds be evenly split. Yet, the ball commanded an auction price of only $450,000, whereas McGwire's 70th homerun ball of 1999 sold for $3.2 million. Fittingly, the $450,000 may not have been enough to cover even the legal fees of the lawyers that each man had employed. And to quote baseball's Yogi Berra, "It was deja vu all over again," when Barry Bond's 700th home run ball was similarly embroiled in a another lawsuit between two disgruntled men.

The biggest opportunity for service in our materialistic culture may well be helping to meet a person's intangible needs as opposed to their tangible ones. Often people are lonely even though they have many material comforts. Yet, poverty can take many forms, material as well as spiritual. We can be materially rich but inwardly bankrupt.

Eric Fromm, psychoanalyst and bestselling author of *The Art of Loving*, put it this way: "The deepest need of man is the need to overcome his separateness, to leave the prison of his aloneness.

We need to experience spiritual and emotional union. Only through loving and giving can we leave the prison cells of our aloneness. We must make someone else's needs as important as our own." St. Paul simply put it this way in Philippians 2:4, "Each of you should look not only to your own interests, but also to the interests of others."

We Serve God Best When We Serve Mankind

Our faith alone in God may assure salvation, but it is our works on behalf of others that most assuredly provide the best evidence of our faith. "Faith without works is dead" (James 2:14–26). I believe very strongly in the words of St. Francis, "Preach the Gospel at all times; when necessary, use words."

At the end of our lives, we will not be judged and rewarded by how many degrees we have, how much money we have made, or how far up the world's ladder we have climbed. When we are judged by God, it will be: "I was hungry and you gave me food; I was thirsty and you gave me drink; a stranger and you welcomed me; naked and you clothed me; ill and you cared for me; in prison and you visited me." We will be rewarded according to what each of us has done (Matthew 16:27).

Two minutes after we have passed from this world and into the next, our regrets will not be that we gave, but that we did not give enough. In *Schindler's List*, Oskar Schindler looks at his gold pin and car, and regrets that he did not give more of his money and possessions to save the lives of more Jews who needlessly died in World War II concentration camps. What we give away in the name of charity is never lost. Only what we hold onto will be lost in time.

We are told that we will always have the poor with us. However, we are still charged with helping these people improve their lives. Care for the poor requires our time, training, and monetary assistance. But the poor must not be seen as a burden—they are to be seen as our neighbors.

In the Old Testament God reveals himself to us as the liberator of the oppressed and the defender of the poor, demanding from people faith in Him and justice towards one's neighbor. In a special way then, the poor present an opportunity to experience the love of God by practicing the virtue of kindness.

In that respect, we ought not to regard material goods as solely our own, but as common, so as to be ready to share them when we see others in need.

"If someone who has the riches of this world sees his brother in need and closes his heart to him, how does the love of God abide in him?" (1 Jn 3:17). Saint Ambrose put it this way, "You are not making a gift of your possessions to the poor person. You are handing over to him what is his. For what has been given in common for the use of all, you have arrogated to yourself. The world is given to all, and not only to the rich."

No one may claim the name of Christian and be comfortable in the face of hunger, homelessness and the injustice found in this country and the world. It is not just about giving to the poor out of a sense of duty around the holidays. It is more about integrating them into our lifestyles in a way that reflects loving God's compassion. We are reminded in 1 Corinthians 13:3 that even if we give away all of our possessions to feed the poor but do not have love, it profits us nothing.

We need to encourage the poor to reconnect with society and become productive participants so that they, too, may share in and be active participants in the common good. But the poor not only lack material goods; they often lack the knowledge and skills to change their circumstances. The principle of solidarity, therefore, is best lived out by helping the poor find the hope they so desperately need.

Habitat for Humanity, a nonprofit, ecumenical Christian housing ministry, provides an excellent example of helping people get back on their feet, while still asking them to walk under their own power. Through volunteer labor and donations, Habitat provides proper housing to partner families at no profit. Such housing is financed with no-interest loans. Partner families, however, do not get a free handout. They must provide the down payment and make the monthly mortgage payments. Additionally, they must also invest hundreds of hours of their own labor—sweat equity—into building their Habitat house and the houses of others.

Habitat has built more than 200,000 houses around the world, providing appropriate housing for over 1,000,000 people in more than 3,000 communities. Habitat's ministry remains a simple one: Christ's love must not be expressed in words alone. It must be true love, which shows itself in action as the "theology of the hammer."

We Are Called to Be God's Visible Hands

Our faith and our concept of religion must not become a club we join merely as idle members. There may well be an "invisible hand" as set forth earlier by Adam Smith which guides our actions toward increasing societal wealth. But sometimes the "invisible hand" is all thumbs. Instead, we are called to be God's visible hands, working in a free enterprise system.

We need to help proclaim that human life is sacred and that the dignity of each person is the foundation of our society and our institutions. People are more important than things, and our institutions need to become more effective at improving life and promoting dignity. They need to reflect concern for others and help bring about social justice.

Our care and use of the environment and its resources need to become more than Earth Day annual remembrances. The challenge for us is to live every day believing that we are one human family, regardless of our national, ethnic, economic, religious, ideological, and other differences. In doing so, loving our neighbor will have global implications as economies everywhere serve the people, not the other way around.

Being God's visible hands can bring about many blessings. On a personal note, shortly after Lori and I married we discovered that it would be very unlikely for Lori to be able to conceive. It was a devastating time for Lori and I felt badly too.

Lori suggested that we consider adopting. With both of us being in our 40s, however, I was more hesitant and felt that if God wanted us to have a child He would have given us one of our own. In truth, I was scared.

It was a difficult decision, especially for me. In coming to a resolution, a thought kept reoccurring to me: "Where would the Holy Family have been had Joseph said 'No'." With much prayer, counseling and consideration we decided to go forward with the adoption.

For me it was an opportunity to give of myself in a way that I never had before. Most of my prior acts of love and charity were candidly done without a long term commitment. Adoption demanded that I jump in with both feet.

In China, we adopted a one-year-old girl and named her Elizabeth ("God's promise"). Through her, God's promise of unconditional love became evermore real for our family. To us, Elizabeth was one of those tangible blessings from the invisible hand of all of creation.

Give Until It Hurts—Not Just Until It Feels Good

Philanthropist Claude Rosenberg, the author of *Wealthy and Wise*, and past chairman of an investment company worth $60 billion, spent many years researching and analyzing America's giving abilities and habits. It is a formidable task since around $250 billion dollars are graciously given on an annual basis.

By his estimates Rosenberg firmly believes that if we Americans were to make charitable donations closer to our comfortable capacities we could invest at least $100 billion dollars more each year in solving societal ills.

Still, one of the hallmarks of this nation is that in times of trouble and communal hardship we give generously. While the Federal Emergency Management Agency (FEMA) may have stumbled badly in dealing with Hurricane Katrina victims the American people did not. Many faith-based groups led the way, functioning as spirited armies of compassion. Overall, 60 million Americans volunteered in some way.

In the absence of a pending emergency, however, we may want to ask ourselves is there anything that we may be holding onto that God may want us to give away? For it is by giving that we are freed from the hold of our possessions and experience financial freedom. In giving, we demonstrably affirm our love for God and neighbor, and in the process discover that it is more blessed to give than to receive (Acts 20:35).

Maybe the most honest and selfish reason for giving is that we experience an emotional emptiness deep inside that needs healing. So often, natural feelings of emptiness are quickly masked by food, television, and other things belonging to the material world. But allowing ourselves to fully feel these voids can present opportunities for holiness and spiritual growth. If we can manage to stay still long enough to pay attention to our emptiness, we will realize our need for God.

Consider that physical hunger through fasting is sought after precisely because it puts us in the position to purify our souls. Every major world religion promotes fasting, because it allows one to discover self-control over the body and its appetites. It also enables us to experience compassion for those who are physically impoverished.

In 2 Corinthians 9, God challenges us to sow bountifully so that we may reap bountifully. By doing so, God promises to supply all that we need in order to provide an abundance for every good work. We will be enriched in every way so that we may continue to be generous in thanksgiving to God. We may not feel moved to give, but being a cheerful giver comes as a byproduct of giving, not a precondition to it.

Learn From Both a Princess and a Pauper

I found it more than a mere coincidence that Mother Teresa and Princess Diana died within five days of one another. The two were friends and perhaps even kindred spirits. But Princess Diana was more like the adolescent student struggling to find love, while Mother Teresa resembled the seasoned teacher who wrote the book on it.

In many ways, Princess Diana lived the fairy-tale life that many of us desire. When Diana became a princess, she was instantly showered with money, elaborate clothes and jewels, celebrity status, and millions of admirers. But as we got to know a little more about the real Diana, we learned that she was desperate to find love.

Money, a mind-boggling wardrobe, and the most photographed face in the world did not provide her with the love for which she yearned. And although Diana experienced love through her children and a few close family members and friends, it was in her moments of selfless public service to the less fortunate that Diana experienced love in the most special way. In particular, she graciously focused the media's attention on worthy causes for humanity, like the elimination of land mines.

After Diana's tragic death, she was honored with a memorial service that was second to none. It included literally tons of flowers, millions of mourners who watched from around the world, and the biggest selling single of all-time, written and sung in tribute by Elton John. When the Arts and Entertainment Television Network (A&E) did a special on the 100 most significant people over the past 1,000 years, they named her number 73. Maybe Diana was so extraordinarily special because she was not only a princess but, in many ways, she was like us.

When her friend Mother Teresa died five days later, the Associated Press first advised us of her death with the headline: "Mother Teresa Dead." They expanded the headline the next day: "Mother Teresa—the tiny saint of the gutters whose untiring ministry to the poor and terminally ill made her synonymous with charity—died yesterday of a massive heart attack."

The local paper in Calcutta carried a cartoon depicting a mosque, a Hindu temple, a Buddhist temple, and a Christian church. Outside each building, members representing these religions stood dressed in their respective religious attire with their hands joined together in prayer as they looked up to heaven. The caption underneath it simply read: "O God, please do not take our Mother away from us."

The memorial service for Mother Teresa was well-attended by dignitaries, but the media's attention paled in comparison with that showered upon Princess Diana's memorial. Surprisingly, the Nobel Peace Prize-winning nun was not included in A&E's list. But something tells me that is just the way Mother Teresa, who owned nothing except three sets of habits made of coarse cloth, would have wanted it.

Mother Teresa lived a life rich with love, because she had many years of bringing joy to the faces of abandoned babies, seeing smiles light up the faces of disabled children, helping the dying poor go home to God in peace, holding the hands of AIDS patients, restoring dignity to leprosy sufferers, and bringing the healing touch of God's love to the sick and lonely.

This saintly woman believed that God used her to accomplish great things because she believed more in her Creator's love than in her own human abilities. Her love for Jesus was not based on what He could give to her. Rather, she loved Him even though He took from her.

Mother Teresa faithfully answered her calling, but not without fear of what her new life might bring. A letter prior to accepting her new calling reveals her apprehension, "I'm so afraid Jesus. I'm so terribly afraid. Let me not be deceived. I am so afraid. The devil can deceive me. This fear shows me how much I love myself. I'm afraid of the suffering that will come from living that Indian life: clothing like that; eating like that; sleeping like that; living with that and never having anything my way. How much comfort has taken possession of my heart."

Mother Teresa would have been unable to experience the depth of Jesus' love without carrying the cross given to her. But she could never have picked up or carried her cross without Jesus.

The weight of her cross was often unbearable, and there were many dark nights in her blessed life that accompanied her until her death. In letters recently released from her spiritual director, Mother Teresa explained the profound contradiction her soul at times suffered: "They say people in hell suffer eternal pain because of the loss of God. In my soul, I feel just the terrible pain of loss, of God not wanting me, of God not being God, of God not really existing."

But Mother Teresa remained faithful throughout and continued to rely on Jesus, regardless of whether or not she felt His presence. Although she often went to bed at 1:00 a.m. and got up just a few hours later at 4:40 a.m., she was always the first one to chapel for forty years.

Mother Teresa willingly passed up the easier road to short-lived happiness; instead, walking the demanding road to eternal joy. To borrow from the words of Winston Churchill, most of us make a living by what we get, but Mother Teresa made a life by what she gave. Selfless acts of service, whether done by a princess or a pauper, are the surest ways to let go and bring more love into the world.

CHAPTER QUESTIONS

1. What are some of the "nets" that you carry, and are you holding onto anything that causes you not to be dependent upon God?

2. When was the last time someone paid something forward to you without expecting something in return? How did you feel? When was the last time you did likewise? How did you feel?

3. Are you in greater danger of having given too much too soon or too little too late? Is it possible to love without giving?

When we are truly serving others,
we are living a rich life.

"If you become a burning light of justice
and peace in the world,
then you really will be true to what the
founders of this country stood for.
This is to love one another
as God loves each one of us."
—Mother Teresa

19

AWAKENING THE AMERICAN DREAM

"...that for your sake he became poor although he was rich,
so that by his poverty you might become rich."
—2 Corinthians 8:9

In its relatively short history, America has experienced several periods of renewal and spiritual reform. They were times of revitalization—a reorientation in beliefs and values toward our founding principles, encouraging faith and civic virtue. These periods, known as awakenings, brought God and our nation closer together.

The Great Awakening of religious devoutness swept through the American colonies between the 1730s and 1770s. A second awakening took place during the period of moral decline after the Revolutionary War. Awakenings also occurred during and after the industrialization and urbanization of America.

As we go forward in this twenty-first century, we are being summoned, once again, to draw from that principled well of our Founding Fathers. We are called to be a nation of strong moral principles—a nation where the pursuit of the American Dream is based on individual liberty, personal responsibility and the promotion of the common good.

Answering the call will require great effort, because people generally prefer to sleep under the balminess of "business as usual." Awakenings, on the other hand, require that we shed our attachments and risk taking an unprotected plunge into icy waters of inspiration, that alone can incite the spirit and stir the soul.

John Steinbeck wrote: "If I wanted to destroy a nation, I would give it too much, and would have it on its knees, miserable and greedy." Awakenings ask that we become agents of divine Providence; that we kneel more before the Author of Liberty and less before the world.

Ronald Reagan's "shining City on the Hill" is only made possible when the people who live there choose to rededicate themselves to an American Dream that is committed to life, liberty, and the pursuit of happiness. As Mother Teresa once remarked, "If you become a burning light of justice and peace in the world, then you really will be true to what the founders of this country stood for. This is to love one another as God loves each one of us."

"Come Follow Me and Think Outside the Box"

To live out the call to be "one nation under God" is a demanding task. We are continually being pulled in contradictory ways. Since the beginning of humanity, God and the material world have seemingly coaxed us in differing directions with the message, "Come follow me." Yet as C.S. Lewis put it, "if you aim at heaven you will get earth thrown in. But if you aim at earth you will miss both."

It would be wonderful to set forth a simple *how-to formula* that would allow us to uniformly claim the wages of both our Creator and the material world. But that is not the way of life. By their intrinsic nature, there will always be some opposing tensions in the pursuit of God's kingdom and a materially based American Dream. Yet, the spiritual should not be viewed as being divorced from the secular, as we are called to be salt and light in our workplace, our communities and our homes.

We each have a body and a soul, which link us with both the material and spiritual worlds. God is the loving force emanating from the world of spirit found in our hearts and souls. The pursuit of money as an end in and of itself tends to keep us bound to the material world. In view of that, it is important to remember that our ultimate citizenship is in heaven. Establishing residency there requires that we set our minds on things above as we seek to faithfully carry out the Gospel while still below.

Jesus' admonition regarding the inability to serve two masters simultaneously makes clear that tough choices often need to be made. Serving God, being a good steward, and improving our standard of living, however, can all be well-founded components in living a rich life.

It is through a reorientation in beliefs and attitudes that we are enabled to find areas of mutual compatibility between "In God We Trust" and the money we bank on. Although money is a miserable master, it can be a skillful servant. New paradigms are continually being shaped that enhance our understanding of the world in which we live. Although the "world" has not changed much since the time of Jesus, our perception and organization of the world has.

Learning to think outside the box is what allows us to continually re-frame our view of reality and improve upon it. Inspiration and imagination are what enable us to prevail over life's problems. Albert Einstein put it this way, "We cannot solve our problems with the same thinking we used to create them."

With this in mind, some religious truths that were initially thought to be incongruent with other approaches to understanding life are now viewed as congruent in a reframed box. For example, many once thought that human intelligence and the ability to reason were irreconcilable with God and Divine revelation—until St. Thomas Aquinas took the logic of Aristotle and applied it to faith.

Aquinas used his inspired intellect to see beyond the widely held traditional religious beliefs of his day. He taught that reason was supportive of revelation and that our common sense was an important part in defining religious virtues. During his time, Aquinas's teachings were undeniably radical, and some viewed him as a heretic. Today, ironically, St. Thomas Aquinas is the favored theologian of many conservatives.

Science and psychology were once thought to be incompatible with religion. Recall that Galileo's "misguided" belief that the Earth revolved around the sun (and not vice versa) was once preached as being in direct conflict with Christian theology. Yet, today, we understand this to be true and wholly consistent.

Science, religion, and psychology are now viewed as three disciplines that provide meaningful approaches to help us deal effectively with the human condition. Today, these three disciplines are generally seen holistically and mutually cooperative with one another, although one may be more appropriate than another in dealing with a specific situation.

If our child is suffering from an infection, for example, we may pray for their health, hold their hand, and talk to them to bring them emotional comfort. But we generally depend the most upon an antibiotic to cure the infection.

The quest for financial and spiritual capital may very well have areas of genuine compatibility. Consider that the noble pursuit of capitalism through self-interest often yields more than increased societal wealth through unintended acts of service. Moral free markets inspire many intended acts of beneficial service. Receiving money as a result of extending constructive goods and service to our neighbors advances God's creation.

Rising standards of living can surely be in concert with the development of human dignity, solidarity and human rights. At times, it may be just as holy to expand and invest in a business, which employs others and provides worthy goods and services, as it is to give to charitable endeavors. Giving to charity clearly is an act of faith, but so, too, is taking the initiative to start your own business.

Business can be a very real and noble vocation. Through business, we as co-creators create new means of wealth. We create goods, services, jobs, and new and better ways of doing things. Engaging in the enterprise of business is virtuous, provided businesses operate as moral institutions. Business in a free market system can be a very effective means of advancing the common good and increasing prosperity.

This is no small point as societal prosperity is what enables the poor to be better served and manufacture their "daily bread." More than providing offerings of fish, the wealth-creating potential of right-minded capitalism can empower the poor to fish for themselves. Many times the most effective way to improve the lot of the poor is to help them realize their own economic initiative through teaching skills that will foster creative enterprise.

Certainly, a bigger economic pie can more effectively feed all participants, particularly the poor. It is economic prosperity that allows our kids to stay in school for a better education, instead of toiling in the fields, factories, and farms as in past generations. The truth is that we need both spiritual and financial capital for our personal well-being and our society's welfare.

Free markets can be the most effective way to use society's resources and the best way to promote the welfare of the family. But we need to be wary of the materialism and consumerism of capitalism, and work toward a moral free market system which places people over profits.

Creating Lasting Wealth by Being Rich in Worthy Values

Here are five examples of what you can do in a practical family setting to think outside the box and create lasting wealth when financial assets are involved:

1. Put Parameters on Allowances

Well-meaning parents often give their children a modest allowance for doing household chores so that they can begin to learn about working for and handling the responsibility of money. The trouble, however, is that children are often free to do what they want with their allowance without any parameters. Without prudent constraints, children usually save their money for a short time to purchase something they want, which often reinforces hastily using money as a consumer.

In addition to putting money aside for near term spending, consider having your children routinely set aside a portion of their allowance for longer term investing, so the children will begin to learn about and appreciate the process and value of compounding interest. Also, your children should learn to give a portion of their allowance to their church and charities. In this way you will be teaching your children to budget, save, invest, and be a responsible consumer and charitable giver.

2. Empower Children to be CEOs of Their Charitable Contributions

While putting sensible constraints on allowances, grant children wide latitude to pick charitable causes important to them. Let them be the CEO in terms of choosing, researching, and contacting the charity. The liberty of allowing your child to give to a cause that they are drawn to is a great freedom of expression. At the same time, it is important to make sure that the charity sends a receipt and acknowledgement to the child, in their name, which will help to reinforce a sense of purposefulness and esteem within the child.

3. Make Formal Loans to Kids

It may seem silly to actually document a loan to a child for a bigger purchase—where the child makes regular payments of principal and interest back to you. But simple formalities can help prepare children for the responsibilities to come. Be sure to celebrate the final payment of the loan where the emphasis should be on becoming debt free. Not only will your children have a greater appreciation for what they buy with borrowed money, but you will help instill in them the importance of paying off their bills on a timely basis. You will be helping them to not become borrowers who are servants to the lender.

4. Consider Becoming a Socially Responsible Investor

Return on investment has become the primary criterion regarding stockholders and corporate America. Yet, decisions about where to invest one's capital have moral and cultural implications too. While ensuring an adequate return on our capital should we not also seek to avoid those companies that participate in harmful activities and invest more often in those that promote the common good?

In furtherance of family and other meaningful values perhaps our investment criterion should favor those companies that protect human life, promote human dignity, preserve peace and the environment, as well as those that pursue economic justice and corporate responsibility. It is worth noting that socially and morally responsible investing is not automatic within index or professionally managed funds. Consider that about 10% of the companies from the S&P 500 index typically get screened out when a socially responsible investment filter is applied. Today, there are a plethora of well-managed socially responsible investment funds that have outperformed the returns of the S & P 500 index.

5. Family Conferences

At some point, all families get together to discuss money. Oftentimes it is in the difficult days following a funeral where there are frequent misunderstandings and confusion. Make it a point to schedule regular family conferences so that you can share your estate and financial plan with your loved ones; learn about and better manage their values, passions, and expectations; and codify/share an ethical will which may encompass your core values, spiritual beliefs, hopes, and blessings, and lessons that you have learned in life.

The focus of these meetings should be more on the transfer of wealth in the broader sense and less on the intricacies of the plan. Passing on wealth is more than passing on money through estate planning vehicles; it is about choosing and preparing the next generations of stewards.

We should be more concerned about giving our loved-ones a heritage of wisdom rather than a heritage of assets. Imparting wisdom should precede the departing of assets. Although wisdom helps create wealth, inherited wealth does not necessarily carry wisdom along with it.

If we leave money to our children but have not left them wisdom, we may well have subverted their need to pray and depend upon God for the truly important things. St. John Chryostom rightly put it this way, "If you leave much wealth to your children, leave them in God's care. Do not leave riches, but virtue and skill."

It has often been said that parents and teachers spend decades preparing children for occupations in the real world, but precious little time preparing children for the issues surrounding the money they will make. Likewise, people spend far more time planning their estates than they do preparing those who will receive it.

In practice, plans need to be beneficiary driven more than they need to be tax driven. It is more important to carefully craft a plan around a prodigal son or daughter than it is to simply minimize taxes. We cannot expect future generations to carryon the torch if we are unwilling to make the time to pass it on.

It is worth noting that a major life insurance company recently surveyed Baby Boomers and their parents about their attitudes on everything from the importance of fulfilling last wishes to passing on real estate and other assets. Surprisingly, 77 percent of Baby Boomers polled said that the most important inheritance they could receive would be values and lessons about life. In fact, values were 10 times more important to Boomers than money.

What Legacy Will You Leave the World?

It was the bleakest winter of Charles Dickens's life. His most recent books were bringing in almost no income and his wife was pregnant with their fifth child. His debts were mounting, and he was under tremendous pressure from his publisher. Experiencing "writer's block" and sleepless nights, Dickens began walking the streets of London.

On many such nights, he witnessed great poverty and the inhumane conditions of factory workers, many of whom were children. The greed and selfishness of those who had, and who took advantage of those who did not, became glaringly apparent to Dickens and moved him to write the classic, *A Christmas Carol*.

Out of adversity, Dickens created a masterful legacy which has touched the heart and stirred the soul of people from many generations. Countless lives have been vicariously changed through Ebenezer Scrooge, who, when visited by the third and final spirit, discovered what his legacy would be: a neglected grave and a death that went un-mourned. Scrooge, determined to change the shadows of what had been shown to him, vowed to alter his life by living out the words, "I will have Christmas in my heart and will keep it there all the year."

Scrooge discovered that the real business of any business person in life is to foremost care for others. As his former business partner, Jacob Marley, and the first spirit to visit Scrooge made plain, being a good person of business is not enough—mankind must be our business. The common welfare, charity, mercy, forbearance and benevolence are our business. The dealings of our trades are but a drop of water in the comprehensive ocean of our business.

An enlightened Scrooge thereafter used his wealth to promote virtue in and out of the marketplace and by doing so created lasting wealth. The intensity of witnessing his self-centered legacy while still living, surely changed Scrooge for the better. Likewise, Alfred Nobel, a Swedish chemist, who made millions by inventing and manufacturing dynamite in the mid 1800s was able to radically alter his legacy when he alarmingly read his own "obituary." Alfred's brother, Ludvig died in France, but the newspaper editor confused the two brothers and mistakenly wrote about Alfred's obituary instead. The headline in the newspaper read, "The Merchant of Death is

Dead!" The obituary went on to describe a man who filled his coffers with material wealth by helping people destroy each another.

Shocked and dismayed, Alfred rewrote that bleak obituary by devising to use material wealth to alter his legacy. At his death, Alfred left more than $9,000,000, over 90% of his estate, to fund awards for those whose work would benefit humanity, not destroy it. These awards, known today as Nobel Prizes, are given to those who during the preceding year shall have conferred the greatest benefit on mankind. In doing so, the lord of dynamite helped transform his legacy into one where he is remembered as a patron for peace.

When Pope John Paul II died he left no material possessions and gave the common instructions that his personal notes be burned. "I leave behind no property to be disposed of. As far as the daily things I need, I ask that they be distributed as seen fit." The last line of his will contained the phrase Jesus said just before he died on the cross, "Into your hands, I commit my spirit." Though his body was racked by Parkinson's and arthritic pain he never quit in seeking liberty through truth and urged us all to "Be not afraid" in the process. Above all his legacy was grounded in conforming his will to Gods.

What will be your legacy? Have you ever thought of writing your own obituary now? Do you have a feel for how it would play out here, or more importantly, in the hereafter? Could you, like St. Thomas More did with his last breath, say that you were the "King's good servant, but God's first?"

By envisioning yourself at your gravesite, with family and friends looking on, you might catch a glimpse as to what they would say about you, and how you would want to be remembered. The whole point of writing an obituary is to focus your life's energy now on creating the legacy you want to be remembered for later.

A legacy is passed on to others during our lives and after we pass on, and it includes both tangible and intangible assets. Legacy planning should not, however, be postponed until near the end of the race in order to finish well. Instead, legacy planning needs to take place in the heat of the race without knowing how far we are from the finish line. In the end, our legacy is not about what we have achieved and left behind when we died. Rather, our legacy is about what we did for God and others while we were living.

When we leave this life, will our legacies show that we invested more in this temporal world than in the eternal one to come? It is wise to remember that whatever financial capital we may acquire, we cannot keep for long; but whatever spiritual capital we may expend, we cannot lose. Martin Luther put it this way, "I have held many things in my hands, and I have lost them all. But whatever I have placed in God's hands, I cannot lose."

In planning for one of life's greatest certainties, death does not allow us to take it with us—there are no hearses pulling U-Hauls. Therefore, it is an exercise in futility to live life with the primary purpose of accumulating financial capital that we can only hold in your hands for a short time. A more prudent course of conduct is to seek spiritual capital that we can send ahead of where we will be going.

Go Vertical and Move from Success to Significance

Being in the world but not of the world is a difficult balance between the competing demands of spiritual and financial capital. What follows is an attempt to visually conceptualize a course of action that leads to lasting wealth.

The following two lines take us in different directions:

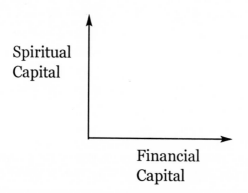

The horizontal line is about spending our life's energy primarily making money and amassing financial capital. Conversely, the vertical line is about developing ourselves as moral and spiritual beings, where God-given resources are used to achieve God-given dreams and desires through spiritual capital. By overlaying a grid onto these two lines the following four quadrants become evident:

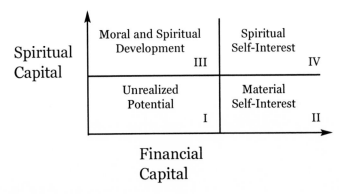

I. Unrealized Potential

This quadrant often reflects those occasions where our actions or omissions are fear-based and our potential is not realized. Characteristics which may be apparent in this quadrant may include a scarcity mentality, a lack of trust and faith, or a slothful attitude. It is here that we can find ourselves feeling spiritually deprived in creative enterprise and in our ability to exploit our potential. The sluggard appearing throughout the Old Testament, or the third servant in Matthew 25 who lost possession of the only talent entrusted to him because he buried it out of fear, might well be found toward the lower left corner of this quadrant. One may surely sin by greed and the desire for power, but here, one may also sin in these matters through fear, indecision and cowardice.

(*Note: The poor, sick, and disabled, who have been disenfranchised and are without hope through no fault of their own, may also find themselves in this quadrant. They may need particular assistance in finding faith and in gaining access to adequate resources so that they can make the most of their own potential and contribute to the common good.)

II. Material Self-Interest

The second quadrant is primarily based on making money where power, prestige, and position essentially define us. Here, we often see ourselves, not merely as stewards or co-creators, but as direct owners of the financial capital we possess. Unhealthy material attachments are not uncommon in our efforts toward becoming successful.

Much of our capitalistic society today helps encourage us to unconsciously gravitate along this axis without going vertical. Yet, the further along we go horizontal without going vertical, the more likely our life will become about living rich for ourselves. Examples of those most likely found toward the lower right corner are the *Rich Fool* described in Luke 12, the stingy Scrooge, John Paul Getty, and Hetty Green.

III. Moral and Spiritual Development

This quadrant is more about spending our life's energy growing as moral and spiritual beings without placing much importance on garnering financial capital in the process. The primary concern is about being rich toward God and others, selfless service, and meeting life's essential needs with a "less is more" mentality. Religiosity is not as important as moral values and virtues which are prized and pursued. The poor widow described in Mark 12 41:44, John Wesley (founder of the Methodist Church), Billy Graham, Pope John Paul II, Mother Teresa and C.S. Lewis would most certainly be examples found toward the upper left corner.

IV. Spiritual Self-Interest

In the last quadrant, God-given gifts, talents, dreams, and desires are faithfully pursued, as we seek financial capital. In this area, however, the focus is more on being an inspired co-creator, with an abundance mindset, where we bring something of value in exchange to the marketplace. Our business is more like a calling, where we take part in the virtuous circle as we move past material self-interest and toward a more enlightened self-interest that promotes the common good and seeks to store up treasures in heaven.

The purpose of money here is not to build affluence for ourselves; rather, it is to be used in serving God and others. It is not as much about increasing our standard of living as it is our standard of giving. In this quadrant the focus is not so much on renouncing wealth as it is on redirecting our efforts regarding wealth. In this context, greater amounts of financial capital could be seen as greater opportunities to enrich others and the world around us. The first Steward in Matthew 25 who doubles the five talents entrusted to him, the virtuous Scrooge, Milton Hershey, J.C. Penny, Truett Cathy (founder of Chick fil-A), and Tom Monaghan (founder of Dominos Pizza) would all likely be examples found toward the upper right of this quadrant.

A Word of Caution: In looking at the eternal picture, there are certain risks that come with greater amounts of financial capital in Quadrant IV: it can become harder for us to live by faith and radical dependence on God; there is a greater temptation to autonomy, pride, and to look to wealth for our security and supply; and there is much greater accountability to God as stewards for the material abundance entrusted to us.

Quadrant III most likely allows one to pursue spiritual perfection more easily since life is often less encumbered by the daily distractions and material attachments that can occur in quadrant IV. But quadrant IV can also be also be a very fruitful quadrant. Consider that it was through the generative efforts of those in quadrant IV that allowed many missionaries, like Mother Teresa in quadrant III, to receive the physical means to provide food, medicine, and shelter in serving the poorest of the poor.

In leaving our legacy, it is true that by progressing along the horizontal axis alone, we will experience a kind of success that may temporarily impress others. However, by making headway along the vertical axis, our lives stand a better chance of experiencing significance, cultivating meaning, and encouraging others.

No matter how hard we may try, we can never accumulate enough along the horizontal to feel secure and significant. That is why we should never wait until we have achieved temporal success before turning our attentions toward eternal significance. Only by going vertical will we find our significance and identity. As we deepen our understanding regarding the vertical nature of work, we can better position ourselves to find fulfillment, which comes from working with a sense of calling, not from the things acquired from work.

To be sure, this graphic illustration has its limitations. There are more forms of capital than just spiritual and financial (i.e. social, intellectual, human, and political capital) that can be plotted, developed and which influence success, significance, and our ultimate legacy. Overall, however, the graph gives us a visual bearing as to what direction we may be heading and also provides a path to redirect our efforts toward a richer life.

Wisely Choose Life's "BIG Things"

The American Dream is best nurtured and kept alive when we are true to ourselves and are willing to explore our personal histories. With this in mind, take some time to do some soul-searching and self-examination. Each one of us has a personal destiny worth uncovering and passing on.

A good example of this is found in the book *Tuesdays with Morrie* written by Mitch Albom. In this true-life story, a former student is reunited with his mentor, a college professor named Morrie, who is dying. In the last months of Morrie's life, the two get together every Tuesday as Morrie openly shares his wisdom about life and prepares to accept death.

In one of his lessons, Morrie candidly talks about the need for us to develop our own subculture. He states: "I don't mean you disregard every rule of your community. I don't go around naked, for example. I don't go through red lights. The little things I can obey. But the big things—how we think, what we value—those you must choose for yourself. You can't let anyone—or any society—determine those for you."

A skilled facilitator can help you uncover your natural behavior, core values, and dreams worth pursuing in accordance with your life's purpose. Ultimately, however, it is up to you to determine what is worth building with your life's energy and what kind of legacy you intend to leave behind. You must choose these things in accordance with your own conscience. But wise choices always stem from an informed conscience. And the key to making wise decisions is that they be based on the notion of virtues—strength of character applied to daily living.

A virtuous American Dream is found in wisely and freely choosing your direction in life. Abiding by laws and imposed rules alone will not result in virtue. We are only complying with what other people have established for us. Virtue, on the other hand, is about developing wisdom, over time, gained through living life and careful reflection. It is about living with compassion and respect for human dignity.

Human freedom and liberty are necessary prerequisites to forming virtue in our lives. Otherwise, we would be like all other animals that are ruled by their instincts or the dictates of their masters. What distinguishes us from other animals is an intelligence and a moral soul which can recognize various degrees of good and evil, and a will, which chooses from among them.

For the wealth to endure, it, like a seed, needs fertile soil in which it can thrive. Yet, as Jesus warns in Mark 4:19, worldly anxiety, the lure of riches and the cravings for other things can prevent wealth from bearing lasting fruit.

Spiritual capital is like the unseen roots of a flower that keep it grounded and nourished. Financial capital is often like the flower's bloom that can be garnered and admired. It is the beauty of the bloom, however, that attracts the eye and tugs at our egos. And if we let financial capital become our primary focus, we tend to neglect the roots, which, over time, cause the flower and bloom to wither and die.

A short-sighted view in business may focus principally on gathering the financial bloom of the sale, instead of creating a lasting relationship with deep-rooted service. It can be as simple as the difference between making a one-time sale to a new prospect versus building a business of satisfied customers over the long-term. Whatever the case, our job is to steadily sow the seeds of spiritual capital; God's job is to bring about the harvest (1 Cor.3:6).

Realize the Dream by Helping Others Achieve Their Dreams

Almost everything we accomplish of importance in life we do with and through other people. Capitalism works only if people remain associative and continue to work to help one another. Therefore, an effective way for you to realize the Dream is to help others accomplish their dreams too.

Bob Littell, author of *The Heart and Art of NetWeaving*, encourages others to look for daily opportunities to "connect people with other people" for their sole benefit, and to provide "gratuitous resources" to them. By doing so, Littell is convinced that "what goes around will come back around" in time to the individual who first made the gratuitous connection.

Helping others reach their dreams is a major building block of capitalism. Network marketing companies and many small organizations, in particular, embrace this principle. Commerce is built on the principle of helping others achieve their aspirations.

Beyond small business and network marketing, many large corporations built their businesses by creating win-win environments. In the book *Loyalty Rules!—How Today's Leaders Build Lasting Relations,* author Frederick F. Reichheld makes the point that companies such as Enterprise Rent-A-Car, Vanguard, Northwestern Mutual Insurance, Cisco, Intuit, Dell Computer, Southwest Airlines, and Harley-Davidson all became successful because they stressed building mutually beneficial relationships.

One standout company in particular, Chick-fil-A, deserves special recognition. Founded by S. Truett Cathy, this fast-food franchise which sells chicken, was built around Cathy's leadership of putting the welfare of others first. By focusing on helping the people around him have better lives, Truett Cathy experienced tremendous success.

He built his business based on biblical principles, and to this day, all the restaurants are closed on Sunday to "ensure every Chick-fil-A employee and restaurant owner has an opportunity to worship, spend time with family and friends, or just plain rest from the work week."

Its corporate purpose is: "To glorify God by being faithful stewards of all that is entrusted to us. To have a positive influence on all who come in contact with Chick-fil-A." Integrating biblical principles with good business practices has yielded some rather impressive results. Today, Chick-fil-A has more than 1,200 restaurants nationwide, with over $2 billion in combined sales.

Seek to Find God in All Things

Lasting wealth is also procured where God is sought in all things, regardless of what we do or our economic circumstances. No job, business, or financial asset has a higher or lower ranking in and of itself. Whatever we do, we are to do for the glory of God. We are all called to be devout and to find God in the ordinary routines of daily life.

Each one of us is but a small part of creation orbiting around our Creator. For a truly meaningful existence, God must be the center of a well-integrated life, involved in all the pieces. Too often, however, God is compartmentalized in a life where we are at the center.

How can people with professional careers and millions of dollars be unhappy and insecure? How could those who have experienced an abundance of material success, near the top of the ladder, not be filled with gratitude that they have received more than their share of blessings? And why is it that people climbing the worldly ladder curse those at the top? In many cases, the main reason is that they are not seeking God in all things.

Discovering how much is enough to keep us happy is a relevant state and a moving target. Instead, we should ask God to take from us everything that distances us from Him and give us everything that brings us closer. Only when we are detached from ourselves and what we own are we then in a position to give our all to God.

Finding God in all things comes through focusing on the inspired dreams that come from our Creator, working on becoming neutral to riches and poverty, and surrendering our attachments to outcomes. We may surely wish for things and circumstances to our liking, but our trust must remain steadfast in God. And although we need to graciously take things as they come, we still need to work hard to make things happen.

Going through life with the principal intention of hastening "retirement," where we will enjoy life and live off the fruits of our labor is naïve thinking. It is like the mindset of the Rich Fool in Luke 12:16–21, who acted richly toward himself, but not toward God. Building bigger barns of our own to store goods for ourselves to take life easy in order to eat, drink, and be merry is unwise. For God may say, "This night your life will be demanded from you. Then who will get what you have prepared for yourself?"

Unfortunately, living out the American Dream today is too often like living out the Rich Fool's dream. Storing up for our future needs frequently takes precedence over serving our neighbor's current needs. Stockpiling assets is increasingly seen as a savvy move in a culture which places great emphasis on how to live richly here and little prominence on what we must do to live richly in the hereafter.

We live in an ebay world where the marketplace for material exchange is now open 24 hours a day. As long as you have the economic means, almost every tangible thing can be purchased for a negotiated price. Yet, nothing that is God's can ever be purchased for money on the spiritual exchange. There is no price that we can pay to buy eternal blessings, and the bidding there starts with the earnest desire to be portals of God's grace.

The desire to seek God for who we are on the inside must outweigh the desire for how we appear on the outside. If only we would take our societies' current obsession for low-carb diets and apply that same fervor to preparing our souls for eternity. In the words of St. Augustine, "We must be caring for our body as if we will live forever, and caring for our soul as if we will die tomorrow."

Fight to Keep the American Dream Alive

Freedom often gets taken for granted as an assumed way of living. Yet, there is always a price to be paid for freedom, whether on Bunker Hill or in Baghdad. Freedom, however, is not a matter waging war; responsible freedom seeks to avoid war, if possible, because of the evils inherent in it.

Still, the demands for freedom and democracy can be great. They are ongoing in a course of action that never gets finished. As President John F. Kennedy said, "Democracy is never a final achievement. It is a call to untiring effort and to continual sacrifice."

Sacrifices of both property and life itself have long been a part of our nation's heritage. The 56 men who dared to sign the Declaration of Independence did so understanding that their property would most likely be confiscated or destroyed, and if captured, they could face execution. Merely signing the document meant that they were committing treason.

Those brave signers, however, lived with a spirit that carried out the promises found in the last line of the Declaration of Independence: *"And for the support of this declaration, with a firm reliance on the protection of Divine Providence, we mutually pledge to each other our lives, our fortunes, and our sacred honor."*

America became a great nation because so many Americans have exhibited great character. Liberty for them was not doing what they impulsively wanted to do; it was finding the courage to do what they needed to do.

Freedom demands a great leap of faith, and once taken, there is no going back. In the Revolutionary War, there was an enormous price exacted in both life and resources in securing freedom. Today, there is an ongoing cost in preserving freedom.

Freedom is great, but the responsibility to maintain it can be even greater. Liberty marches to an unhurried drumbeat. Of this Thomas Jefferson remarked,

"The ground of liberty is to be gained by inches. It will not be won overnight."

But freedom is never a sure thing, whether a new way of life, or an integral part of everyday life. At any point, free people can choose not to pay the price—regardless of the sacrifices made by prior generations or the responsibilities owed to future ones.

In the moment, freedom presents an opportunity not to be squandered, but to be cherished and exploited. Regarding this, John Quincy Adams declared, "Posterity—you will never know how much it has cost my generation to preserve your freedom. I hope that you will make good use of it."

Posterity may not be so kind to us should we squander the freedom that was paid for by prior generations of Americans. The freedom to pursue our dreams in a way that our Creator intended exists only as long as we are willing to fight for those principles and moral values of liberty that will help keep the Dream alive. After all, true freedom is the power, rooted in reason and will, to act or not to act, in truth and goodness, with God as our ultimate end.

Reconnect with America's Founding Spirit

Our Founding Fathers believed that the American Dream depended upon the strong character of its many diverse individuals. They understood that the Creator, who gave us our inalienable rights, requires virtue and vigilance as the price for freedom and liberty.

For our Founding Fathers, America was an emerging market economy, and capitalism a new-born babe. If they could return today, they would most likely be amazed by the economic and military might that America has achieved some 230 years later. On the other hand, they would most likely be taken aback by the enormity of government, its swelling deficits and the waning level of spiritual capital found in today's American Dream.

From our country's inception to the present, our republic has depended upon virtue, both private and public, for its survival. But as both George Washington and Thomas Paine pointed out long ago, "Virtue is not hereditary." Virtue must be taught, nurtured, and consciously passed on from one generation to the next.

In his first Inaugural Address, President Ronald Reagan spoke of a man, named Dr. Joseph Warren, and referred to him as "one of the greatest" among our Founding Fathers. Dr. Warren was a Harvard-educated medical doctor who became a Major General at the outset of the Revolutionary War. Instead of giving orders from a distance at Bunker Hill, he volunteered to fight alongside his men against the British onslaught. Dr. Warren became the first high-ranking officer to fall in the war when he was struck in the head by a musket ball that killed him.

The night before Bunker Hill, Dr. Warren, as the President of the Massachusetts Congress, said to his countrymen, "Our country is in danger, but not to be despaired of.… On you depends the fortunes of America. You are to decide the important questions upon which rest the happiness and the liberty of millions yet unborn. Act worthy of yourselves."

The tragic events of 9/11 awakened Americans to the sober reality that geographical invulnerability is now history. And although we should prudently take steps to shore up homeland security, there is only so much that can be done in a democratic and free society. At some point, national security depends upon more than sophisticated intelligence and defending our borders. We should heed the words of President John Adams who said, "It must be felt that there is no national security but in the nation's humbled acknowledged dependence upon God and His overruling Providence."

The heartrending beginning of the War on Terror also awakened Americans to the greatness of that founding spirit and our slumbering sense of patriotism. In part, I wish every day could be another 9/11—never in respect to the dramatic loss of innocent human life, but for the inspiration to the human soul that reaches out to care for others in need. Our challenge, however, is to hold onto that selfless spirit of 9/11, not only during wartime but long after the war has ceased. Ultimately, we need to find a peaceful way to live together as one human family with our brothers and sisters around the globe.

Winning the War on Terror will at some point require more than just decisive military action. If we are to truly win the War, we must also fight to eradicate global poverty, educate humanity on the sanctity of life, and act in ways that support human dignity. Families, communities, marketplaces and government must work together to overcome poverty, pursue the common good, and care for all of creation. So long as glaring economic and social imbalances persist it will not be possible to preserve lasting peace.

The principles of democracy, particularly in the Middle East, must also be carefully molded around diverse cultures with great respect for native traditions and religious beliefs. The American Dream, grounded in love, is not America's message to the world; it is our Creator's message to humanity. In the end, love is the only light that can illuminate the present dimness of the American Dream, both here and abroad.

As we seek lives that are rich, we do so with the firm belief that we are God's greatest creation, and that we are here to make the world a better place. Love is the power necessary to do that, and our Creator is the source of all love. And despite all of its shortcomings, religion is a tremendous teacher and guardian of essential virtues that keep us allied to God. One could write a book about the negative things concerning religion as an institution, but one could more easily fill a library with all the good it has done for the people of America.

If we are to achieve a rich life and pass on the American Dream from one generation to the next, it will be because of our commitment to virtues and the production of spiritual capital in a free market system. We do not really own material possessions anyway. We merely have use of them for a while. "For we brought nothing into this world, just as we shall not be able to take anything out of it." (1 Timothy 5:6–7)

We only have possession of what is inside our souls, where the values that became our life's virtues were first conceived. And when we are successful in this regard, we will have passed on a principled legacy and a sacred part of our heritage to the next generation of disciples who live on and for the millions yet unborn. We will have rescued the American Dream and acted in a manner worthy of ourselves.

The magnificent fresco on the ceiling of the Sistine Chapel of the Creation of Adam, as set forth in Chapter One, gives us much to consider today. The parody on this book's cover poignantly depicts the dilemma of a 21st century Adam grasping for financial wealth and spiritual health.

For all of us as contemporary Adams, creating lasting wealth and cultivating spiritual capital means that we have to loosen our grasp and decisively put America and the American Dream back in God's hands. In the final analysis, lasting wealth is what God does through us and in us. What we do with our own hands does not last. Only in this way can we properly pursue spiritual and monetary prosperity in what truly matters and live a life that is rich where it counts.

CHAPTER QUESTIONS

1. What are the "Big Things" in your life and whose voice are you following in the pursuit of your dreams?

2. In 100 words or less, write out your own obituary. Are you happy with that person? Is God?

3. How much is enough for you, and what is one thing that you can do better to pass on a principled legacy?

Lasting wealth is procured by steadily sewing the seeds of spiritual capital with enlightened self-interest.

ABOUT THE AUTHOR

Charlie Douglas, J.D., AEP, CFP® is a nationally recognized expert, author and professional advisor in the estate and wealth management industry. As an attorney and financial planner, Charlie has been resourcefully counseling corporations and high-net-worth individuals for over 20 years regarding wealth-related issues. Today, he often helps his clients build, protect, and pass on a rich legacy of wealth through values-based and multi-generational planning.

As a member of the National Speakers Association™ and certified through the Christian Financial Professionals Network™, Charlie is a frequent lecturer and keynote speaker for professional organizations, church groups, and other associations.

He lives in Atlanta, Georgia with his wife Lori and their daughter Elizabeth.

Contact Charlie @ www.richwhereitcounts.com

—FREE BONUS—

DOWNLOAD FREE, professional articles and audios regarding how to realize financial wealth and spiritual health by going to www.richwhereitcounts.com. Also receive, while the supply lasts, a FREE BONUS BOOK** from the *Walking With the Wise* series by Mentors Magazine™ where Charlie Douglas and other influential mentors and millionaires, including Bill Gates, Jim Rohn, Brian Tracy, Mark Victor Hansen, Donald Trump, and Suzie Orman teach the secrets of prosperity in business and in life.

*(**Excludes shipping and handling charges of $4.95)*

BIBLIOGRAPHY

Adams, Marilyn. "Broken pension system in crying need of a fix" USAToday.com
17 Nov. 2005
<http://www.usatoday.com/money/perfi/retirement/2005-11-14-pensions-usat_x.htm>

"Affluence hasn't gone global: World consumption is up but few enjoy the boon, UNDP
Report says". CNN Money.
http://money.cnn.com/news/economy/wires/9809/09/un_wg/ (9 Sep 1998).

A' Kempis, Thomas. Imitation of Christ., Nashville, Tennessee: Thomas Nelson, Inc.,1999.

Albom, Mitch. Tuesdays with Morrie: an old man, a young man and life's greatest Lesson.
New York: Doubleday Dell Publishing Group, Inc, 1997.

Alcorn, Randy. The Treasure Principle. Oregon: Multnomah: 2001.

Alcorn, Randy. Money Possessions and Eternity. Wheaton, Illinois: Tyndale: 2003.

Alcoholics Anonymous: The Story of How Many Thousands of Men and Women Have Recovered
from Alcoholism, 3rd ed. New York: Alcoholics Anonymous World Services, Inc. 1976.

Andrew Carnegie: Prince of Steel, VHS, 50 mins., 1995, (A&E Television Networks), 1996,
distributed by New Video Group, New York.

Appelbaum, Alec. "Bridegroom Revisited". SmartMoney.com.
http://www.smartmoney.com/mymoney/index.cfm?story=20000712 (13 Jul 2000).

Auchmutey, Jim. "Death of a Day Trader". The Atlanta-Journal Constitution 24 Feb 2002,
pp. A1.

Aversa, Jeannine. "Analysts: Growing deficit hobbles economy" USAToday.com 15 Jan. 2006
<http://www.usatoday.com/money/economy/2006-01-15-fiscal-fitness_x.htm>

"Greenspan says trade deficit may prove costly" USAToday.com 15 Nov. 2005
<http://www.usatoday.com/money/economy/trade/2005-11-14-greenspan_x.htm>

Barry, William A., SJ. Finding God in All Things: A Companion to the Spiritual Exercises of
St. Ignatius. Notre Dame, Indiana: Ave Maria Press, 1991.

Barton, David. Original Intent: The Courts, the Constitution, & Religion". Aledo, Texas:
WallBuilder Press, 1996.

Bellesi, Denny and Leesa. The Kingdom Assignment. Zondervan: Michigan, 2001

Bennett, William J. The Death of Outrage: Bill Clinton and the Assault on American Ideals.
New York: The Free Press, 1998.

Bennett, William J., ed. The Book of Virtues: A Treasury of Great Moral Stories. New York:
Simon & Schuster, 1993.

Bennett, William J., ed. The Broken Hearth: Reversing the Moral Collapse of the American
Family. New York: Doubleday, 2001.

Bennett, William J.: "Paige's 'values' are America's values". The Washington Post 14 Apr. 2003 <http://www.empoweramerica.org/stories/storyReader$720>

Biblical Financial Studies. Gainesville: Crown Financial Ministries Inc., 2002.

Bill Gates, VHS, 50 mins., (A&E Television Networks), 1996, distributed by New Video Group, New York.

Blouin, Barbara and Katherine Gibson. *Inheritors & Work: The Search for Purpose.* Blacksburg, Virginia: Trio Press, 1996.

Blouin, Barbara and Katherine Gibson. *For Love and/or Money: The Impact of Inherited Wealth on Relationships...* Blacksburg, Virginia: Trio Press, 1997.

Blouin, Barbara and Katherine Gibson, eds. *The Legacy of Inherited Wealth: Interviews with Heirs.* Blacksburg, Virginia: Trio Press, 1995.

Blouin, Barbara, Katherine Gibson and Margaret Kiersted. *The Inheritor's Inner Landscape: How Heirs Feel.* Blacksburg, Virginia: Trio Press, 1994.

Blouin, Barbara, Katherine Gibson and Margaret Kiersted. *Passing Wealth Along to our Children: Emotional Complexities of Estate Planning.* Blacksburg, Virginia: Trio Press, 1995.

Blouin, Barbara, Katherine Gibson and Margaret Kiersted. *Working with Inherited-Wealth Clients: A Guide for Professional Advisors...* Blacksburg, Virginia: Trio Press, 1995.

Blue, Ron with Jodie Berndt. *Generous Living: Finding Contentment through Giving.* Grand Rapids, Michigan: Zondervan Publishing House, 1997.

Blue, Ron with Jeremy White. *Master Your Money.* Chicago: Moody Publishers, 2004.

Bryant, Adam. "They're Rich (And You're Not)". Newsweek. 5 July 1999, pp. 37–43.

Catechism of the Catholic Church: With Modifications from the Editio Typica. New York: Doubleday, 1995.

Cauchon, Dennis and John Waggoner. "Solutions for debt crisis go far beyond tinkering." USAToday.com http://www.usatoday.com/news/nation/2004-10-04-debtsolutions-cover_x.htm (5 Oct 2004)

"The looming national benefit crisis." USAToday.com 4 Oct 2004 <http://www.usatoday.com/news/nation/2004-10-03-debt-cover_x.htm>

Cava, Marco R. della. "In Katrina's wake, generosity." USAToday.com 7 Sept. 2005. <http://www.usatoday.com/life/2005-09-06-katrina-generosity_x.htm>

"After Katrina, a wave of gratitude." USAToday.com 23 Nov. 2005. <http://www.usatoday.com/life/2005-11-22-katrina-thanks_x.htm>

CNN. "Elders, Boomers and Their Inheritance" June 28, 2005 <http://money.cnn.com/2005/07/28/retirement/legacy_survey/.

Chernow, Ron. *Alexander Hamilton.* New York: Penguin Press, 2004.

Chopra, Deepak. *The Seven Spiritual Laws of Success: A Practical Guide to the Fulfillment of Your Dreams.* California: Amber-Allen Publishing and New World Library, 1994.

Comby, Jean. *How to Read Church History, Volume 1: From the Beginnings to the Fifteenth Century.* New York: Crossroad Publishing Company, 1995.

Comby, Jean with Diarmaid MacCulloch. *How to Read Church History, Volume 2: From the Reformation to the Present Day.* New York: Crossroad Publishing Company, 1995.

Covey, Stephen R., A. Roger Merrill and Rebecca R. Merrill. *First Things First: To Live, to Love, to Learn, to Leave a Legacy.* New York: Simon & Schuster, 1994.

Crutsinger, Martin. "Greenspan Says the Bill for Soaring Deficits Will come." AOL.com http://aolsvc.news.aol.com (7 May 2004)

Dampier, Philip, prod. The Gettys: A Tragedy of Riches. 100 mins. (A&E Television Networks) 1995, distributed by New Video Group, New York. Videocassette

DeMar, Gary. America's Christian Heritage. Broadman and Holman: Tennessee, 2003.

DeMuth, Christopher. "Guns, Butter, and War on Terror." American Enterprise Institute for Public Policy Research. May 2004, pgs 1–4

Dent, Harry S. *The Roaring 2000s.*, New York: Simon & Schuster, 1998.

Despeignes, Peronet. "Two years in a row, more in poverty." USATODAY.com http:www.usatoday.com/news/nation/2003-09-26-poverty-usat_x.htm (26 Sept 2003)

Drinkard, Jim. "Poll: Many say U.S. deeply divided." USAToday.com 23 Nov 2004 http://usatoday.printthis.clickability.com/pt/cpt?action=cpt&title=USATODAY.com

Dominguez, Joe and Vicki Robin. *Your Money or Your Life: Transforming Your Relationship with Money and Achieving Financial Independence.* New York: Penguin Group, 1992.

D'Souza, Dinesh. "The Billionaire Next Door". Forbes. 11 Oct 1999, pp. 50–62.

Durning, Alan Thein. *How Much is Enough?: The Consumer Society and the Future of the Earth.* New York: W.W. Norton & Company, 1992.

Dychtwald, Ken, Ph.D. Age Wave. Audio Renaissance, 1989.

Dyer, Wayne W. *There's A Spiritual Solution to Every Problem.* New York: HarperCollins Publishers, 2001.

Dyer, Wayne W. *Your Sacred Self: Making the Decision to Be Free.* New York: HarperCollins Publishers, 1995.

Edwards, Chris and Tad DeHaven. "War between the Generations: Federal Spending on the Elderly Set to Explode." Policy Analysis. No. 488. 16 Sept 2003.

Federer, William J. *America's God and Country: Encyclopedia of Quotations.* Coppell, Texas: Fame Publishing, Incorporated, 1996.

Finkelman, Paul, ed. *Religion and American Law: An Encyclopedia.* New York: Garland Publishing, January 2000.

Fithian, Scott C. *Values-Based Estate Planning: A Step-by-Step Approach to Wealth Transfer for Professional Advisors.* New York: John Wiley & Sons, Inc. 2000.

Forbes, Steve: *"The Moral Basis of a Free Society".* The Heritage Foundation http://www.policyreview.org/nov97moral.html (November-December 1977).

Frankl, Victor. *Man's Search for Meaning.* Boston: Beacon Hill Press, 2000.

Fromm, Erich. *The Art of Loving.* New York: HarperCollins Publishers, 2000.

"Galbraith: Help the Weak". <u>CNN Money</u>. 15 Oct 1998
http://money.cnn.com/1998/10/15/markets/moneyline_intv/

Geary, Leslie Haggin. "Riches to rags: millionaires who go bust". <u>CNN Money</u>. 14 May 2002
<http://money.cnn.com/2002/05/08/pf/saving/q_gonebust/index.htm.>

"Generation X Examined in Major Study: Media habits, beliefs about morality, religion, work, technology revealed". <u>ASNE News Release</u>. 14 Dec 1998
<u><http://www.asne.org/kiosk/news/genx.htm></u>

Gilbert, Jersey with Trevor Delaney, Dagen McDowell and Odette Galli. "Where to Invest in 2001". <u>SmartMoney</u>. January 2001, pp. 89–99.

Gibney, Alex and Barbara Sears. <u>David Halberstam's The Fifties</u>, Vol 1–Vol 6. 540 min., (A&E Television Networks, directed by Tracy Dahlby and produced by W. Paterson Ferns and Richard Heus). New York: distributed by New Video, 1997, Videocassette.

Gilbert, Matthew. " 'Born Rich' reveals privileged information." <u>Boston.com</u> 13 Jan 2004
<http://boston.com/news/globe/living/articles/2003/10/27/born_rich_reveals_privilege>

Gingrich, Newt. "A Campaign about Values." <u>AEI.org</u> 2 Sept 2004
<http://www.aet.org/include/news_print.asp?newsID=21116>

Glassman, James K. " "Greatest Generation" May Be the Newest." <u>AEI.org</u> 6 Jul 2004
<http://www.aei.org/include/news_print.asp?newsID=20847>

Gokhale, Jagadesh and Kent Smetters. *Fiscal and Generational Imbalances: New Budget Measure for New Budget Prioritie*s. Washington D.C.: The AEI Press, 2003

Gongloff, Mark. "Are Americans too far underwater?" <u>CNNMoney.com</u> 29 Sept 2003
http://money.cnn.com/2003/07/28/news/economy/balnace¬sheets/index.htm

"Are we too deep in debt?" <u>CNNMoney.com</u> 7 Apr 2004
<u><http://cnnmoney.printthis.clickability.com/pt/cpt?action=cpt&title=Are+we+too+deep+in+debt.html></u>

"Do deficits matter?" <u>CNNMoney.com</u> 2 Feb 2004
<http://money.cnn.com/2004/02/02/news/economy/budget/index.htm>12

"Greenspan's changing tune: Despite its Chairman's recent claims, the Fed noticed a stock-market bubble six years ago". <u>CNNMoney.com</u> 19 Sep 2002
<http://money.cnn.com/2002/09/18/news/economy/greenspan_story/index.htm>

Gordon, John Steele. *The Great Game: The Emergence of Wall Street As a World Power 1653–2000*. New York: Scribner, 1999.

Gordon, Marcy. "Pension Agency Reports $22.8 Billion Shortfall" <u>AOLNews.com</u> 15 Nov. 2005
<http://articles.news.aol.com/business/article.adp?id=20051115132309990036>

<u>Great Events of the 20th Century (1900–1995), Vol 1–Vol 7</u>. VHS 6 Hours.
Eugene, Oregon: Marathon Music & Video, 1997.

Grossman, Cathy Lynn. "Pope's encyclical on love avoids controversy." <u>USAToday.com</u> 26 Jan 2006.
<http://www.usatoday.com/news/religion/2006-01-24-papalencyclical_x.htm>

Gunderson, Edna: *"Madonna's epiphany"*. USA Today
    < http://www.usatoday.com/life/2003-04-17-madonna-main (April 17, 2003)>.

Guss, Alison, producer and director. The Rockefellers. 50 mins. A&E Television, 1996.
    Videocassette.

Hagenbaugh, Barbara. "Great debate: Could Fed have deflated stock bubble?" USATODAY.com.
    http://www.usatoday.com/money/economy/fed/2002-09-23-bubble-debate_x.htm
    (23 Oct 2002).

Hamilton, Joan O'C. "The Dark Side of Silicon Valley's Wealth". BusinessWeek Online.
    http://www.businessweek.com/1999/99_28/b3637069.htm?scriptFramed (1 Jun 2000).

Hampson, Rick, Martha T. Moore, Kevi McCoy and Dennis Cauchon. "One day seared
    into memory". USA Today, 17 Sep 2001, p.6A.

Hampton, Rick. "The Day Before". USATODAY.com.
    http://www.usatoday.com/news/sept11/2002-09-09-last-day_x.htm. (10 Sep 2002)

Henriques, Diana B. "Spitzer Casting a Very Wide Net." NYTimes.com
    http://www.nytimes.com/2003/10/12/business/yourmoney/12mutu.html (14 Oct 2003)

"House votes to strip Supreme Court of authority in pledge cases." USAToday.com
    http://www.usatoday.com/news/washington/2004-09-23-house-pledge¬_x.htm
    (23 Sept 2004)

"How the rich kids live." CNN.com
    http://www.cnn.com/2003/SHOWBIZ/TV/10/27/apontv.bornrich.ap (13 Jan 2004)

Howe, Neil and Bill Strauss. *13th Gen: Abort, Retry, Ignore, Fail?*. New York: Vintage Books,
    April, 1993.

Hubbard, R. Glenn. "The Social and Medicare Morass" AEI.org 6 Jul, 2006
    http://www.aei.org/include/pub¬_print.asp?pubID=20844

"Hunger Basics—FAQ". BREAD.org http://www.bread.org/hungerbasics/index.html
    (27 Jan 2003).

Huntington, Samuel P. *Who Are We? The Challenges to America's National Identity*. New York:
    Simon and Schuster, 2004

Hutson, James H. *Religion and The Founding of the American Republic*. Washington: Library
    of Congress, 1998.

"In Search of The Spiritual." NEWSWEEK 29 Aug. 2005.

Jackson, Sammy, prod. Milton Hershey: The Chocolate King. Directed by Don Horan. 50
    mins. (A&E Television Networks) 1995, distributed by New Video Group, New York.
    Videocassette.

J.C. Penney: Main Street Millionaire VHS, 50 mins., (A&E Television Networks), 1995,
    distributed by New Video Group, New York.

J. Pierpont Morgan: Emperor of Wall Street, VHS, 50 mins., (A&E Television Networks),
    1995, distributed by New Video Group, New York.

John, David C. " The Top 10 Myths About Social Security Reform." Executive Summary
    Backgrounder No.1802 (2004)

Johnson, Spencer, M.D. *Who Moved My Cheese?: An A-Mazing Way to Deal with Change in Your Work ad in Your Life.* New York: G.P. Putnam's Sons Publishers, 1998, 2002.

Johannesburg, South Africa AP. "U.N.: World failing to meet targets for reducing poverty." 7 Sept. 2005. <http://www.usatoday.com/news/world/2005-09-07-un-poverty_x.htm>

Kahn, Kim. "How does your debt compare?" MSNMoney.com http://moneycentral.msn.com/content/SavingandDept/P70581.asp?special=0401debt (7 Jan 2004)

Kiyosaki, Robert T. with Sharon L. Lechter, C.P.A. *Rich Dad, Poor Dad: What the Rich Teach Their Kids About Money—That the Poor and Middle Class Do Not.* New York: Warner Books, 1998.

Knox, Noelle. "Religion Takes a Back Seat in Western Europe." USATODAY.com 11 Aug. 2005 <http://www.usatoday.com/news/world/2005-08-10-europe-religion-cover_x.htm

Koch, Wendy. "Americans interrupt lives to help hurricane victims." USAToday.com 30 Sept. 2005 <http://www.usatoday.com/news/nation/2005-09-29-record-volunteers_x.htm>

LaBarre, Polly. "How to Lead a Rich Life." Fast Company Magazine. 2 February 2003

Levin, Gary. "Rather to Quit." USA Today. http://www.usatoday.com/life/television/news/2004-11-23-tv-rather_x.htm (23 Nov 2004)

Lewis, C.S. *Mere Christianity.* San Francisco: Harper, 2001.

Lewis, C.S. and compiled by Arthur Owen Barfield. *The Four Loves.* Orlando, Florida: Harcourt, Brace & Company, 1988.

Lewis, C.S. and compiled by Lesley Walmsley. *C.S. Lewis on Faith.* Nashville, Tennessee: Thomas Nelson Publishers, 1998.

Lieber, Jonathan and Richard Lowery. " The Bush Spending Cuts Are Missing in Action" AEI.org http://www.aei.org/include/news¬_print.asp?newsID=19992 (25 Feb 2004)

Loconte, Joseph. "Why Religious Values Support American Values." Heritage Lectures NO. 899

Limbaugh, David. *Persecution: How Liberals Are Waging War Against Christainity.* Washington D.C.:Regnery Publishing, Inc., 2003.

Manning, Brennan. *Abba's Child: The Cry of the Heart for Intimate Belonging.* Colorado Springs, Colorado: NavPress, 1994.

McBride, Alfred. *The Story of the Church: Peak Moments from Pentecost to the Year 2000.* Cincinnati, Ohio: St. Anthony Messenger Press, 1983.

McGeary, Johanna. "Can the Church Be Saved?: Catholicism in Crisis". Time. 1 April 2002, pp. 28–38.

Meacham, Jon. "Beyond the Priest Scandal: Christianity at a Crossroads". Newsweek. 6 May 2002, pp.22–33.

Mears, Bill. "Supreme Court backs municipal land grabs." CNN.com 22 Jan. 2006 <http://www.cnn.com/2005/LAW/06/24/scotus.property>

Memories of 1960–1969: The Fabulous 60's—Vol 1–Vol 5. VHS 5 Hours. Madacy Entertainment, 1997. Videocassette.

Meyer, Phillip. "Pearl Harbor's deeper lessons for today's crisis". USA Today, 17 Sep 2001, p. 25A.

Miller, Lisa. "Religion: Rebels With A Cause". The Wall Street Journal. 18 December 1998, pp. W1.

Mitchell, Susan. American Generations: Who they are. How they live. What they think. 2nd ed. Ithaca, New York: New Strategist Publications, Inc., 1998

Mitchell, Susan. Generation X: The Young Adult Market, 2nd ed, Ithaca, New York: New Strategist Publications, Inc., 1999.

Mitchell, Suzanne, prod. Biography of the Millennium: 100 People—1000 Years, Vol I–Vol IV. VHS 200 mins. (A&E Television Networks) New York: New Video Group, 1999. Videocassette.

"Moral Values: A Decisive Issue?" CBSNews.com http://www.cbsnews.com/stories/2004/11/03/60II/printable653593.shtml (5 Nov 2004)

Morley, Patrick M. The Seven Seasons of a Man's Life: Examining the unique challenges men face. Nashville, Tennessee: Thomas Nelson, Inc., Publishers, 1995

A Nation Adrift: A Chronicle of America's Providential Heritage. VHS 92 mins. (New Liberty Video) Shawnee Mission, Kansas, 2003.

Nicholi, Dr. Armand. The Question of God. New York: The Free Press, 2002

Noonan, Peggy. "You'd Cry too if it happened to you". Forbes. 14 Sep 1992, pp.58–69.

Novak, Michael. The Catholic Ethic and the Spirit of Capitalism. New York: The Free Press, 1993.

Business is a calling: Work and the examined life. New York: The Free Press,1996.

"Farewell to a Great: There Was a Man." AEI.org 14 Apr. 2005 <http://www.aei.org/publication22289>

"John Paul the Great: Reminiscences and Reflections" AEI.org 11 Apr. 2005 <http://www.aei.org/include/pub_print.asp?pubID=22279>

"Pain, Power, Passion. AEI.org (25 Feb 2004) <http://www.aei.org/include/news_print.asp?newsID=19998>

"The Blind-Obedience Myth: There's No Virtue in Being an Unquestioning Sheep." AEI.org 27 Apr. 2005 <http://www.aei.org/include/pub_print.asp?pubID=22378>

"Troubled Continent: The Crisis of Demography- and of the Spirit." AEI.org 9 Feb. 2006 < http://www.aei.org/publications23776>

O'Hearn, Deirdre. The Du Ponts: America's Wealthiest Family, produced by John Griffin and Molly Thompson, 50 mins. A&E Television, 1996. Videocassette.

Page, Susan. "State of the Union? Not so good, most say." USAToday.com 30 Jan. 2006 <http://www.usatoday.com/news/washington/2006-01-26-bush-sotu-cover_x.htm>

Parker, Kathleen. "God, country gain fragile new toehold". USA Today, 1 Oct 2001, p. 15A.

Pearne, Dennis, Ed.D. with Barbara Blouin and Katherine Gibson. *Wealth Counseling: A Guide for Therapists and Inheritors*. Blacksburg, Virginia: Trio Press, 1999.

Pearson, John. *Painfully Rich: J. Paul Getty and his Heirs*. New York: MacMillan, 1995.

Pennock, Michael Francis. *This is Our Faith: A Catholic Catechism for Adults*. Notre Dame, Indiana: Ave Maria Press, 1989.

Peterson, Karen S. "Ringing in an uncertain New Year". USATODAY.com. http://www.usatoday.com/life/2002-12-25-nervous-new-year_x.htm (25 Dec 2002).

Perterson, Peter G. *Running on Empty: How The Democratic and Republican Parties Are Bankrupting Our Future and What Americans Can Do About It*. New York: Farrar, Straus and Giroux, 2004.

Peyser, Marc and B.J. Sigesmund. "Heir Heads" MSNBC.com http://msnbc.com/news/978291.asp (16 Oct 2003)

Pilzer, Paul Zane. *God Wants You to Be Rich: How and Why Everyone can Enjoy Materialand Spiritual Wealth in Our Abundant World*. New York: Fireside, 1995.

Riedl, Brian M. "$20,000 per Household: The Highest Level of Federal Spending Since World War II" Heritage.org http://www.heritage,org/Research /Budget/BG1710.cfm (23 Mar 2004)

"Restrain Runaway Spending with Federal Taxpayers' Bill of Rights." Backgrounder No. 1793 (2004)

"State of the Union 2006: The President's Call for Spending Restraint" Heritage.org 3 Feb. 2006 <http://www.heritage.org/Research/Budget/wm975.cfm?renderforprint=1>

"The President's Budget: Strong on Short- Term Spending, But Long- Term Challenges Remain" Heritage.org 7 Feb. 2006

Reflections: U.S. Catholic Bishops. Excerpts: Sharing Catholic Social Teaching: Challenges and Directions. Washington, DC: United States Catholic Conference, Inc. 1999.

Rowland, Mary. "Fastow in handcuffs: A surprise glimpse at ourselves". MSNMoney.com. http://moneycentral.msn.com/content/P31268.asp?special=msn (8 Oct 2002).

Rugy, Veronique de. "The Republican Spending Explosion" Cato Institute Briefing Papers. 23 Jan. 2004.

"Remedial Math for the President: The Only Thing Missing from the 2007 Budget is Fiscal Responsibility" AEI.org 13 Feb. 2006. <http://www.aei.org/publication23842>

Russell, Cheryl. *The Baby Boom: Americans Aged 35 to 54, 2nd ed.* Ithaca, New York: New Strategist Publications, Inc., 1999.

Sachs, Jeffery D. "The End of Poverty." TIME 14 March 2005 pp. 42–54.

Sahadi, Jeanne. "Money and happinees: How tight the bond?" CNNMoney.com 6 Jul. 2005. http://money.cnn.com/2005/07/01/commentary/everyday/sahadi/index.htm

Sanoff, Alvin. "Half of teens say school's unsafe" USATODAY.com 8 Aug. 2005. http://www.usatoday.com/news/education/2005-08-16-school-safety_x.htm>

Samuelson, Robert J. *The Good Life and Its Discontents: The American Dream in the Age of Entitlement* 1945–1995. New York: Random House, Inc., 1995.

Shaviro, Daniel. "How Tax Cuts Feed the Beast." NYTimes.com http://www.nytimes.com/2004/09/21/opinion/21shaviro.html (21 Sept 2004)

Sheler, Jeffery L. "Faith In America: In troubled times, how Americans' views of Religion are changing". U.S. News & World Report. 6 May. 2002, pp. 40–49.

Sher, Barbara. *It's Only too Late If you Don't Start Now.* New York: Delacorte Press, 1998.

Shnayerson, Michael. "Madcap with a Twist". Vanity Fair. December 1999, pp. 336–366.

Sirico, Robert A. *The Soul of Liberty.* Michigan: Action Institute, 2002.

Towards a Free and Virtuous Society. Michigan: Action Institute, 1997.

Snow, Kate, Jim Clancy and Martin Savidge. "Atlanta Looks for Answers in Wake of Mass Killing". CNN.com. http://cnn.com/US/9907/31/atlanta.shooting.02/(31 Jul 1999).

"Socially Responsible Investment Guidelines." USCCB.org 8 Jan.2006 <http://www.usccb.org/finance/srig.htm>

"Spitzer: Investors Fleeced billions." CNNMoney.com http://money.cnn.com/2003/11/06/markets/spitzer_ldt/index.htm (6 Nov 2003)

"Spitzer sues broker, insurers." CNNMoney.com http://money.cnn.com?2004/10/14/news/fortune500/spitzer_marsh.reut/index.htm (14 Oct 2007)

Spalding, Matthew. *The Enduring Principles of the American Founding.* Washington, D.C.: The Heritage Foundation, 2000.

Stanley, Thomas J. *The Millionaire Mind.* Kansas City, Missouri: Andrews McMeel Publishing, 2000.

Stanley, Thomas J and William D. Danko. *The Millionaire Next Door: The Surprising Secrets of America's Wealthy.* Marietta, Georgia: Longstreet Press, Inc,. 1996.

Strauss, William and Neil Howe. *Generations: The History of America's Future, 1584 to 2069.* New York: William Morrow & Company, Inc., 1991.

Strauss, William and Neil Howe. *The Fourth Turning: An American Prophecy.* New York: Broadway Books, 1997.

"Study: More know 'The Simpsons' than First Amendment Rights." USATODAY.com 1 March 2006 <http://www.wnd.com/news/article.asp?ARTICLE_ID=45021>

"Supreme Court spanked for confusion." WorldNetDaily 28 Jun. 2005 <http://www.wnd.com/news/article.asp?ARTICLE_ID=45021>

Tarshis, Peter, producer & director. Henry Ford: Tin Lizzy Tycoon. 50 mins. (A&E Television Networks) 1994, distributed by New Video Group, New York. Videocassette.

Taylor, Guy. "Supreme Court backs eminent domain." The Washington Times.com 22 Jan. 2006 <http://www.washtimes.com/functions/print.php?StoryID=20050624>

"Terror fears, economy spur U.S. voters." USAToday.com
http://www.usatoday.com/news/politicselections/nation/polls/2004-11-03-exit-
polls¬_x.htm (2 Nov 2004)

The Astors: High Society VHS, 50 mins., 1996, (A&E Television Networks), 1995, distributed by New Video Group, New York.

The Story of Wall Street. (A CNBC World Premiere hosted by Sue Herera. An original
Two-hour documentary event that spans the 200-year history of American Capitalism.)
CNBC 2000.

The Vanderbilts: An American Dynasty VHS, 50 mins., 1995, (A&E Television Networks),
1995, distributed by New Video Group, New York.

Towers, Jonathan, prod. The Great Depression, Vol 1–Vol 4. 200 min., (A&E Television
Networks). New York: distributed by New Video, 1998, videocassette.

Ty, Brother, Christopher Buckley and John Tierney. God is My Broker: A Monk-Tycoon Reveals
the 7 1/2 Laws of Spiritual and Financial Growth. New York: Random House, 1998.

Updegrave, Walter. "Gambling our future away?" CNNMoney.com
http://money.cnn.com/200411/05/pfexpert/ask_expert/index.htm (5 Nov 2004)

Vanderbilt, Arthur T. Fortune's Children... The Fall of the House of Vanderbilt: Quill, 1991.

Vergano, Dan. "Water Shortages will leave world in dire straights" USATODAY.com
http://www.usatoday.com/news/nation/2003-01-26-water-usat_x.htm (27 Jan 2003).

"Venture- A season of Vengeance." CBCNews.com
http://www.cbc.ca/venture/worlcom/man2.html (28 Sept 2004)

Ward, Nathaniel. " The 2,770,000,000,000 question" MyHeritage.org 7 Feb. 2006
<http://my.heritage.org/Features/EmailArchive/2006/020706.asp>

Walt, Vivienne. "Drought, hunger won't relent in Ethiopia". USA Today, 8 May 2000, p. 1A.

Warren, Rick. The Purpose Driven Life: What On Earth Am I Here For? Michigan:
Zondervan, 2002.

Washinton AP. "Court splits on Commandments cases." USAToday.com 27 Jun. 2005
<http://www.usatoday.com/news/washington/2005-06-27-scotus-commandments_x.htm>

Watson, Noshua. "Generation X: Generation Wrecked". Fortune.com.
http://www.fortune.com/fortune/investing/articles/0,15114,373330,00.html. (23 Oct 2002).

Wealth & Power, Vol 1–Vol 2. VHS 200 mins., (A&E Television Networks). New York:dis-
tributed by New Video, 2000.

"Wealth Survey: How Do You Stack Up?" CNNMoney.com
http://money.cnn.com/2003/01/22/pf/banking/q_consumerfinances/index.htm
(22 Jan 2003).

Wessel, David. "To Slash U.S. Budget, Republicans May Need to See the Issue in Moral
Terms." New York Times 4 Nov. 2004, natl. ed.: A7

Westbrook, Kay. Enter Into the Joy: Living as God's Steward. Boston: Pauline Books & Media,
1996.

Wilkinson, Bruce H., PhD. *The Prayer of Jabez: Breaking Through to the Blessed Life.* Sisters, Oregon: Multnomah Publishers, 2000.

"What is the American Dream?" The Library of Congress: American Memory Fellows Program. http://online.sfsu.edy/~kferenz?syllabus/dreams/thedream.html (26 Apr 2004)

Wolf, Richard. "A fiscal hurricane on the horizon" USAToday.com 15 Nov. 2005

Yntema, Sharon, ed... *Americans 55 & Older: A Changing Market, 2nd ed.* Ithaca, New York: New Strategist Publications, Inc., 1999.

Zevin, Dan and Carolyn Edy. "Boom time for Gen X". US News & World Report, Vol. 123, 20 Oct 1997, pp. 68.

BUY A SHARE OF THE FUTURE IN YOUR COMMUNITY

These certificates make great holiday, graduation and birthday gifts that can be personalized with the recipient's name. The cost of one S.H.A.R.E. or one square foot is $54.17. The personalized certificate is suitable for framing and will state the number of shares purchased and the amount of each share, as well as the recipient's name. The home that you participate in "building" will last for many years and will continue to grow in value.

Here is a sample SHARE certificate:

YES, I WOULD LIKE TO HELP!

I support the work that Habitat for Humanity does and I want to be part of the excitement! As a donor, I will receive periodic updates on your construction activities but, more importantly, I know my gift will help a family in our community realize the dream of homeownership. **I would like to SHARE in your efforts against substandard housing in my community!** *(Please print below)*

PLEASE SEND ME _____ SHARES at $54.17 EACH = $ $_____

In Honor Of: _____

Occasion: (Circle One)   HOLIDAY   BIRTHDAY   ANNIVERSARY

OTHER: _____

Address of Recipient: _____

Gift From: _____ *Donor Address:* _____

Donor Email: _____

I AM ENCLOSING A CHECK FOR $ $_____ PAYABLE TO HABITAT FOR HUMANITY <u>OR</u> PLEASE CHARGE MY VISA OR MASTERCARD *(CIRCLE ONE)*

Card Number _____ Expiration Date: _____

Name as it appears on Credit Card _____ Charge Amount $ _____

Signature _____

Billing Address _____

Telephone # Day _____ Eve _____

PLEASE NOTE: Your contribution is tax-deductible to the fullest extent allowed by law.
Habitat for Humanity • P.O. Box 1443 • Newport News, VA 23601 • 757-596-5553
www.HelpHabitatforHumanity.org

Printed in the United States
76419LV00004B/25-99

9 781933 596631